★★★ THE ★★★ GREAT REVOLT

★ ★ ★ THE ★ ★ ★
GREAT
REVOLT

INSIDE THE POPULIST COALITION
RESHAPING AMERICAN POLITICS

Salena Zito and Brad Todd

CROWN
FORUM
NEW YORK

Copyright © 2018 by Salena Zito and Bradley Todd

All rights reserved.
Published in the United States by Crown Forum, an imprint of the
Crown Publishing Group, a division of Penguin Random House LLC, New York.
crownpublishing.com

CROWN FORUM and colophon is a registered trademark of
Penguin Random House LLC.

Library of Congress Cataloging-in-Publication Data is available upon request.

ISBN 978-1-5247-6368-8
Ebook ISBN 978-1-5247-6369-5

Printed in the United States of America

Jacket design by Dan Donohue and Josh Smith
Jacket photograph by Stacy Kranitz
Maps by Shannon M. Venditti. Used by permission. All rights reserved.
Map design on p. 286 by Tim Saler (Grassroots Targeting)

10 9 8 7 6 5 4 3 2 1

First Edition

With a smile, a tear, and an abundance of love,
this book is dedicated to my children, Shannon and Glenn,
who fill my days with all three;
to my parents, Joan and Ron, whose guidance surrounded me
with love, family, and tradition;
to my sisters and brother whose dedication to family
and community inspire me;
to my virtuous son-in-law, Michael;
and to my granddaughter, Eleanora.
—Salena Zito

For dad, Ron Todd, my first editor,
who hauled me around when I got my first writing job
at age fourteen and could not drive myself.
And for Elizabeth, who has the patience to endure
the first oral draft of everything,
long before it's worth hearing.
—Brad Todd

Contents

Authors' Note

The best analysis marries smart empirical research with on-the-scene, shoe-leather reporting. That's the premise behind the collaboration that brought this book to life.

We first met more than a decade ago—a reporter covering national politics from Pittsburgh, far outside the Beltway, and a political strategist whose roots were at the other end of the Appalachian mountain chain in Tennessee. Populism is not just a subject to study for us; it's a worldview we understand genetically. When a populist wave swept an unconventional candidate into office in 2016, we gravitated to each other to combine our expertise and analyze the unique moment in American political history.

Like most professionals in our respective businesses—journalism and Republican campaign strategy—we did not predict Trump's rise from the start. One of us, Brad Todd, even predicted his coming demise, wrongly, multiple times in the course of the Republican nomination fight. But in the general election campaign, we each had front-row seats to the tidal wave as it formed far out in the political ocean.

Salena Zito lived on the road, reporting for the *New York Post* and the *Washington Examiner,* while contributing pieces to publications such as *The Atlantic.* For a long article in the *Post,* Zito traveled the length of the old Lincoln Highway, highlighting the record surge of support for Trump far off the beaten path. In his role as a strategist and ad-maker advising Republican campaigns and conservative groups including the National Rifle Association, Todd watched focus groups of undecided voters, especially in the Midwest, process their hesitations about Trump and their overriding anxiety about globalism and traditional politics.

These experiences witnessing real, and largely forgotten, people process the choices in this election led to the conclusion that this election might be more than a single event and perhaps a whitecap in an ongoing tide. It is our hope that the combination of our expertise not only brings a unique method to telling the story of one election but also introduces the faces of a movement that may well go beyond it.

1
Hidden in Plain Sight

Jefferson, Ashtabula County, Ohio—It is 1:45 in the morning and Bonnie Smith's alarm has just gone off. That alarm is a reminder that, seven days a week, she is living her lifelong dream of owning a bakery.

"I come in at two-thirty in the morning. We start making doughnuts from scratch. After that, I go into the breads and pies or whatever I have going out—like right now I need to do cupcakes, and I have a couple pies I have to put out, but I also have to check what orders are going out. Then we start soups, and by eleven o'clock we start lunch," she explains.

At sixty-three, she is two years into her second career in the small town of Jefferson, running a Chestnut Street bakery that is a throwback to simpler times: pretty pink-and-green wallpaper decorated with cupcakes surrounds a fireplace and tables and chairs that fill the front of the bakery.

By 9:00 a.m., already half of her sugar cookies, tea cakes, cream wafers, brownies, mini tarts, and thumbprints are gone. With the help of her grandson, a fresh batch of sugary glazed doughnuts makes its way from the kitchen to a tray in the display case.

The aroma is irresistible and intoxicating and gently teases the senses.

A young mother enters with her three-year-old daughter, Evelyn, who immediately makes a beeline to the display case filled with colorful cookies and pastries and, with the willfulness and determination only a toddler possesses, plants her face against the case to get a closer look at the cupcake with rainbow sprinkles on top.

To the girl's delight, Smith hands her the confection, and minutes later Evelyn's face and fingers are covered in pink icing. The imprint of her little face on the display case—a smudged outline of a tiny nose and lips—makes Smith smile broadly.

As Smith started making soup for the anticipated lunch crowd, the diminutive brunette was sporting a white apron with LEGALLY SWEET embroidered across the front, the name of her shop and a hat tip to her thirty-plus years at the Ashtabula County Sheriff's Office.

She started working as a cook in the sheriff's department when the youngest of her three children was five years old. It was the same job her mother had.

But Smith wanted more.

So she went back to school for criminal law while she worked as a cook in the courthouse. She then moved over to dispatch and up through the ranks in the sheriff's department until she made deputy, all the while raising her three children with her husband, an electrician for Millennium Inorganic Chemicals—one of the last big blue-collar employers in the once-mighty manufacturing county of Ashtabula, wedged between the shore of Lake Erie and the Pennsylvania state line, northeast of Cleveland.

Smith was raised a Democrat, her parents were Democrats, she is married to a Democrat, and she worked for elected Democratic sheriffs in a county that had not voted a Republican into local office for as long as anyone you find can remember.

Until 2016, that is, when Ashtabula picked Donald Trump over Hillary Clinton and swept in a local ticket of Republicans underneath him.

Bonnie Smith was one of the unlikely participants in that unforeseen realignment that happened across the Great Lakes region in hundreds of communities like Ashtabula County, flipping Michigan, Wisconsin, Pennsylvania, Ohio, and Iowa into the Republican side of the electoral college after serving as what journalist Ron Brownstein dubbed the reliable industrial Democratic "Blue Wall" for decades.[1]

How Democratic was Smith, and how recently? In March 2016, she voted for Bernie Sanders over Hillary Clinton in the Ohio primary contest. Voting Republican wasn't even on the table for her, until suddenly it was, just a few months later.

"I am not sure what happened, but I started to look around me, and my town and my county, and I thought, 'You know what? I am just not in the mood anymore to just show up and vote for who my party tells me I have to vote for,'" she says.

She was not alone. Ashtabula County had given its votes to John Kerry, Al Gore, Bill Clinton, and Michael Dukakis. It gave Barack Obama a 55 percent majority share of its vote twice—before turning 180 degrees to prefer Trump over Hillary Clinton by a margin of 57 percent to 38 percent, a 31-point swing from one election to the next.

At first look, the numerical magnitude of Ashtabula's swing, in a nation presumed frozen in partisan polarization, is what seems notable. At second look, the remarkable aspect is just how common that kind of change was in 2016 in the states that make up the Rust Belt.

Thirty-five counties in Ohio, long the nation's premier presidential bellwether, swung 25 or more points from 2012 to 2016. Twenty-three counties in Wisconsin, thirty-two counties in Iowa, and twelve counties in Michigan switched from Obama to Trump in the space of four years.

With few exceptions, these places are locales where most of America's decision makers and opinion leaders have never been. Trump only carried 3 of the nation's 44 "mega counties," places with more than one million in population, and only 41 of the country's 129 "extra large" counties with more than 400,000 but less than one million. Those 173 sizable counties are home to 54 percent of the U.S. population, and in 135 of them Trump even lagged behind the net margin performance of losing 2012 GOP nominee Mitt Romney. Trump crawled out of that mathematical hole in the all-but-forgotten communities—thousands of them.

It took a lot of Bonnie Smiths, in a lot of places like Ashtabula County, to wreck political expectations—and if their political behavior in 2016 becomes an affiliation and not a dalliance, they have the potential to realign the American political construct and perhaps the country's commercial and cultural presumptions as well.

For Smith, who lives with her husband, George, on a working

farm in nearby Saybrook, the political tipping point—even more than the job losses and the decay of the area—was a result of her faith and her growing disconnect on cultural issues from the candidates she had previously supported.

"I had looked the other way for far too long, had accepted that I was supposed to be more modern in my views when I wasn't comfortable with the views my party started to take," Smith says, making clear that this was a difficult decision to have made and to discuss publicly. "And I took a stand for myself, my beliefs, for life, and for my country."

She says she also took a stand for her community: "All of this decay has happened under their [the Democrats'] watch."

The shopping district where Legally Sweet sits is struggling; a Family Dollar store is around the corner, and the majestic Ashtabula County courthouse, where she worked for years, is across the street. Shuttered businesses dot both sides of the street.

"The town closes up about three o'clock on the weekdays and, like, one o'clock on Saturday. There's nothing here. The people come in and . . . you're making it but you're not. You know? You've got enough to skimp by for the next day, but that's it," she says.

The statistics on the area's own economic development website paint a picture of an Ashtabula County stuck in transition and trying to creatively reinvent itself to get out of the Great Recession, from which the wealthier America on the East and West coasts recovered years ago. As of May 2016, the local economic partnership wrote that the county's employed workforce level was still stuck under 42,000 people—nearly the same figure as at the bottom of the national recession in 2010, a fall from 46,000 in its pre-recession high.[2] Nationally, the number of employed Americans had bounced back to pre-recession levels by 2014.[3]

The physical reality of the county's industrial footprint tells the same story. Empty, idle, hulking coal-fired power plants line the lakeshore, and the docks that once attracted waves of Italian and Scandinavian immigrants to unload coal and iron ore now see little activity. The county's population, according to the Census Bureau's 2016 estimates, is 98,231, almost exactly what it was after the 1970 census, a span that saw the country as a whole grow by 59 percent.[4]

A Democrat for decades, Smith didn't quite know what to expect when she went home one day and told George she was thinking about supporting Trump. He told her he was already there. "So there was that," she says, laughing.

———

America's political experts, from party leaders to political science professors to journalists to pundits, did not expect the Smiths, or enough people like them, to vote for Donald Trump. Virtually every political and media expert missed the potential of Donald Trump because they based their electoral calculus on assumptions that they hadn't bothered to check since the last presidential election. To recognize the potential of the Trump coalition, analysts would have had to visit places they had stopped visiting and listen to people they had stopped listening to.

"I am kind of that voter that was hiding in plain sight that no one saw coming. I was right here all along. I've seen the job losses here, the rise in crime, the meth and heroin problem, society essentially losing hope; something just gave in with me," Bonnie Smith says.

The political experts called the 2016 election wrong—not because they took too few polls or studied too many census trends, but because they assumed American elections were immune to the same changes wreaking havoc in every other part of American society.

Amazon is in the process of destroying Walmart and what is left of Main Street at the same time. Streaming services such as Netflix and YouTube are fragmenting and democratizing the creation and delivery of video entertainment. Person-to-person payment systems like PayPal and Venmo, and crowd-sourced funding communities like GoFundMe and Kickstarter, are reshaping the movement of private capital. In virtually every sphere of American society, institutional loyalty and expert filtering are being discarded in favor of direct communication and deliberate silo-ing. Similarly, Donald Trump's electoral coalition is smashing both American political parties and the previously impenetrable political news media, often in spite of Trump himself.

In the wake of the 2016 election surprise, the political experts have continued to blow it—looking to predict the coming demise of the president without pausing to consider the durability of the trends and winds that swept him into office. Even if Netflix disappears, traditional cable providers will never have the monopolistic hold on viewers they did twenty years ago. Similarly, after Trump, traditional political parties will not have the same sway with voters they've had for past election cycles.

The history of the American electorate is not a litany of flukes; instead it is a cycle of tectonic plate–grinding, punctuated by a landscape-altering earthquake every generation or so. This movement is not dissimilar to that of any other American consumer category; it should come as no surprise that electoral choices float and change in the same manner as other voluntary behaviors in the most open and dynamic market in the world.

Analysts of consumer-product marketing make a distinction between category killers and category builders. Disruptive brands that merely reorient a single category are category killers: think Miller Lite beer, or diet soda. Meanwhile, products that are category builders do more, starting an entirely new marketplace: think Federal Express or Apple's iPad.

Political analysts across the spectrum have given Trump credit for being a category killer, reshaping Republican politics in his image. But the characteristics of his rise and the unique new coalition he fused in the Rust Belt argue that he should be viewed as a category builder, the first success of a coalition that is not likely to soon separate.

Employing direct marketing to the consumer instead of relying on referrals is a hallmark of category builders. Trump's favored message delivery mechanisms—Twitter, dominance of cable news even when it required self-stoked controversy, and television-friendly rallies—not only cut against the normal practices of the professional campaign industry, they enabled him to outflank, and simultaneously own, his critics in the news media as well. Trump used the red-hot scrutiny of journalists to polarize and galvanize a plurality of voters in primary after primary, and then in the general election's key battlegrounds.

Attacking all existing brands with equal ease and success is another trait of category builders. Trump drove a wedge between voters and the existing brands simultaneously, making the case that both parties were incapable of delivering his attributes. Trump's campaign was arguably the least partisan in recent memory, because from the start he aimed his fire at both political trenches. By Election Day, Trump had vanquished not only the stale institutional hierarchy of the Democratic and Republican parties, exemplified perfectly by the gasping legacy brands of Jeb Bush and Hillary Clinton, but the entire national press corps as well.[5]

In his first campaign announcement speech in the lobby of Trump Tower in June 2016, Trump said: "I've watched the politicians. . . . They will never make America great again. They don't even have a chance. They're controlled fully—they're controlled fully by the lobbyists, by the donors, and by the special interests, fully."[6] Trump, previewing his stamina for a slashing campaign that would leave him with few elected allies, said, "This is going to be an election that's based on competence, because people are tired of these nice people. And they're tired of being ripped off by everybody in the world."

Trump bore out his differentiation on the primary campaign trail for a year through Iowa, New Hampshire, South Carolina, and subsequent primaries, even creating a months-long melodrama around the prospect that he might mount a third-party bid if his effort at the GOP nomination was thwarted. Trump deftly used Republican elites, exemplified by the well-off and well-connected backers of Jeb Bush and Mitt Romney, as foils, even daring to attack the donor-heavy, in-person audiences sitting just feet from him at the GOP's primary debates. What struck many as thin-skinned rants turned out to be brand-building, proving to Trump's most loyal followers that he was a different kind of Republican, one that wasn't much of a Republican at all.

For nearly a century, American politics has put the New Deal coalition of government takers on one side, opposed by the fusion of affluence and evangelicalism of the modern Republican Party. The coalition that elected Donald Trump—and the one that opposed him—fit neither of those blueprints.

James Carville, the architect of the first Clinton campaign in 1992, famously said that after five Republican victories in the prior six presidential elections, he and the Clinton team engineering what was then a novel Democratic victory "didn't find the key to the electoral lock here. We just picked it."[7]

The question of whether Trump's unconventional bid merely picked the lock of a different era of Republican politics or whether his new fusion of populism with conservatism is a remaking of the American political axis entirely, is a central question of this book.

———

Any discussion of the populist-conservative Trump coalition has to start with crude demography, because that winning coalition of voters was not one anyone in politics considered to be a possibility.

In the wake of two crushing Republican presidential defeats, the mantra that "More White Votes Alone Won't Save the GOP"[8] was an article of faith (and the headline of a 2013 piece in *The Wall Street Journal* by uber-strategist Karl Rove). The Republican National Committee's postmortem of Mitt Romney's loss to Barack Obama in 2012 concluded the same thing in many more pages of copy, bathed in census information. "The nation's demographic changes add to the urgency of recognizing how precarious our position has become," wrote the authors of the widely cited report.[9]

Even neutral pundits such as *The Cook Political Report*'s Dave Wasserman postulated that "it's no wonder that some pundits have suggested Democrats have an emerging 'stranglehold on the Electoral College.' "[10]

Democratic strategists echoed this theory, and it underpinned every strategic decision they made. Fresh off their second consecutive presidential victory by a wide margin with Barack Obama carrying their banner, Democratic campaign pros were confident of their new enduring majority. Veteran journalist Ron Brownstein of *The Atlantic* dubbed this new amalgam of fast-growing demographic groups such as Latinos, socially liberal young voters, energized African American voters, and left-leaning women as the "coalition of the ascendant," and the moniker stuck.[11]

In 2015, the liberal think tank Center for American Progress wrote a de facto obituary of the GOP. "For years Republicans could rely on white voters—and, in particular, working-class whites—to constitute a decisive proportion of the electorate and deliver victory. This is no longer the case."[12]

It was a mantra Republican mega-donors, suffering with post-traumatic stress syndrome from Romney's loss, were eager to advance. They pushed freshman senator Marco Rubio's proposal to reform immigration laws and create a pathway to legality for the more than ten million illegal immigrants in the United States. They backed RNC chairman Reince Priebus's remaking of the party's staff structure around the concept of year-round field-staff outreach to minority communities, instead of saving up dollars for advertising in the last weeks of the election season. This article of faith quickly spawned an order of clergy, the political operatives who enforced discipline around the post-Romney takeaway: the only possible winning future Republican coalition must, by dint of math, become less white, less old, less rural, and more educated.

But quietly, many conservative data nerds began to analyze exit polling data from the 2012 election and drew a different conclusion. They saw signs that Romney had not fully exercised his own voting base on Election Day. One of the first among these analysts was Sean Trende, who writes for the popular polling aggregation website RealClearPolitics .com. Just days after the election, Trende calculated that the Romney-Obama election might have included fewer than 91 million white voters, down from the 98 million who had participated just four years before, while African American and Hispanic raw voter numbers increased slightly. The Democrats' insistence on the inevitable rising power of minority voters was premature, according to Trende, and not an explanation for Romney's loss. "In other words, the reason this electorate looked so different from the 2008 electorate is almost entirely attributable to white voters staying home," Trende wrote.[13]

Notably, Trende did not hail from, or work for, the Republican Party's committee-based power structure in Washington, freeing him to suggest that Romney, beloved in the inner sanctums of professional GOP politics, had failed, rather than been failed by, the electorate available to him.

Trende, and those who furthered his analysis, were widely derided by Official Washington.

Romney's strategists, including veteran adman Stuart Stevens, regularly shot back at theories like Trende's, saying, "The myth survives that there are these masses of untapped white voters just waiting for the right candidates."[14]

But at least one person in the political pantheon of the country was listening: Donald Trump.

From the start of his campaign, Trump crafted an issues matrix that was as far from Romney's as one could be and still fit nominally under the Republican tent. The capitalist free-trade consensus that Romney, Clinton, and every Bush on the national scene had endorsed was ridiculed by Trump, even in his announcement speech.

"The problem with free trade is you need really talented people to negotiate for you. . . . Free trade can be wonderful if you have smart people, but we have people that are stupid," Trump said in his announcement speech. "We have people that aren't smart. And we have people controlled by special interests."[15]

Attacking trade and multinational agreements was at the core of Trump's campaign—and a linchpin for his antiestablishment coalition—from the start. Trump assailed U.S. agreements with China just minutes after he descended the escalator for his debut as a candidate, in the second paragraph of his announcement speech, saying, "We used to have victories, but we don't have them. When was the last time anybody saw us beating, let's say, China in a trade deal? They kill us."[16]

And he segued seamlessly into his second primary angle on the topic, and one more suited to the Republican primary audience, illegal immigration. "When do we beat Mexico at the border?" Trump asked. "They're laughing at us, at our stupidity. And now they are beating us economically. They are not our friend, believe me. But they're killing us economically. The U.S. has become a dumping ground for everyone else's problems."[17]

Trump's nationalist argument was economically pragmatic from the start, devoid of the ideological language of the trench warfare that had stalemated presidential politics for the preceding thirty-five years. Treated as a gadfly when he dropped into the race, the uniqueness of Trump's opening argument was largely unnoticed. Since the Reagan era, virtually every Republican presidential aspirant until Trump had made arguments with a coherent libertarian anti-government ideology at its core, the intellectual heirs to failed 1964 nominee Barry Goldwater, waging war on behalf of the international private sector against the creep of socialistic government. Republicanism itself became consumed with the "big government versus small government" argument. Trump's premise rested on a different axis and picked different battles.

Trump's announcement speech spanned 6,342 words, and not one of them was "conservative" or "liberal." But the speech was not devoid of issues. Saving a few odd rambles into commentary on his personal wealth and his business trophies, Trump homed in on the themes that would animate his seventeen-month campaign: infrastructure spending, immigration reform and a wall on the southern border, protection of Medicare and Social Security benefits, a proactive and ruthless approach to the Islamic State terrorists, an unyielding support for Second Amendment gun rights, and a pledge to use the White House's bully pulpit to shame American corporations into on-shoring future manufacturing jobs.

Trump's populism found an immediate positive reception in both curmudgeonly New Hampshire and the antiestablishment South, setting him up for key early primary victories, overpowering the conservative appeals of his rivals. And more than just setting the pace in the primary phase, Trump gained a foothold with the same rural and industrial voters in economically challenged Rust Belt states who had either stuck with Obama in 2012 or stayed at home.

These voters represented the last, and most overlooked, clause in Brownstein's description of the coalition of the ascendant. The subhead of Brownstein's dispatch coining the moniker in November 2012 said: "A combination of the young, minorities, and women joined with just enough blue-collar Midwestern whites to put the president over the top."[18]

Without Trump's victories over a crowded field in New Hampshire and South Carolina, he likely never would have been able to overcome the mass of elite donors aligned against him. And without the twin sympathetic platforms of Twitter and live rally speeches on Fox News, which spoke directly to the non-Republican voters in forgotten small and midsized communities in rural Pennsylvania,

Ohio, Michigan, Wisconsin, and Iowa, he certainly never would have won the general election.

Trump's candidacy would not only defy conventional labeling; the coalition it attracted would be forged on an entirely new axis, welding together the conservative bloc that had become almost chemically opposed to Hillary Clinton with an emerging populist cohort that voted based on its assessment of its own economic and cultural condition, when it bothered to vote at all.

A few observers in the center-left press toyed with the mathematical possibilities presented by Trump's appeal, but ultimately could not project its efficacy.

Data-loving columnist Nate Cohn of *The New York Times* wrote, presciently, in the summer of 2016, "Whatever you think of Donald J. Trump, it is clear that this election has the potential to reshape the allegiances of many white working-class voters who have traditionally sided with the Democrats and many well-educated voters who have sided with the Republicans. . . . The potential for him to break through among white working-class voters isn't merely theoretical. . . . There are more white working-class voters than is generally believed, and Mr. Obama was stronger among these voters than typically assumed."[19]

But by November, Cohn had talked himself out of the radically correct projection of the Trump coalition that he had made five months before. On election morning, Cohn's team of data modelers at the *Times* gave Clinton an 85 percent shot to win the election, and Trump only an 11 percent chance to win Pennsylvania, a 7 percent chance to win Wisconsin, and a 6 percent chance to win Michigan.[20]

The architecture of this new coalition, essentially a realignment, was made possible by technological changes that Trump was the first to fully exploit. The Internet, and the rise of social media's prominence in reporting, has made the national landscape of journalism both more fragmented and more pack-oriented at the same time. The rise of Twitter and other aggregators, such as DrudgeReport.com, have empowered consumers to pick and choose not just their favorite news outlets but favorite individual reporters and commentators. The prevalence of aggregators and the ubiquity of Twitter use among writers and editors have created a national virtual newsroom, simultaneously giving every journalist an instant feedback loop on the stories their competitors are chasing, incentivizing them to do the same.

Trump's preference for making his newsworthy—and often outlandish and almost always candid—statements via his Twitter account enabled him both to speak directly to his audience and to command the full attention, and agenda, of the press corps. That dominance of the spotlight, even when the spotlight turned negative, was a crucial component of Trump's primary victory in a crowded field subject to a ruthlessly low campaign donation limit of $2,700 per person. If every candidate's ability to advertise is limited artificially by legal donation caps, then the candidate with the most free media attention, however harsh it might be, has an advantage. Trump's ability to go around the filter of analysts was even more critical because his coalition was novel.

Had Trump's candidacy arisen in an earlier era, with just three networks and two wire services dominating and imposing a rigorous traditional filter on information reaching the consumer, his paradigm-bursting message might never have gotten through to its intended audience.

But in the age of the smartphone, Trump's audience could not only find him, and recirculate his content to their peers on Twitter and Facebook; it could organically grow large enough to fuel the ratings success that made him a dominant presence on the cable news shows throughout the Republican primary process, starving a dozen major GOP candidates of any spotlight at all.

Even voices in the proud *New York Times* newsroom now cede that Facebook, not the Old Gray Lady itself, now drives the national conversation with the horsepower of its search traffic and algorithms providing traditional media its best chance to be seen. "Measured by web traffic, ad revenue and influence over the way the rest of the media makes money, Facebook has grown into the most powerful force in the news industry," wrote *Times* media columnist Farhad Manjoo in the heat of the 2016 campaign.[21]

By the midway point of the GOP nomination process in March 2016, when Trump had romped through the early primaries to become the clear front-runner, the analytics firm mediaQuant and

The New York Times calculated that Trump had earned $1.9 billion dollars' worth of exposure on news programs, nearly triple the amount Hillary Clinton had received to that point and six times the amount of his closest Republican rival, Senator Ted Cruz, or Democratic challenger Senator Bernie Sanders.[22]

Trump got booked onto cable news shows because he was good for ratings—driving eyeballs to morning gabfests like *Fox & Friends* and MSNBC's *Morning Joe,* and evening staples like Fox's *Hannity.* Conservative commentators and hosts who bucked Trump saw their ratings drop, while those who gave him an audience saw their ratings soar.[23]

Trump deliberately used this muscle of his loyal audience to incentivize more favorable coverage for his campaign, punishing hosts and outlets critical of him and rewarding those who gave him free rein. An extended spat between the candidate and Fox News Channel's Megyn Kelly, in which Trump hurled what most observers saw as crude, thinly veiled sexist slurs at the prime-time host after her questions during the first GOP primary debate, in August 2015, led to a temporary Trump boycott of the entire network.

When Fox's brass caved in the standoff and subtly picked a newsmaker over its own on-air talent, Trump returned to its airwaves and brought his ratings back with him.[24] Trump dominated the pregame and postgame coverage of the Republican debates, which drew ratings previously unseen in nomination contests. Trump even dominated coverage of the two debates he skipped, including one in the week before the first nomination votes were cast in the Iowa caucus.[25]

As Trump's star and his TV ratings rose in the Republican nomination process, he drew the fire of the party's intelligentsia, mostly expressed in the print media.

Magazines such as *The Weekly Standard* and *National Review,* long house organs of the ideological Right, devoted entire issues to making the case against Trump's ideological apostasy.

With the Iowa caucuses and the onset of the actual nomination process less than two weeks away in late January 2016, the editors of *National Review* pleaded with American conservatives to reject Trump and his hybrid message of populism fused to rhetoric that appealed in tone, if not in substance, to the rebellious conservative heart. "Donald Trump is a menace to American conservatism who would take the work of generations and trample it underfoot in behalf of a populism as heedless and crude as the Donald himself," wrote the magazine's editors.[26]

The Weekly Standard's founding editor, Bill Kristol, an influential Republican thinker for decades since his days on the staff of Vice President Dan Quayle, remained a Trump critic from the earliest primaries throughout the fall election, penning articles with titles ranging from "Donald J. Obama" (as Trump was sewing up the nomination in April) to "Dump Trump Now More than Ever" (a month before the general election).[27]

Kristol's last pre-election piece, on the eve of voting in November, titled "A Populist-Nationalist Right? No Thanks!," pointed squarely at Trump's realigning of the consensus on the American political Right. Kristol's rational laments pointed not only to the lack of ideological coherence of his party's nominee, but to an angst that perhaps the voters among the electoral coalition of the Right were suddenly more interested in triumph than tribe.

The pleas of the Washington conservative salons urging the base to eschew Trump's often crudely expressed ideological apostasy leapt from the theoretical to the pragmatic in the final month of the campaign.

On a Friday night in early October 2016, *The Washington Post* released a video recording of a lewd behind-the-scenes conversation between Trump and television host Billy Bush in which Trump talked obscenely of grabbing women by the genitals.

The revelations, and the nonstop media frenzy they triggered, pushed many Republican leaders who had reluctantly held on to their party's unconventional nominee to finally let go of the rope—from dozens of congressmen to the chair of the Republican Governors Association, Governor Bill Haslam (R-TN), to 2008 presidential nominee Senator John McCain (R-AZ), to embattled rising stars Senator Kelly Ayotte (R-NH) and Representative Joe Heck (R-NV), with McCain, Ayotte, and Heck engaged in difficult Senate campaigns.[28]

The fallout from the tape brought prominent conservative women who had thus far kept silent on Trump to step out in opposition to him, from former secretary of state Condoleezza Rice to popular evangelist Beth Moore, who chastised male Christian leaders still clinging to Trump: "Try to absorb how acceptable the disesteem and objectifying of women has been when some Christian leaders don't think it's that big a deal," Beth Moore said, joined by Dr. Russell Moore, the leading political voice of the nation's largest Protestant denomination, the Southern Baptist Convention, who announced he could support neither Trump nor Clinton.[29] Russell Moore chastised Protestant evangelical leaders who stuck with Trump: "Convictional evangelicals who are pro-life and pro-family know Hillary Clinton is not with us and we cannot go that way but that doesn't mean we have to follow another way that is reckless and horrible. . . . Many of the people who for years have warned us about situational ethics and moral relativism are now asking us to practice it."[30]

Pollsters on both sides of the political aisle predicted a record low performance for Trump in the looming election among women, the college-educated, and the religiously pious, hollowing out any potential Republican majority and imperiling down-ballot candidates as well. Journalist Ron Brownstein summed up the angst of Republican handicappers in a column released the weekend the scandal broke, titled "How Trump Could Become a 'Political Black Hole' for the GOP," delineating a consensus fear among party strategists that Trump might not only go down, but take scores of other Republican candidates with him.[31]

But when the votes were counted it was not Trump who was a black hole for Republicans, but rather opposition to Trump.

Heck, who before his renunciation of Trump held a small but steady lead in his Senate race in Nevada, wound up losing by a slightly wider margin than Trump lost Nevada to Clinton. Ayotte was similarly unable to separate from Trump, losing by just over 100 votes in New Hampshire, a state Trump lost by 3,000 out of 700,000 cast.[32]

Trump's coalition on Election Day obliterated the article of faith among experts in both parties that a Republican could not win largely on the strength of his margins among white voters.

It is possible that no other candidate in the 2016 Republican field could have assembled that coalition, precisely because too many of the party's thinkers and donors were wedded to the inaccurate, quasi-religious belief that the GOP's existing demographic base could not stretch far enough to encompass a winning coalition in 2016. The Trump campaign, devoid of any donors in its earliest stages and including few of the party's Washington-based strategists, was untethered to the totems that constrained the Romney and McCain campaigns—a blind fear of expressing skepticism about trade deals, an unwillingness to take an edgy approach to border security, and an inability to use the unpolished language that could inspire confidence in the GOP's most unreliable and skeptical voters.

Trump's candidacy proved that a radical reshaping of the axis of decision-making, from one of ideology to one fusing aspiration with agitation, could build a governing majority in the electoral college—something short of a national majority or even a plurality, but more than enough in both traditional swing states like Ohio and Florida, and the "Blue Wall" of Democrat-dominated states in the Great Lakes region.

In assembling his new Republican margin in the critical Rust Belt states carried by Obama—Pennsylvania, Ohio, Michigan, Iowa, and Wisconsin—Trump built a robust new voter base that included the ideological secular Republican conservatives that Kristol and the editors of *National Review* sought to dissuade, far more evangelicals than Russell Moore hoped for, and millions more women and college-educated men than pollsters predicted.

In this book, we will explore seven archetypes of the most surprising voters who make up Trump's coalition—voters who broke ranks to back Trump and voters who by all expectations should have broken ranks to desert him, based on the course the campaign took.

We will focus on the voters that Trump's novel argument—coinciding with the decade-long leftward cultural drift of the Democrats—brought into the Republican fold, and those who stuck with him when their demographics indicated they might not. Some stayed with Trump, or were attracted to him, because of his platform, others because of their opposition to Hillary Clinton, others because of his polarizing style.

The specific voters who exemplify these seven archetypes of the Trump coalition and are profiled here were discovered in ten pivotal counties in the five Great Lakes states that tipped the electoral college to Donald Trump: Pennsylvania, Ohio, Michigan, Wisconsin, and Iowa. All ten of these counties had been in President Barack Obama's column in 2012, and most of them gave Trump a larger margin than any other Republican in this era.

From farm counties in Iowa and Wisconsin, to the suburbs of Detroit, to fading industrial centers on the shores of Lake Erie and the Mississippi, we spent time in diners, watering holes, bed-and-breakfasts, and coffee shops, finding Trump voters where they live and work. We avoided interstates and chain restaurants, looking for the places that make these communities authentic so we could better trace the journey of the voters who shook the American political system.

Our reporting was supported by empirical data analysis and survey research. The Great Revolt Survey was conducted exclusively for this book. The survey was fielded by the respected Republican opinion research firm OnMessage Inc. in August 2017, among a group of 2,000 self-reporting 2016 Trump voters, with 400 each coming from Ohio, Pennsylvania, Michigan, Iowa, and Wisconsin.

Some of these archetypes fit the familiar portraits of lower-income whites painted by journalists routinely since the election, but far more are hidden in plain sight and emblematic of wide swaths of voters whom analysts least expected to find in Trump's column.

To understand the potential staying power of this new populist-conservative coalition, and to decide if its marginal elements are likely to ever return to voting Democratic in future elections, one must walk with these voters, in their own places and within the imperfect textures of their angst and aspirations.

This is the story of the people behind the electoral earthquake.

2

Red-Blooded and Blue-Collared

The postmortems from the 2016 campaign painted a simple picture of the coalition that elected Donald Trump—it was economically distressed, uneducated, and angry. CNN host Fareed Zakaria wrote that Trump won by "speaking openly to people's economic anxieties, cultural fears, and class rebellion," naming specifically "those Americans who feel frustrated, anxious, angry—even desperate."[1]

A headline in *The New York Times* a month after the election blared, "Where Were Trump's Votes? Where the Jobs Weren't."[2] The *Chicago Tribune*'s headline barked: "How Trump Won the Presidential Election: Revenge of the Working-Class Whites." The author of that piece, Jim Tankersley, accurately linked exit polls showing that Trump had won whites without a college degree by 39 points, according to exit polls, far outdistancing Mitt Romney's margin of 25 points. "They were the foundation of his victories across the Rust Belt, including a blowout win in Ohio and stunning upsets in Pennsylvania and Wisconsin." Tankersley called it "a rejection of the business-friendly policies favored at various points by elites in both parties" and a "raw outburst at the trends of rising inequality and economic dislocation."[3]

Most of these postmortems summoned edgy words to assign emotional impulsiveness to the motives of Trump's voters. They were painted as an angry mob that either was incapable of making a reasoned decision between Clinton and Trump, or one that willingly acted out of rage. Their economic status was said to be hopeless and their outlook angrily pessimistic. The pundits got that motivation and attitude wrong.

The Great Revolt Survey of Rust Belt Trump voters conducted for this book reveals a more complicated picture. It defines the Red-Blooded and Blue-Collared archetype as a Trump voter who had worked a blue-collar, hourly wage, or physical-labor job after the age of twenty-one, and had experienced a job loss in the last seven years either personally or in their immediate families. Among this group, a full 84 percent were actually optimistic about their own future career path or financial situation, regardless of how they felt about their community's prospects as a whole.

This inherent optimism about their personal situation, paired with concern about the community's economic status, is a nuance missed by many analysts—and one that perfectly matched Trump's optimistic and forward-looking slogan, "Make America Great Again."

Voters in this archetype ranked Trump's promise to bring back manufacturing jobs as more important than his promises to protect safety-net programs or his pledges to build a wall on the Mexican border or put conservative judges on the Supreme Court.

Like the rest of the Trump coalition, they took a decidedly skeptical view of multilateral international agreements, reflecting a full reorientation of the partisan approach to globalism over the last decade. Eighty-five percent of Red-Blooded and Blue-Collared voters agreed that "the United States should make our own decisions on major issues and challenge other nations to follow our example" instead of "the United States should follow the example of European nations on major issues and cooperate fully in multi-national organizations like the United Nations."

Similarly, this group of voters is at the vanguard of the new Republican orientation of hostility toward large corporations—with 79 percent agreeing that "large corporations don't care if the decisions they make hurt working people." Mirroring the Trump pool as a whole, almost everyone in this archetype, 83 percent, believes Trump "stands up for working people against powerful corporate interests."

Ideologically, it's a conservative group of voters—with 61 percent self-identifying as conservative—but not quite as conservative as Trump's coalition overall. It's slightly less educated than Trump's total voter base and has a lower reported income. Fully half of this group reports that they know someone personally who has battled drug addiction.

Trump's appeal to this group has been thoroughly examined in other realms, but understanding where these voters' electoral journeys might take them next is the goal of this chapter.

Ed Harry

Wilkes-Barre, Luzerne County, Pennsylvania

Within moments of meeting Ed Harry, you understand he is the kind of guy you want on your side.

His impression is blunt and immediate; you also understand that if he were to become an adversary, he would be a relentless opponent.

Harry sits in the last booth of D's Diner, a Plains Township eatery just over the border of Wilkes-Barre's city limits. He is leaning against the tiled wall facing the dining room and the broad rectangular windows that look out onto the parking lot; white eyelet lace curtains and red-white-and-blue stars in the windows add to the charm of the diner.

Up front, the place is filled with customers at a chrome lunch counter as waitresses busily fill coffee cups, take orders, and greet regulars with a warm hello and the universal diner question that implies familiarity: "The usual?"

"The usual" repeatedly is, of course, the answer.

A double-layered white cake with whipped white icing and toasted coconut sits on the counter covered in a glass cake dome. It is 7:30 in the morning and already two pieces have been served.

For twenty-nine years D's Diner had been Eddie's Place; when the owner fell ill in late 2016, it closed. But unlike most businesses that close in this county, this one reopened with a new owner and a remodel.

But the menu, the hospitality, and the servers remained, as did the loyal customers. The waitress explains there is a line to get a seat at the counter or in a booth on most days; that was certainly the case on this day.

Outside on Fox Hill Road, some businesses are gone or vacated; there is a Ford dealership, a pet cemetery, and a spattering of homes.

Overlooking the diner on a hillside less than half a mile away is Pennsylvania's first casino, the Mohegan Sun Pocono.

For generations the Wyoming Valley—where Luzerne sits along the banks of the mighty Susquehanna River—has been the home of the quintessential blue-collar worker, the sons and daughters of the sons and daughters of immigrant coal miners and factory hands.

Today, Luzerne County is one of the sweet spots for finding the kind of Trump voter who has received the most public attention—the Red-Blooded and Blue-Collared voter.

Harry, like so many others in Pennsylvania with a lifetime of loyalty to the Democrats now disrupted by globalism and Donald Trump, fits the bill—and he's quick to spot others who do too.

On this day, seven men under the age of thirty, dressed in utility uniforms and hard hats, take seats across from Harry in an oversized booth. They squeeze a chair in on the end. He nods and smiles; they nod and smile.

"You see all of those young men," he says, loud enough for them to hear, "they probably all voted for Trump. They were all Democrats and they all voted for Trump," Harry says.

Harry orders the ham-and-cheese omelet with white toast; he doesn't notice that they heard him.

As Harry makes his way toward the restroom, one of the young men grins sheepishly, leans over, and says, "Shhhhhhhh, you know we can't talk politics when we have our company uniforms on," pauses, and then pulls out the familiar red MAKE AMERICA GREAT AGAIN ball cap from his back pocket.

His friends laugh, as he hurriedly stuffs the ball cap safely back into its hiding place.

For most of his life, Harry was a Democrat. He still is. "I wasn't just a guy who voted straight Democrat up and down the ballot, it was religion to me, it was my identity, and it was also an essential part of my job," he says.

Harry's father worked the coal mines here in Luzerne County for thirty-three years, as did his father before him and his father before that, four generations to be exact, part of the great Welsh migration that came to this part of the country in the mid-nineteenth century.

When Harry was a senior in high school, his father almost died in a mining accident. "I don't know how he didn't die, but his belt got caught on his buddy's there in a shaft hanging from a sixty-degree angle. At that time, he weighed like 260 pounds, so my dad's weight brought him against the side of the shaft, saved his life," Harry says.

"He came home and walked in the house when he wasn't supposed to be there. He was working the afternoons, so I wouldn't expect him home until after eleven. He was there like seven, seven-thirty. I'm doing homework. He comes in and gets a glass and fills it up with whiskey and drinks it straight down, which was quite unusual since he normally drank beer. He filled another glass up and drank half of it and then sat down and started crying.

"First time I ever saw my dad cry, and he told me what happened. His biggest concern was, 'How am I going to support my family now, when I can't go back in the mines because I'm afraid?' "

His father eventually took a Republican patronage job at the Pennsylvania Department of Transportation (PennDOT). His son called that moment the time his father "sold his soul."

Harry's mother was first-generation American, and his maternal grandfather was Russian: "He worked on the railroads, spoke broken English up until the day he died," he explains.

After high school, Harry went to college "mostly to satisfy my parents," but then the Vietnam War got in the way. Harry spent four years in the U.S. Air Force, two years rotating between Thailand and Vietnam and two years working for the NSA.

Harry says his unit's primary function in Southeast Asia was to cancel attack flights. "If the pilots gave out their strike coordinates in the clear and they get canceled, chances are they're going to get shot out of the sky, because the Vietnamese had a very sophisticated communications-intercept system. They knew exactly where they were going to come in.

"I rotated back just after we broke the whole Laotian war. Our commander was given twelve hours to get to the Philippines to tell them how and where we get that information, because it was top, top, top, top secret. When he came back he said that they had every intelligence organization that existed [in] 1968 and '69; from the

White House intelligence to the Defense Department to the CIA, the NSA, all of them there."

In the end, he wound up on a different assignment. "I had been scheduled to go to train the CIA operatives in Laos on how to use the equipment they never used before. Me, a kid from Allentown.

"The funny thing is, when I rotated out, they rotated another kid from Allentown in to do the training. He ended up getting shot, but he survived okay. That's a long time ago," Harry says.

When Harry came home, the experience left him with the ability to do only two things for an entire year. "I went to night school and I drank. I drank a lot."

But college didn't really stick, "and drinking has no good end-game," he says.

So he got a job locally, working for a supermarket service, but lasted only a year before he got laid off. "Then I took a job in a state facility, in a mental institution, as a custodian, and honestly, I loved it."

It was there he discovered his calling: persuasion.

Harry became part of the organizing force during the explosive rise of public-sector unions in the United States in the early 1970s, which was very similar to the previous rise of industrial-based unions during the Great Depression.

Teachers, firefighters, sanitation workers, police officers, as well as secretaries and custodians, beefed up the union membership rolls in record-breaking numbers in the early '70s.

Harry's job was part of an extensive campaign to turn public-sector facilities in Florida into union facilities.

"I would go to mental health centers at five in the morning, stand outside that gate, and pass out notices of a meeting for maybe that night or the next to test the interest of the workers," he says.

Beforehand, he would go in and meet with the management to find out where he should be, or shouldn't be. "Usually nobody showed up in the beginning, so it's a process."

He was there for a six-month assignment that turned out to take two years, ending up at the University of Florida in Gainesville. "I was there to win over the custodians, all the maintenance people, all of the assistants to the deans, etc.

"It turns out I was very good at winning over the trust and

confidence of people. It wasn't an easy job, you know, these guys understand that if the shop they work in doesn't become unionized they might be risking their jobs. But I was taught at a young age your work ethic was your word, and whatever you did in your life you were only as good as your word," he says.

After two years he left Florida and brought his skills to work in his hometown. "My job switched to being someone who did contract negotiations, and I also handled arbitration cases and labor board stuff," he says.

When he returned home he found that his father's patronage job was gone, the Republican governor had termed out of office, and a new Democratic governor, with Democratic patronage hires, was now in charge of PennDOT.

"So I am registered as Democrat, which pissed everybody off; I was sort of disowned. To make a long story short, I ended up helping Dad get a job back with PennDOT because of all the Democratic friends I had. I did not participate in my sister's wedding. I wouldn't be an usher because we had words over politics."

Eventually they made peace.

Politics for him became part of the job; he always voted Democrat; so did his friends. As he rose up in the ranks he became deeply involved in national politics, eventually serving as a delegate at the national convention for Bill Clinton in 1992.

From 1980 until he retired he was in charge of the eight or nine northeastern counties in Pennsylvania for the Democrats. "I coordinated all the phone banks, the door-to-door knocks, anything that was related to any election, from gubernatorial elections, to presidential, to local."

Harry also spent much of his time as a union arbitrator, representing members of his union—a position that earned him their trust, a critical relationship to have to convince voters which candidate for office would have your back.

Harry adjusts his navy blue Penn State ball cap. At seventy, he looks fifteen years younger despite his bushy gray hair; his eyes are dark and piercing, his beard trimmed neatly, his voice deep and commanding. If anyone went to central casting looking for blue-collar union boss type and Harry was in line, he would be the first man picked.

The job eventually started to take its toll.

"I can remember one arbitration case I had, a PennDOT driver, drunk. Didn't think anything of it. I go to the arbitration case, he comes in drunk. In our position, you can't say no to anybody. You have to represent the people—which a lot people thought, 'How could you?' "

He pauses, rubs his deep-set eyes, then continues. "I represented pedophiles, rapists, bookies. I had to. I don't have any other choice. When you are an arbitrator, that is no different than being an attorney. You have to fulfill that requirement. You're taking their money, so you have to defend them; good, bad, and the ugly.

"I've been in the middle of an arbitration case when I find out the evidence that gets presented by the other side and I'm not aware of it, and I should be because my people should be telling me, so I'd call a time-out and say, 'Let's go talk' to the person I am defending.

"And I ask them: 'Did you know about this? Why didn't you tell me? Well, just so you know, we're going back in there and the case is over.' Boom, so I've done that, gone back in and said, 'My apologies for wasting everybody's time.' Then I withdraw my grievance and leave. Because that is the right thing to do."

In 2003, he retired after twenty-five years. "I didn't want to work any longer. I was burned out. I ended up protecting people who shouldn't have been protected. They should have been fired. The whole workforce changed from people who looked forward to going to work, to people who make excuses not to," he says.

Even after his retirement, he served as the president of the Greater Wilkes-Barre Labor Council, serving as the powerful business agent for the American Federation of State, County and Municipal Employees (AFSCME). He was still the face of the labor movement in Luzerne County, he was still the guy who met with the local politicians, negotiated events, helped folks find jobs, and led protests when Washington stopped listening.

But when the establishment Democrats stopped caring about his people, he stopped caring about them.

Harry's fracture from the Democratic Party started with the trade agreements that he says are structured in such a way that they incentivize corporations to base themselves overseas. "Outside of our country they don't have to worry about paying decent benefits, living wages, and providing salaries as a worker moves up the ladder," he says.

"My party, the party that was supposed to be the party of the working guy, the guy I stood up for and worked for all of my career, was no longer part of this new ascending Democratic coalition. Blue-collar America essentially had the door shut in its face," he says.

Traditionally, Luzerne County has been emblematic of the heart and soul of the working-class wing of the Democratic Party. Its residents personified the character traits of the New Dealers; they supported government social programs that served as a safety net for the residents, they were pro-life, pro-gun, they joined unions and churches alike, they were multidenominational but were likely found in someone's pew most Sundays.

Drive through Wilkes-Barre, or Hazelton, or the dozens of coal-patch towns that make up this Wyoming Valley county, and you will see churches of all denominations clustered in every corner. Each one was built to accommodate the wave of immigrants that flooded this region a hundred years ago, and each represented a different ethnic group that established footholds in tight-knit city blocks.

Today, those ethnic churches stand like stone sentinels guarding parishioners who have long been gone; most have closed. In the past decade, dozens of churches have been shuttered, some demolished or left vacant. The once glorious stained-glass windows have been sold or vandalized, their prized artifacts spread to other parishes across the country.

The small groceries, movie houses, diners, taverns, and schools that surrounded them are also gone. Many of the homes are worn away by decay, neglect, or abandonment. When the jobs left, the people left.

This area thrived during the country's first industrial revolution. It is sputtering during the technological revolution. Automation and technology are its enemies.

"Economically, we have been struggling for a generation, probably two; the mills, factories, and coal mines are essentially all closed, the labor unions have weakened, we don't have the members or the power to persuade or punish big corporations if they cut jobs or benefits or threaten to pack up and leave if we don't concede," he says.

Even when the unions did concede, the final humiliation was that those companies left Luzerne County anyway, according to Harry.

When this region was nothing more than a frontier settlement, a new form of coal, anthracite, was found along the riverbanks of the Susquehanna all throughout the valley. But that discovery presented a problem: anthracite was so hard and dense, it could not sustain a fire. Tradesmen could use it for forging, and they did during the Revolutionary War, but little else; and no one had yet figured out how it could be used for commerce. It wasn't until a couple of decades into the nineteenth century, when Judge Jesse Fell invented an iron grate capable of maintaining a fire using anthracite, that the Wyoming Valley found its way into the center of the Industrial Revolution.

That invention changed the course of the Wyoming Valley in the final decades of the nineteenth century; it brought commerce, great wealth, and a massive migration of European immigrants to the county. Coal-patch towns, unincorporated towns, and company towns all sprung up and began to dot the valley at a rapid pace.

The coal brought the canals, the canals brought the railroads, and the railroads brought the rapid transportation of commerce that lured the immigrants, hundreds of thousands of them, including Harry's ancestors.

At the turn of the twentieth century, it is estimated that as many as 100,000 immigrants ended up in the coalfields and coal towns of Luzerne County. The first wave came from Wales and England, like Ed Harry's family; then came the Germans, Poles, Italians, Slovaks, Russians, and Ukrainians. By 1930, immigration had taken Luzerne County to its peak population of 445,109 souls. Today, with only 316,383 people in residence, evidence of the immigrant influence is everywhere, from the architecture to the old ethnic clubs, to the current heritage festivals that dot the county's calendar.[4]

"They were mostly poor people, peasants from the Old Country who came here to make a better life, to become this great thing called 'an American,' and to work. Oh, did they work," says Harry.

One hundred years ago, miners here produced nearly 100 million tons of coal—ten years ago that number had tumbled to 1.7 million tons.[5] But even though for decades coal has had barely an echo of its former impact, the people of Luzerne still identified with the life.

"It was that promise of a better life that became their identity, and that identity has been passed down generation after generation; even if you never stepped in the same coal mine your father or your grandfather did, you still identified as that being part of who you are," he says.

In an irony only nature could produce, the same high-heat geological forces that made Luzerne's coal eons ago ensured it would not cash in on the region's economic boom of the twenty-first century—fracking. The Marcellus Shale formation that has revitalized much of northern Pennsylvania with oil and gas production ends before it reaches the Luzerne County border, along what one prominent geologist called a "line of death."

The same heat that made the coal "cooked out" whatever gas existed in prior millennia.[6] So while counties just north or west move on to a new fossil-fueled economic era, Luzerne must stare at its past.

The enduring self-identity of the mining life is part of the mystery of Luzerne that reporters and pundits and national Democrats missed when calculating who a Luzerne County voter is, according to Harry. They made the same mistake in places like this around the country.

Throughout and after the 2016 campaign, national news outlets were full of derision for this easy-to-spot hard-core type of Trump voter. "Trump owes his victory to the uniformed," screamed a piece in *Foreign Policy* magazine two days after the election, under the un-nuanced headline "Trump Won Because Voters Are Ignorant, Literally."[7] It became formulaic for analysts who did not understand the Trump voter to ascribe their motivations to either economic desperation or a lack of intelligence, or both. "Why are white, uneducated voters willing to vote for Trump? Job unhappiness to be sure, but I would posit that it is also because they have not been adequately educated to understand just how dangerous a President Trump would be to the Constitution," wrote one *Newsweek* pundit.[8]

Those insults say more about their writers than the Luzerne County voters who too many journalists, sitting an easy drive away in their New York bureaus, did not come to meet. The common analytical inaccuracy of describing Trump supporters as unthoughtful rubes is driven as much by the lifestyles of the analysts as the intellect of those analyzed.

Luzerne County might be just 135 miles from the heart of New York City, but it is light-years away from many of America's cultural influencers who live there, and that disconnect made it difficult for most of those analysts to crack the code on the Red-Blooded and Blue-Collared voters.

"They were not able to understand that you didn't have to work in a factory or a coal mine to identify with the sentiments of that worker, it was part of your legacy, your heritage, if you grew up here. So you would see someone who spent their whole life in a factory and a young person who was college-educated and doing okay sharing the same sentiments about how the system needed an overhaul," Harry says.

In 2008, Barack Obama beat Republican nominee Senator John McCain of Arizona by 9 percentage points in this county; he beat Mitt Romney in 2012 by 5 points.

Four years later, Trump crushed former secretary of state Hillary Clinton in Luzerne by a whopping 20-point margin. Not since Ronald Reagan had Luzerne County voted for a Republican for president by *any* margin, much less a runaway. More important, Trump's 26,237-vote edge in Luzerne alone accounted for nearly 60 percent of his margin statewide in the Keystone State.[9] He had similar rock-star status in the Pennsylvania primary in Luzerne County, racking up 77 percent of the local vote over Senator Ted Cruz and Governor John Kasich, compared to 57 percent statewide.

The state and federal governments are the top two employers here now. The third largest is perhaps the best metaphor for the new economy in which Luzerne County struggles to find its place. It's the Internet giant Amazon.com, which has a monstrous fulfillment center in Pittston Township, where the average annual salary for warehouse work is $27,040, well below the standard of living paid by the smokestack jobs it replaced.[10]

"That salary makes it difficult to support a family, people start losing hope, especially people who aren't book-smart but excel at working with their hands. We just don't have room for them anymore," Harry says. "We have cut them out."

Harry saw the rise of discontent years ago. "This did not happen overnight, people just didn't wake up on election night and say, 'I am going to do something different,' " he says.

"And this did not end on election night either. I would argue that the election of Donald Trump wasn't about him, but about those of us who want something more from Washington. Maybe we just wanted to shake things up. Maybe we wanted to send a message. Maybe it was a lot of both," he says.

Unlike the 3,832 Democrats in Luzerne County who changed their party registration to Republican, ostensibly so they could vote in the closed 2016 Republican primary, Harry did not.[11] He didn't formally leave his party at the beginning of the election—but his eye did wander.

At the diner, Harry dusts the crumbs from his white toast off of his deep-navy Penn State sweatshirt and switches from coffee to pop. As the young utility workers at the next table leave, he tips his hat, and they return the gesture.

"I made a promise to myself, four years out, after Obama won his second term, that I would never vote for a Bush or a Clinton. That was absolute. Nothing would ever change that. I thought they were both corrupt," he says of the former Democratic nominee and Jeb Bush, son and brother of a former U.S. president.

"When Trump first announced, I laughed. I just couldn't believe that he even had a chance," he says, but Harry was dead set on someone outside of the establishment so he started to look at the other choices.

"The only other nonpolitician was Dr. Ben Carson. Everybody else, outside of [Kentucky senator] Rand Paul, I didn't really have any use for. Put them in a bag and shake them and they all come out the same."

As the campaign went on he wasn't committed to anybody. "The one I liked the best was Jim Webb," Harry says of the Democratic ex-senator from Virginia and former secretary of the navy, "and I thought he was probably the best candidate out of everybody, but he didn't last except for a couple of months."

The more he listened as the campaign went on, he explains, the better he understood that the Democrats definitely hated Trump, and the Republican establishment hated Trump. All the lobbyists on K Street hated Trump. The Chinese came out against him. India came out against him. Mexico came out against him.

"I figured I must have a candidate, because everybody who's coming out against him are all corrupt, and he's an outsider. So, I said, 'I think I found my candidate,'" says Harry.

Then he made the announcement. "I had decided to go to the rally he held here in Wilkes-Barre and I ran into a local radio reporter who knew me as a Democrat union official. She said, 'What are you doing here?' I said, 'I guess I saw the light. I'm going to support Trump.' She said, 'You want to get interviewed?'"

He told her bluntly, "Actually, I don't care."

During the course of the interview she asked him if he was involved in the labor community in the area.

"I said, 'I just happen to be president of the labor council.' When we got done, I said, 'Well, that should get me a resignation tomorrow.' Sure enough, I got a phone call from them the next day," he says. He voluntarily resigned, and he did it in person, in front of the entire council.

Harry has lost trust in everything big in this country. "Big banks, big Wall Street, big corporations, the establishment of both parties and their lobbyists, and the big media corporations; gone are the days of the network news just delivering the news," he says.

"This Russian shit day-in and day-out is just absolute nonsense, as far as him being in cahoots. I watched ABC last Thursday; the first ten minutes dealt with nothing but the allegations that he was in bed with the Russians. The big storms that hit the Midwest got a minute. Nothing else got any time. It was just all this bullshit."

Harry is optimistic about Trump. "But it is going to be a hard slog, he has to work against the Democrats and the Republicans.

"In his heart I know he wants to do well. But Washington's culture is so embedded that it may be a year before he gets a handle, or eighteen months before he gets a handle on everything," he says.

And no, he does not care about what Trump tweets. "We knew exactly who he was when we voted for him, tweet and all."

Harry is looking forward to watching Trump negotiate and spar with Washington. He'd like to see him bring them to their knees, but is realistic. "I used to hate to negotiate labor contracts," Harry admits. "Absolutely worst job in the world. Time-consuming, petty, you had to play games, it's a tough thing to do, and you've got a responsibility for everybody you represent to do the best you could, and you got to be good to the employers because you don't want them to go out of business," he says.

"It's a fine line that you walk, and you had to be conscious of all of that. I think he's learning that right now, because what he was used to doing as a CEO, and he can't do that now.

"What I liked about Trump was that it was more than about Trump, it was about people, it was about being part of something bigger than just me, I felt as though I was part of something important and worthy of accomplishing something better than what have had," Harry says.

As long as Trump stays away from becoming a Bush or a Clinton and stays tough, Harry is in for the long haul with this new alliance. "If he becomes one of them, then I think this movement continues, without him."

Joe Keenan

Viroqua, Vernon County, Wisconsin

Joe Keenan looks like a guy who has spent his entire life working with his hands. They are callused, faintly smudged—not because they are unclean, but because years of tinkering, plowing, and bailing have left their marks. And they are muscular, a sign of the constant use of them over a lifetime.

"Oh yeah, I grew up on a farm," Keenan says, and subconsciously rubs his hands together.

At around five-eleven, he has a stocky build. His sandy brown hair and beard are sprinkled with gray, and while both are cropped short, the humidity from a fresh rain causes wiry curls to emerge.

He is wearing blue jeans and a royal blue pocket T-shirt with a JOE'S REPAIR logo over his left breast pocket; he is a quick-witted, to-the-point, pure no-nonsense Midwesterner who loves to laugh at his own puns.

Keenan is sitting with a group of acquaintances at the VFW in Viroqua on a shiny red barstool; he is a stone's throw from his home and the small business he owns.

This is *the* place to get a drink in this town of four thousand souls.

Located in the southwest corner of Wisconsin, surrounded by the lush Driftless region, with the Mississippi to the west and the Kickapoo River running through the center, Vernon County includes a latticework of throwback small farms in an era of large conglomerate-farming enterprises.

"The geography of the area helped us keep our farms smaller and family-owned," says Keenan of the Driftless region, which is known for the hilly topography that is a hallmark of much of the Upper Mississippi River Valley, a quirk that happened when glaciers that formed ten thousand years ago never reached the area to flatten it.

"I grew up here. We moved into the Volk area when I was five. Before that, we were down on the rural edge of Vernon County on the De Soto area. My folks came from Iowa, basically followed their parents from Iowa to Wisconsin. I always like to say only one came across but there's a lot of us here now," he says.

"I own a repair shop, farm machines and so forth," he explains. He mostly makes house calls to repair the farm machinery, essential to local farmers to get their crops out of the ground and out the door in the most expedient way possible. "You break down and can't move your crops, you don't get paid; you don't get paid, you can't feed your family, your livestock, you are dead," he explains of the vital work he does to keep area farmers' businesses rolling when something breaks down.

There is a diversity among farmers here; the descendants of the Germans who migrated to the area over a century ago, a robust Amish settlement, and a new wave of organic farmers.

Keenan is one of eleven kids; his mother was one of sixteen, his father one of eight. He started doing serious farm chores at around six years old. "We milked the cows. I also was involved in loading hay bales off the wagon. In those days, we didn't have a thrower and so everything was by hand. We backed the wagons into the haymow and unloaded them by hand and stacked everything. The time-consuming part of it taught you a lot about work. I came from a family that was all about pride in your work," he says.

The social side of Keenan's life followed true-to-form for a dairy farm kid in western Wisconsin. "When I graduated from high school I married my high school sweetheart." True to his working-class Catholic roots, Keenan grew up in a Democrat family. "Although I always thought my mom may have been a closet Republican," he says, laughing.

Keenan is not afraid to say who he voted for in 2016; he is also not afraid to say who he voted for in 2008 and 2012.

"I voted Obama, Obama, Trump," he says.

Why did he vote for Obama? "Well, in politics change is a potent message and he had a potent delivery. I thought the country needed something different, he was poised, confident, and had a good message and I bought it the first time," he says.

Keenan's support for Obama was not unusual in Vernon County. The Democrat won 60 percent of the local vote in 2008, beating Senator John McCain by 23 points in this rural rectangle that is home to 30,814 people—a wider margin than he scored statewide.

Joe Keenan's vote the second time for Obama was more personal; he did not care for Mitt Romney, the 2012 Republican nominee.

"I have a sister who married into the Mormon religion and I find the religion too secretive and controlling for me. I was concerned that might influence how he governed, and so Obama got my vote again," he says. And again in 2012, Keenan's vote mirrored the total vote of his rural county on the Mississippi River, which picked the incumbent Democrat over Romney by 15 points.

By 2016, Vernon County had flipped to support Donald Trump—both in the presidential primary and in the general election—one of twenty-three counties in the Badger State to swing from Obama to Trump. Only Iowa saw more localities change hands, as both states moved hard to the GOP. Wisconsin hadn't been painted red in the electoral college since 1984.

Hillary Clinton's inability to repeat Obama's victories in Wisconsin, Pennsylvania, and Michigan alone denied her the electoral college majority she needed to become president. She needed only 38,875 voters across those three states to choose her instead of Trump—and she left plenty on the table, getting 598,012 fewer votes in those three states than Obama had, including almost 2,000 fewer in Vernon County alone.[12]

Vernon's history of voting for Democrats is not just a past-tense assessment. In 2016, even as Trump carried it by 5 points, incumbent Republican senator Ron Johnson lost the county to Democrat Russ Feingold, despite carrying the state. Johnson lost Vernon County in his 2010 race too, as did Republican governor Scott Walker in 2014.[13]

Keenan finds it comical that some people are embarrassed to admit they voted for the Manhattan businessman, and he uses it to needle them.

"Trust me, I am the only person in my family who is not afraid to say I voted for Trump."

He and his relatives are devout Catholics. "It is an important part of who we are, who I am." They were also devout Democrats.

Viroqua is an interesting mix of rural and hipster, or perhaps the better word is "hippie."

On one hand, there are the descendants of farmers who have worked the rich soil for over a century; on the other, there is an evident counterculture on the county seat's Main Street that seems more Vermont than Vernon County.

During the 2016 Democratic Party primary contest between Hillary Clinton and Bernie Sanders, Viroqua was plastered with Sanders signs everywhere.

The hippie lifestyle here is legit. The local farmers' market on a warm spring Saturday has tie-dyed shirts, pottery, and organic everything from honey to beets to chocolate. Kickapoo Coffee, an austere shop just across the street with pour-over coffee and organic pastries, has two young men in flannel shirts and full beards playing the fiddle as young people line up for the organic coffee.

La Farge, a tiny Vernon County town located along the Kickapoo River, is home to the second-biggest employer in the county behind the medical center: the Coulee Region Organic Produce Pool (CROPP), the farming co-op that makes Organic Valley brand dairy products, and claims to produce four in every ten gallons of organic milk sold in the United States.[14]

Organic Valley was born when the small farmers of Vernon County recognized there was power in numbers and formed CROPP. It began as just a seven-farm collective, but today it includes more than a thousand farmers nationwide.[15]

Downtown Viroqua is sprinkled with antique stores, trendy shops such as the art gallery that specializes in local artists, and a fair share of closed businesses as well. And the city has received a modicum of national recognition for its "food scene," with local restaurants serving farm-to-table dishes to draw in customers.

An elderly woman outside of the art cooperative sits on a bench watching the crowd of younger families file past her with their organic vegetables, honey, and Amish jams and fruits, and remarks forlornly, "By three p.m. no one is on this street; not that way when I was a young woman."

Her reflection expresses part of the complexity of Viroqua—the past of a downtown Main Street filled with shoppers frequenting local stores now struggles to reemerge. The new movement has had some successes, but there are still gaps in the Main Street storefronts.

Vernon County's population after the 2000 census was essentially no different from its head count in the 1900 census—but the decade and a half since 2000 has seen modest growth and, more significantly, the county is now younger than either the state or nation as a whole, the holy grail of statistics for localities in the graying upper Midwest. Twenty-six percent of Vernon Countians are now under the age of eighteen, increasing the chances that the county can replace its population sustainably.[16]

Keenan's extended family has done its part in that; he grew up with lots of grandparents, aunts, uncles, and cousins living all around him.

"Yeah we spent quite a bit of time together. It was always looking forward to the big family gatherings. There was never a shortage of food. Regardless of how many people you had, there was never a shortage of food. You know, it's funny because when they would do that, it wasn't just family showing up, it was always the neighbors too," he says.

After high school and a youthful marriage, "I went into the repair business. Farm repair, started at an implement dealer. I always sort of had that knack, of course I followed an older brother who only could break things. So, naturally I learned how to fix the things he broke on the farm," he says.

His wife has a similar background. "We both were basically five miles from each other. It was funny, because we'd taken over both family farms; and when we were dating, ten miles back and forth wasn't that far, but when you're hauling feed, ten miles is a long ways," he says.

Keenan raised a family on the farm repair work over the decades. "I made house calls, raised three boys from that business," he says.

His middle son now lives in Japan, teaching English to Japanese students; his youngest son is a nurse and lives in La Crosse. "And my oldest son is thirty-one and lives with his wife on the family farm. He is really good at breeding cattle."

Going back to his vote for Obama, he repeats: "You know, in politics 'change' is a very good line, but I don't think any of it really meant anything. My vote ended up going for a guy who went back and apologized for everything we have done in our history, that is something that I know I can't do because I don't look back on anything that I've done. Because if you know that you're doing right, you can't go back and apologize," Keenan says.

"So here's what I haven't told you: my firstborn was a stillborn child, and she was the little girl. And I know that everything that we go through in our lives makes us who we are today. And that's for the whole nation. And I can't imagine going back and apologizing for everything in our lives, because it makes us become stronger for everything that we go through. And the bad things actually make us better, if you aren't bitter."

They strengthen your character, he adds. "The biggest disappointment with Obama was the direction of the country, it just tanked and I don't mean the recession, I mean where he took the country in the face of that. I kept hoping he'd get it right, I kept hoping he was going to change, the simple fact is he did want to change the country, but not in the right direction.

"Why I liked Trump was because he is going to clean out Washington," Keenan says. "You know, when I was little I remember going to visit my grandpa and grandma, I got to stay down there for a week. They had just taken this farm property over, which that eventually became the family farm. They were clearing rats out of a building, and I'll never forget how they got the rats out of the building. It's the same concept—they have to want to leave. Trump is the kind of guy who is going to make the rats in Washington want to leave, he is going to be so disruptive, so outside the norm, that the swamp will drain because the swamp can't stand him and how he is running things.

"That is how you really change things. You make it so offensive for the swamp rats to be there, so unlike anything they had experienced, rip their power out from under them, and that is what he is doing. But that, that gets the country going in the right direction.

"In 2015, when they first walked out on the stage, I truly wanted Ohio's governor," Keenan says of eventual third-place finisher John Kasich. A friend sitting three barstools away spits his beer out: "You got to be shitting me!" he says, then apologizes for the mess.

"Not when they first walked out, now come on now, think in the moment," Keenan replies, trying to explain his motives as they both break out into laughter. The Kasich moment, he says, lasted a week; then he went to Trump. By the following spring, when the Wisconsin primary rolled around, Keenan and Vernon County gave Trump a big 11-point margin over his nearest competitor. That support happened even as Trump was losing the state overall by double digits to Senator Ted Cruz, in his biggest stumble on the way to the GOP nomination.

"The one thing you saw with Trump is he didn't pretend to be anything else but himself. Nothing stuck to him. To me, you know, if you aren't afraid of the skeletons in your closet, you can do a lot of things," he explains.

Since Trump has been in office, Keenan has not regretted his vote, taking the president's side in his ongoing battles. He has been disappointed in the press and other elected officials, both Democrats and Republicans, in their reactions to Trump. "Well, I think they're more concerned about destroying him and they have no concern about the country," he says.

"Look, I am never going to blindly support someone again, but I will tell you this: I do like how he is taking on the establishment since becoming president. I like that he doesn't back down, no matter how exhausting it is; if he is standing up for us, I will stand up for him. It really is just that simple. He is a reflection of our frustrations, but he is also a force that makes people want to be part of, like working together and you accomplish something, part of thing.

"It is like when I finish a job and fix something that no one said could be fixed, or if we are all working together on the farm and accomplishing something, it is being part of that, is what it is like to support Trump, because honestly you are supporting yourself and your country."

Dave Rubbico

Erie, Erie County, Pennsylvania

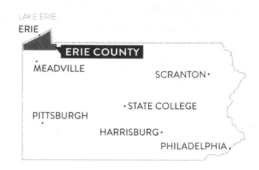

LAKE ERIE
ERIE
ERIE COUNTY
MEADVILLE
SCRANTON·
·STATE COLLEGE
PITTSBURGH
HARRISBURG·
PHILADELPHIA·

The scene outside Sara's at the mouth of Presque Isle Bay in Erie is chaotic, noisy, and colorful, filled with families, teenagers, older couples, and motorcycles all vying for one of the popular eatery's tasty milkshakes, ice-cream cones, or foot-long hot dogs.

The red-and-white color scheme of Sara's is everywhere. It's on the numerous pieces of Coca-Cola memorabilia that adorn every crevice of the building, on the flowers, on the historic gas pumps, and on the vintage telephone booths and old road signs. There are mannequins dressed up in period costumes, historic traffic lights, and vintage railroad signs too.

"You ain't nothin' but a hound dog / Cryin' all the time," Elvis Presley croons from eternity. Or perhaps it is from the speakers pumping nostalgia outside to the people sitting on the cherry-red picnic tables. Or perhaps it is coming from someone's car. It's hard to tell.

Adjacent to Sara's is Sally's Diner, a perfectly preserved classic 1957 Mountain View Diner, the second-to-last one built by the famed Singac, New Jersey, company that perfected the American diner that became the retail icon of the mid-twentieth century.

The perfect sterling-silver streamline style is enhanced, you guessed it, with eight-inch red-and-white ceramic checkerboard tiles along the front.

Sally's Diner was moved to the Sara's lot in 2003, in two pieces.

In its previous two lives, Sally's was first called Serro's Diner in Westmoreland County, Pennsylvania; then, when it was moved to Butler, Pennsylvania, it was called Morgan's Eastland Diner. The owner of both Sara's and Sally's, Sean Candela, says he named it Sally's after his mother's nickname; it still has its original booths, tables, tiles, and countertop inside.

There is a colorfully painted vintage billboard for Erie's beaches outside Sara's; GREETINGS FROM PRESQUE ISLE, PENNSYLVANIA, it beckons, its artwork showing 1950s-era families sitting on beach towels, under oversized umbrellas.

It looks like a scene to draw people to Cape May, New Jersey, on the Atlantic Ocean, rather than to the lakeshore of a Rust Belt city known for its heavy industrial production. The other side of Erie's history is this miniature tourist mecca; it has long been a destination for blue-collar families in Pennsylvania and surrounding states, where they can spend a long weekend on a sandy shore, of sorts, with typical roadside, beach-town attractions like Sara's.

David Rubbico, sixty-four, is sitting on a bench in front of the billboard; he is gulping an oversized drink.

"I got the peanut butter milkshake," he says with a broad smile. "Come on, come here, you have to check this out."

He makes his way through Sara's front entrance and out the back. The crowd is thick; the noise is both deafening and joyful, the kind of moment a grandfather would enjoy during a visit with his grandchildren.

As Rubbico makes his way through the crowd, no one blinks at his ensemble: he is dressed in full Trump-logo regalia. He has the classic red MAKE AMERICA GREAT AGAIN ball cap on. The back of his baby-blue T-shirt reads, in bold red, THIS IS THE USA. WE EAT MEAT. WE DRINK BEER. WE OWN GUNS. WE SPEAK ENGLISH. WE LOVE FREEDOM. IF YOU DON'T LIKE THAT, MOVE. An image of Donald Trump appears along with the quote. On the front of the T-shirt is a simple American flag, a small decal over his left breast pocket; under it, it says, MAKE AMERICA GREAT AGAIN.

Once out in the parking lot on the other side of Sara's, he points to his black 4x4 Jeep; if you had any doubt as to how he feels politically by his clothing, the decals on his vehicle erase that doubt.

Three things are clear: Rubbico loves the Pittsburgh Steelers, loves Donald Trump, and despises Hillary Clinton with a vengeance.

The last part is the most interesting, because this lifelong Democrat voted for Barack Obama—twice.

STEELERS runs across the top of his back window in large bright gold decals—and the taunt THIS PATRIOT IS FULLY INFLATED AND DOESN'T CHEAT runs across the bottom in the same gold decals.

In between are bumper stickers reading HILLARY FOR PRISON and INFOWARS, with others, marking every Super Bowl the Steelers have won, filling up the rest of the window. Seven more bumper stickers fill his tailgate, from BENGHAZI MATTERS to MAKE AMERICA GREAT AGAIN, all along the back.

He beams—this is clearly his pride and joy, his work of art, his way to finally express how he feels politically after years of supporting Democrats and being let down.

Forty thousand people ago, Erie was the third-largest city in Pennsylvania behind Philadelphia and Pittsburgh; when it shrank from 140,000 in the late 1960s, it lost its third-place status to Allentown, on the other side of the state. Job losses between 2010 and 2016 alone forced 10,000 people to leave Erie County, according to the Erie County Redevelopment Authority.

It's a city that is scarred by change, on one hand—empty factories, deteriorating city neighborhoods, abandoned homes, abandoned businesses—and trying to adapt, on the other hand, via the "Eds and Meds" approach, which utilizes the assets of five local universities and research hospitals (including the largest osteopathic medical school in the country), to draw new employers to the area.

Three new building projects, valued at more than $100 million, are in the beginning stages in 2017, including expansion projects at Erie's two hospitals—UPMC and Saint Vincent's—as well as a 600-job expansion at Erie Insurance, a company founded here in 1925 that has become an ever-more-important pillar of the economy as the smokestack legacy firms of the same age die away.

The city has recently invested in a strategy that might surprise those who stereotype Trump Country—it's bringing in refugees to help rebuild the dwindling population. They are betting on a new set of locals, scrambling side-by-side with their more established neighbors to put lives and a city back together.

A drive past the hub for refugees, the Multicultural Community Resource Center on East Tenth Street, located in an old schoolhouse, finds it bustling with activity in midafternoon.

Of all the voters who made up the Trump-coalition patchwork, former blue-collar Democrats were the ones who were stereotyped by parachuting journalists the most. Often tagged as angry, bitter or stuck in another time, the language used to describe them often mirrored the elitist disdain that fueled their unhappiness in the first place. This mass-media reaction to their political expression deepened their distrust.

These are the voters who have gone through the most traumatic economic and cultural change in America in the past thirty years; technology, global wage competition, and a nationalizing, secularizing culture have upended the way of life of the American blue-collar manufacturing worker more than they have for any other subgroup. In their eyes, they have lived by the rules and done everything they were supposed to: they worked hard, prayed hard, raised their kids to do the right thing, coached their kids' softball games, served as ushers at their churches, were civically engaged, and asked only to watch their favorite team play football on Sundays and to have a chance to give their offspring a slightly better economic situation in their hometowns when they were done.

But the world did not return the favor. Big companies did not cater to them to earn their business anymore, big media did not share their values, big Hollywood made them the butt of their jokes, and big business and big government showed them the door when technology replaced their job skills.

"There was some excitement here the other day," says Rubbico. "You sure you want to know?

"There's a shed right over there at the entrance to Waldameer Park," he says, pointing over his shoulder to the family-run amusement and water park. "They found a body in it. The poor girl, she just came back from rehab, and she overdosed," he explains.

The body was that of Michelle Howland, an Erie mother of four, who was found in an unlocked storage shed at the Village Trailer Park, just east of an entrance to Waldameer Park. She had returned to Erie only two days earlier, after spending six months as a patient in a drug treatment facility in Altoona.

"Opioids are a big problem here," he explains. In the most recent year with statistics available, 2015, both Ohio and Pennsylvania racked up more than 3,000 overdose deaths, and Michigan nearly 2,000. All three states saw double-digit-percent increases from 2014.[17]

The Great Revolt Survey of Trump voters in the five swing states

of the Rust Belt indicates that more than one in three report personally knowing someone who has struggled with addiction to narcotics
such as opioids or methamphetamines—but half of the Red-Blooded
and Blue-Collared voters say the scourge has hit close to home. The
epidemic is often painted as a rural crisis in the popular press, but
Trump voters in all county sizes reported its personal impact almost
equally. Those in mega counties with populations over one million, such as Cleveland, Philadelphia, and Pittsburgh, report just as
high an incidence—40 percent—as those in medium-sized counties
with populations of 100,000 to 200,000. Rural county respondents
clocked in at a similar 36 percent.

Rubbico moved to Erie in 1985, "after I got hurt and got out of
the army." He says he injured his back on a mission at Fort Bragg.
"That is all I can say about that."

Rubbico joined the army on August 21, 1978; he enlisted after
college when jobs were nowhere to be found in Erie, and served for
eight years.

On September 19, 1977, a few months after Rubbico graduated from college, more than 10,000 well-paying jobs were lost in
the steel industry from Erie to Youngstown to Pittsburgh—along
with supporting jobs: engineers, technicians, construction workers,
fabricators—the day became known regionally as Black Monday.

"I went to Duquesne University in Pittsburgh, graduated in 1977,
and enlisted in the army a year later because of 22 percent unemployment up here. I came up here, I met somebody in Pittsburgh,
and I'm up here and we ended up getting married, and I went in the
service so I could support my family," he says.

He was accepted into a New Jersey graduate school program to
pursue a master's in public administration, but switched gears instead. "For some stupid reason I decided I was tired of school and
wanted to work. We didn't have any kids, but I felt guilty because
unemployment was so bad, so I enlisted in the service the day after
my first wedding anniversary."

After the service he worked for the United States Post Office for
a short time. "When they found out I was a disabled veteran, they
fired me the Friday before Christmas. December 1985. They said

they considered most veterans drug addicts from the Vietnam era. Even though I wasn't Vietnam era. Then I worked for the VA hospital in Lyons, New Jersey. We had a two-thousand-bed nursing home facility. Underground tunnels connecting the three main buildings. My parents lived in Jersey, so I stayed with them," he explains.

He flew back every other weekend to see his wife and kids, who had stayed in Erie with his wife's mother. He finally got a job with the Pennsylvania civil service. "I quit my VA job on a Friday, drove to Erie on a Saturday, and started here on Monday, June 6, 1986," he says.

Rubbico's roots put the "blue" in blue-collar. "I was born in Somerville, New Jersey . . . My father worked at a factory with asbestos; they made brakes for cars. I was born and raised Democrat. You didn't talk Republican in my parents' household. They were very strict and I figured I just continued the tradition and voted Democrat all of my life," he says.

Including Barack Obama.

Rubbico is stout, his hair is gray; he has a pleasant smile and a very quiet tone to his voice, explaining to surprised ears why he voted for Obama twice.

"Back then I just didn't have any other choice. It's just that things got progressively worse and with Obama's second term, instead of being a . . . How can you say it? Instead of being someone who does a job, he was being someone pussyfooting around, and he was too much with delicate diplomacy and not enough for action, like our current president is," he says, comparing Obama to Trump. "That's what turned me off, and I switched."

His job in Pennsylvania was as an income-maintenance caseworker at the Pennsylvania Department of Public Welfare. "I also used to be a statewide union official in the Pennsylvania Social Services Union for Chapter One, which is all of northwestern Pennsylvania, about one-fourth of the state," he says.

He retired at the age of fifty-nine. "I was forced into early retirement almost three years ago. I can give you an answer why, or I can give you an honest answer as to why.

"It got harder and harder to accept the administration, it got harder and harder to accept everything. The clients were encouraged to defraud the system. There was corruption. Harrisburg said they're more interested in making clients happy instead of the accuracy of taxpayer-funded benefits. It got harder and harder to deal with that. There was too much fraud and corruption, yeah."

What turned him against the party he was part of for his entire life?

"The policies of Barack Obama. I really wanted him to live up to those speeches he gave. They were perfect. I gave him a second chance too. I figured he wasn't succeeding because the Republicans were trying to stop him at every turn. That was maybe part of it, but honestly it was because his values and vision of the country are much different than mine. And I am a union Democrat!" he exclaims.

Rubbico was not alone in his defection. Clinton earned 63,833 votes fewer than Obama had in 2012 in Pennsylvania, 238,449 fewer in Wisconsin, and 295,730 fewer in Michigan. She needed only 77,744 more votes, if scattered perfectly, to win all three states and the presidency.

Rubbico wears his support for Trump very much the way he wears his support for his beloved Steelers. It's on his clothes, it's on his car, it is everywhere.

When his daughter graduated from Liberty University in May 2017, he had MAKE AMERICA GREAT AGAIN written in white letters on red fabric on top of the cap that all the parents wore at commencement along with the graduates; the other parents had messages of encouragement to their children or expressing their faith in God. Not Rubbico.

"Look, this isn't that complicated, in fact it is pretty simple. I wanted Barack Obama to succeed. He ended up hurting us. He was weak. Donald Trump? Well, we finally have someone who has the balls to say what needs to be said and then goes out and does what he says."

Trump's outspokenness, which caused many suburban Republicans to blush, blanch, and perhaps even defect from him to vote for Clinton or a third-party candidate, was an asset for voters like Rubbico who mince few words themselves. It's these voters, in this new coalition more because of style than ideology, who could either turn hard against the congressional GOP during the 2018 elections or swing back to voting Democratic once Trump is done.

"My support for Trump isn't going anywhere. I haven't found a thing he has done that I don't like. From firing Comey, to firing Reince Priebus, draining the swamp is going to take time, and that's okay, I've got all of the time in the world."

3

Perot-istas

Before Donald Trump upended the general election and broke the expectations narrative that surrounds politics in America, he smashed the Republican Party's own nominating process—and he had a lot of help in doing it. With the GOP's donor class, operative corps, party volunteer apparatus, and ideological brain trust all lined up almost uniformly against him, Trump had only four weapons at his disposal—a compliant media hungry for the ratings he could bring; a debate process set up and policed by the Republican National Committee that heavily favored his unique situation; enough personal wealth to run a campaign without outside donations; and a base of voters outside the Republican primary universe who were willing to crash the party with him.

Trump's unlikely path to the Republican nomination was aided by an influx of new voters in the Republican caucuses and primaries. In states with open primaries, such as New Hampshire and many Deep South states, in which voters who are not registered Republicans are allowed to participate, Democrats and independents flooded in to help choose the GOP delegates. In northern states like Pennsylvania, with strict primary rules that confine the process to only Republicans, voters switched allegiances, even if only temporarily, to participate. In both cases, Trump was the beneficiary.

The energy behind Trump's campaign also produced new voters for the Republican side, voters who were not inspired to vote for Mitt

Romney or John McCain or Barack Obama. These voters, nonideo-logical and drawn to the maverick candidate from outside the political system, we labeled "Perot-istas" for their similarity to the group of voters who in 1992 propelled another iconoclastic billionaire candidate for president, Ross Perot. That first candidacy by the nasal-toned Texan fell short in a three-way race against Bill Clinton and President George H. W. Bush, but it helped drive turnout that year to 55 percent of the voting-age population, the highest in that era since 1968 and a share surpassed since only in 2004 and 2008.[1]

Typically, Democrats dominate campaign metrics around new voter registration. Their base voters are more transient and more erratic in their voting behavior, and the party devotes significant mechanical resources to registration and turnout efforts—more than Republicans do. But in 2016, organic enthusiasm for Trump cut into that gap. The Republican analytics firm Grassroots Targeting found notable pockets in Pennsylvania of Republican dominance in new registrants, centered in areas such as Luzerne County that swung hard to Trump on Election Day.

Democrats normally expect to reap the benefit of increased turn-out, but in the Great Lakes states it was Donald Trump who gained. Pennsylvania's turnout was up 6.7 as a percentage of citizen voting-age population, including a 4.6 percent increase in the urban center of Pittsburgh and a 4.1 percent increase in urban Philadelphia.[2] Clinton's efforts to crank up the Democratic-base vote worked—but they couldn't offset Trump's harvesting of rural and industrial Obama voters. In states where Clinton's campaign was caught flat-footed and paid attention only in the waning days, urban voting decreased—by, for example, 11.4 percent in Milwaukee County among the voting-age population, and by 4.9 percent in Detroit's Wayne County.[3]

This movement of infrequent voters and late-in-life registrations supporting the Republican ticket formed a notable and important slice of a winning coalition in a close election. Utilizing vote-history records, the Great Revolt Survey of Rust Belt Trump voters defined Perot-istas as those older than thirty who registered for the first time in 2016, or those eligible to vote but not voting in 2008 and 2012, or those with no history of primary participation. This group comprised 6 percent of the Trump coalition in the states surveyed, according to survey returns; and they were, as expected, significantly less conservative, less ideological, and less religious than the rest of the Trump pool. Only 48 percent of this group identified as conservatives, compared to 64 percent of the Trump coalition in the Midwestern battlegrounds entirely. They were the least likely Trump voters to say that the Supreme Court was Trump's most important campaign promise, and the most likely to cite his pledge to bring manufacturing jobs back to the U.S.

Among the Trump voter archetypes, Perot-istas were the least likely, by a significant margin, to have been married or to have participated in civic clubs and other local service organizations—and they were the most likely to have been hunting or fishing in the last ten years, also by a significant margin.

As analysts project the future of the populist-conservative coalition that elected Trump, this group of voters seems to be the most difficult to keep engaged without the glue of a politically inexperienced, unpredictable, nonideological personality like Trump's.

Connie Knox

Fort Madison, Lee County, Iowa

Shirley Chisholm, Barack Obama, Ross Perot, and Donald Trump.

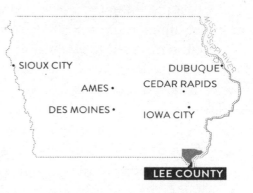

The first two are African American Democratic trailblazers, and the last two are billionaire white men—all were political mavericks and they all ran for president. Chisholm was a Texas congresswoman in the 1970s and '80s and the first viable black presidential aspirant; Obama was the freshman senator who dared challenge the already-coronated Democratic front-runner before paying his dues; Perot was the iconoclastic Texas electronics mogul who made the two strongest independent showings for president in modern history, in 1992 and 1996; and Trump was the interloper who crashed the Republican Party in 2016.

It's such an unlikely grouping of people that it could only be the answer to one trivia question: it's a list of national candidates who've been supported by Connie Knox of Fort Madison, Iowa.

At sixty-nine, she's furious at a political establishment she believes has forgotten people like her who live in the middle of the country.

"I suggest that on the East Coast Governor Cuomo and on the West Coast Governor 'Moonbeam' [Jerry Brown] get their heads out of their collective anal openings and listen to what regular people are thinking," she says. "I am beyond mad."

Knox was a member of the United Automobile Workers union while working at Sheaffer Pen Corporation in Fort Madison, a town of 10,597 people on the banks of the Mississippi River in the state's southeastern-most county. The company, begun by local jeweler Walter Sheaffer in 1912, grew to become not just the anchor of the local economy but also one of the world's best-known fountain pen manufacturers.[4] The Sheaffer family eventually sold the company, leading to a string of transactions that put it in the hands of the French conglomerate that makes the Bic brand of pens. In 2008, Bic closed its Iowa factories, which had once employed 1,000 people.[5]

"I started in the 1980s and they were already shipping [production] lines to Mexico," Knox says. "I worked in every department except repair and molding—I drove a truck for six years, mostly local, between the plants."

Active in her local union as a onetime steward, Knox recalled the strikes and labor strife that others in the community say contributed to the multinational ownership's decision to close the Fort Madison factory. "I was in on the first strike [negotiations], and after a couple of sessions they put me in the basement answering telephones because they were afraid I was going to hurt someone," she says, leaning across the table in the market café at the local Hy-Vee supermarket to make her point.

"I don't like scabs. I told them don't hurt the office workers . . . but when they bring a busload of workers from somewhere else, don't think you are crossing this [picket] line." Knox punctuates her words with an imaginary line drawn by her hand.

That wasn't the last strike at the Lee County operations of the pen company, and Knox says that over time she began to distrust the UAW's national leadership. "I thought the strikes were a joke. I questioned whether we got the support we needed from the higher-ups in the union. I asked our rep: 'How come every time we sign a contract you show up in a new Cadillac?' "

Knox believed in the union movement, but is a populist and a contrarian even in her opinions of the union leaders. "It was the feeling that they were just about as much on the company's side as they were on the people's side." Knox explains the drift in allegiances of her union as a parallel to the corrosive effects she sees in government and in corporate America. "A bureaucracy is a self-fulfilling entity. Once it is created, it will say or do anything to keep the money coming in," Knox asserted.

About to complete her seventh decade, Knox is now "on husband number four and the last one." She is just as outspoken and feisty about herself as she is about the powers that be—and that is exactly the trait that drew her to Trump. "I was supporting Trump before my Republican friends were."

"My three presidential heroes are Thomas Jefferson, Andrew Jackson, and John F. Kennedy, and Trump just may be in that running," she says. "I like that he's not owned by the lobbyists and owned by the establishment—I hope," she adds, with a caveat that echoes what many other maverick-loving voters like her say.

Cynical about politicians in general and critical of both parties, Perot-istas like Knox abide in a no-man's-land in America's two-party system. Making up only a small percentage of the electorate overall, these voters, who ricochet wildly between attraction to mavericks on both ends of the political spectrum, or don't vote at all, make up a key archetype of the Trump coalition. Perot-istas are the modern-day equivalent of electoral shock troops, ready to elevate a political gadfly or rebel precisely because they do not conform.

Usually the maverick flames out, starved of the institutional support needed to get through the state-by-state gauntlet of the party nominating processes, or the tremendous legal hurdles required to get on some state ballots as an independent or third-party candidate. But in the case of 2016, the maverick crashed the party and won—pummeling a large and deep field of Republicans with the help of Perot-istas like Knox.

Knox is a registered independent—but she did switch to Republican for a short time in 2016 so she could participate in Iowa's first-in-the-nation presidential caucuses and support Trump. The New York billionaire finished a strong second in Iowa's caucuses and then swept to victory in the next contest in New Hampshire, where independents are allowed to participate in the primary. As the nomination process then turned mostly to Southern states with largely open processes, Trump's troops showed up in record numbers—people who don't typically participate in primaries—to elevate him above the pack and put him on the path to become the nominee.

Knox spent most of her adult life, forty-three years, as a registered Democrat—though she has consistently supported one Republican, Iowa senator Chuck Grassley. "I think he does a wonderful job for the people of Iowa," she says.

"I'm in agreement with Republicans on fiscal responsibility, small government, and most definitely the Second Amendment, but I agree with the Democrats on things like making sure the people who can't take care of themselves are taken care of," she says. It's clear, however, that Knox has no intention, even in the Trump era, of becoming a card-carrying Republican. "I also have a problem that the Republicans can't keep their nose out of people's bedrooms."

She's nobody's religious conservative. "I was raised in the Methodist church, but I would consider myself to be more spiritual than religious," she says. "It's probably the one thing I agree with Karl Marx on: religion is the opiate of the masses. If you are focused so much on the next life, you are not worried about what is happening in this life, and that's sad."

In a state that has plenty of religious conservatives, socially center-left voters like Knox are exactly the kind of voters a Democrat needs to persuade to win, but she has nothing but contempt for the 2016 Democratic nominee, Hillary Clinton.

"There were two 'Hillary for Prison' signs on the road to West Point [Iowa], and we said 'Yes, you betcha!' " Knox says enthusiastically. "I think it's time she got the consequences of her actions."

Knox, who had previously voted for Barack Obama, believed that Clinton took communities like Lee County—which still relies on a manufacturing economy that includes a meat products plant, a windmill-blade maker, a DuPont paint factory, and one of the country's largest fertilizer plants—for granted. "She thought she had the blue-collar vote tied up. She didn't even bother campaigning in those states," Knox says of Clinton.

ABC News calculated that Clinton made just seven visits to Iowa, Wisconsin, and Michigan combined, while Trump came to those three states eighteen times—becoming the first Republican to carry all three of the Midwestern battlegrounds in the same election since 1984.[6] Lee County was one of the places that helped tip the Hawkeye State to the GOP for only the second time since the Reagan era.

The voters of this aging riverfront populace, who had given Barack Obama a 16-point cushion in 2012, gave Trump a cushion of the same size in 2016. Only 41 other counties among the more than 3,000 in America proved as volatile as Lee County between those two elections—and 11 of them were also in Iowa.

Like many of its rural peers in the upper Midwest, Lee County is bleeding population—its current census estimate is 34,615, which is down 3.5 percent from the 1990 number. Its historical population peak came at 44,207 in 1960, as the postwar manufacturing boom ramped up the county's factories situated not just near the Mississippi River but on a major railroad crossing of that river.

Lee County is 94 percent white—even slightly whiter than the state as a whole—with only 15.5 percent of its residents having obtained a bachelor's degree. Iowans as a whole have more formal education than Lee Countians on average, but the state share with bachelor's degrees or higher, at 26.7 percent, is still below the national average of 29.8 percent.

The Clinton campaign's national strategy of appealing to minorities, young Millennial voters, and Republicans in highly educated locales who were turned off by Trump, did not leave much room to fit Iowa's six electoral votes under her tent—even though her husband and Obama had both won it handily twice. Any kind of winning Democratic coalition in Iowa includes not just liberals and Democrats—and the younger demographics that fit in those definitions these days—but also the cranky antiestablishment populists who mistrust large corporations and Republicans both.

Knox falls into that category—but her colorful political profile shows the electoral challenge for Democrats who are becoming ever more urbane and homogenously liberal in their national platforms.

Spry and opinionated, Knox has little love for the Republican brand but is as far from politically correct as a voter can get. Sitting at the grocery store café, she taps her purse and says she's got a .380-caliber pistol tucked inside, with the Iowa Concealed Carry permit that allows her to have it. "If somebody has a sign posted they don't allow guns on their premises, I don't shop there," she says, safe today because the Hy-Vee chain of grocery stores, which is based in West Des Moines and covers eight mostly Midwestern states, allows its local managers to make those decisions in states where concealed carrying is allowed.

She's drawn to Trump's attitude more than his issue positions— she looks for independent streaks and saw more of that in him than in Clinton or the more conventional Republican choices in 2016.

"If you've read *Art of the Deal,* he is so cagey," she says, alluding to Trump's autobiography. "I think he's smarter than people give him credit for. You can't be as successful as he is without being smart . . . and I also think he's a patriot."

Knox once admired Obama but turned on him during his administration. "I foolishly campaigned for him because I thought Martin Luther King would have loved to see this day when a black man could be president," Knox says, shaking her head, noting that Obama, too, started out on the national stage as somewhat of a maverick who was not content to politely wait his turn.

Her last disappointment with Obama came over the one issue that has perhaps realigned the most between the two parties in the last two decades—international trade. "I was jumping up and down [mad] when he signed off on TPP [the Trans-Pacific Partnership], because I think that was going to be worse than NAFTA [the North American Free Trade Agreement]," Knox says. In a heartland county like this one, NAFTA is no longer an acronym—it's a noun, and a profanity. Whether it's in the textile belt of the Deep South or the smokestack states of the interior North, the international trade deal negotiated by President George H. W. Bush and pushed to completion with the help of President Bill Clinton, is viewed as the single biggest culprit in the loss of manufacturing jobs to Mexico with its cheaper labor pool.

That animosity toward NAFTA's legacy bubbled up on the campaign trail in 2016, stoked by Trump—who pledged not only to revoke Obama's endorsement of TPP but also to renegotiate NAFTA's terms with Mexico. For her part, Clinton also backed away from TPP, but the center of gravity of anti-trade-agreement politics has clearly shifted from the Democratic Party to the Republican Party. Many journalists tried to claim that Trump's anti-trade-deal stances were hypocritical, since so many of the products that bear his own company's brand name are made offshore—but Trump, who owed nothing to the GOP's capitalist donor class, shrugged off the criticism and kept the edge on his anti-globalist, anti-trade-deal messaging.

Knox's expectations of Trump focus mostly on his outsider standing and not around any set of policies. "He's got a lot of housecleaning to do," she says, noting that too many of the government employees he inherited are closer to Hillary Clinton than to him.

And in the end, she says, she's likely to stick with Trump, unless he, too, becomes a creature of the swamp.

"The only person that is able to turn me against Trump is Trump."

Rose Zuba

Kingston, Luzerne County, Pennsylvania

At first Rose does not want to give her last name; she hesitates for a day, then decides it is okay. That is just her way.

At age seventy, Rose Zuba is trim, her silver hair perfectly coiffed, her eyes a sparkling blue. Her demeanor moves between humble and shy; she is always sweet and well-mannered.

She's been "going with" the same gentleman for forty-six years, and lives in the same area where she used to pick coal off the ground to heat the family's "company home" after her father died due to "an incident, something" that happened at the local coal mine. She was only three years old.

She does not elaborate on what that something was, saying only that her mother was just twenty years old when her father died. "Let's just say it was related to the coal," she says of his passing.

That is the end of that conversation, and Zuba leaves no doubt it will not be reopened.

"We were very poor. After my father died it was just my mother and my older sister. We lived in what they used to call a company house next to the coal mine," she says of the small home typical of those built to house miners who made northeast Pennsylvania one of America's important coal-producing areas for a century.

Today, Zuba lives in Kingston in Luzerne County, a tree-lined bedroom community of Wilkes-Barre, Pennsylvania. The municipality hugs the broad Susquehanna River and sits just outside the city.

Economically, times are not easy in this area, and they have not been in quite a while. But that economic depression is not what drove Zuba to vote in the 2016 election. Her provocation was something more, something deeper—it had to be—because in the fifty years she's been eligible to vote, the country and her community have seen worse turmoil than they are experiencing today.

But nothing ever motivated her to vote for president of the United States until the political emergence of Donald J. Trump.

"We used to pick our own coal and everything. You know, to have heat and all. We lived in a company home. I guess you'd say it was a four-room: two bedrooms, a kitchen, and a living room–parlor. And, well, mostly two bedrooms upstairs. They were very, very small."

Her mother became gravely ill after her father's death. "She had a partial stroke at the time he died."

It took a while, but her mother eventually recovered and went to work at the local hospital.

"And my uncle, my father's brother, he lived right down the street from us. So he more or less took care of us," she says.

Her uncle was also impacted by the treachery of lax midcentury mining safety practices in this country.

"He lost his arm in a mining accident," she says bluntly. "He was only a boy when it happened." She then becomes quiet. The miners' necessary reaction to those practices made Pennsylvania, Ohio, and West Virginia the buckle of the United Mine Workers labor union belt—and reliably Democratic bases at the ballot box.

But Donald Trump changed that, carrying all three old coal states—the first Republican to do that since Ronald Reagan—and accelerating a gradual realignment in the region. He won Pennsylvania by just 44,292 votes, and he did it by converting lifelong Democrats in small industrial places like Luzerne, and by motivating the irregular voters who lean right but couldn't get excited about more typical Republicans such as Mitt Romney or John McCain.

With a population of 316,383, Luzerne County was one of the ten largest counties in the country to swing from supporting Obama to supporting Trump. Just three counties in Pennsylvania, including Luzerne, switched their local pluralities from an Obama victory in 2012 to a Trump victory in 2016. Trump's margin in those three counties alone was 33,658, in terrain Romney had lost by 31,153.[7] Had Hillary Clinton been able to repeat Obama's margin in just Luzerne, Erie, and Northampton Counties, she'd have kept Pennsylvania's twenty electoral votes in the Democratic column. She would have needed to not only keep more of Obama's votes, she also would have needed to offset new participants like Zuba.

Zuba never left the Luzerne area; after she graduated from high school she went immediately into secretarial work, and then office administration. "I just had a natural knack for it," she says.

Politics was always a very big turnoff for her. "I just didn't like and I never ever liked anyone who ran for office. I didn't like the local politicians, I didn't like the national politicians. None of them ever motivated me to vote for them."

Political corruption runs deep in northeastern Pennsylvania; especially here in Luzerne County and in neighboring Lackawanna. A former Luzerne County commissioner is serving prison time for accepting thousands of dollars from a developer to steer his vote. Three former judges from this county are also in jail for a buffet of different corruption crimes, and a federal grand jury indicted a former longtime state senator for accepting bribes.

All in all, in the past few years, more than thirty government officials were toppled in the Luzerne County public corruption probe, underscoring Zuba's mistrust of politicians.

"I have had no interest in any of them locally because they were all in it together," she says. "They were all cut from the same cloth. No matter what party they were from, well, they were all the same to me. And they were all more or less to me bought and paid for. They listened to whatever the ones that would pay for them, what they wanted them to do."

The buildup to her decision to finally register and cast her vote for Trump had been percolating for eight years, she says.

"Along comes this guy who pays his own way. He was his own man. He was not beholden to any party, or any special interest other than his own interest. He was his own man. I admired that. I liked that. I was finally ready to vote." Zuba was first eligible to vote in 1968. Since then, she demurred from voting for or against Presidents Richard Nixon, Gerald Ford, Jimmy Carter, Ronald Reagan, H. W. Bush, Bill Clinton, George W. Bush, and Barack Obama.

She has watched the region around her go from devastated— when the Knox Mill closed in the 1950s—to some economic peaks, with the building of textile companies. But those soon went south for cheaper labor, before decamping again in the 1990s and 2000s to Mexico and China. So mostly the economy in Rose Zuba's backyard has eroded. The hard truth is this region peaked almost a hundred years ago, when anthracite coal from the Wyoming Valley heated the homes of Americans across the country.

"The politicians kept getting rich, the people in the region were barely getting by," she says.

Still, she insists, Trump's appeal was not based on economic promises, nor on social issues, but something more esoteric. "It was his striking independence. That was really appealing to me. His willingness to not be ashamed of patriotism or speaking his mind."

Obama's eight-year effort to make amends with historic enemies such as Iran, and to back away from the projection of American force abroad, drove voters like Zuba to the brash-talking Trump. The Great Revolt Survey found that 78 percent of Trump voters in five Rust Belt states believed Trump to be more patriotic than Obama, with only 5 percent choosing Obama and 17 percent saying both are equally patriotic.

Zuba says part of her frustration in the past decade or so is her weariness of people not doing an honest day's work or at least trying to better themselves; a scar she carries from her meager upbringing.

"What really gets me is the attitude of people. Here you had my uncle who had one arm and he did have relief, but I think it was twenty dollars per month, and what he got for food from relief was like a pound of processed beef and one pound of butter and powdered eggs and powdered milk, and that was about it for the month.

"He had one arm and he went out and worked. Whether it was cut the weeds, you know, from the highway or even into different institutions to work. Like as a janitor and things like that. And what really is annoying, I think, is people who are able-bodied to work and don't," she says.

"My mother worked hard for years, you know. And everyone around her really didn't get paid a lot, you know. But they worked hard and they had pride in their work, and I see this culture changing around us in that no one values hard work. No one gets something out of it and that is a shame, because there is something great about pulling together and working for a single cause, in whatever you do in your job."

Zuba's mom went on to live until she was eighty-five years old. "She was no cook, because she worked since she was young. So my uncle was the one that took care of us and cooked for us and all. He was a good cook."

On Election Day in 2016, Zuba could not contain herself. "I was really excited to finally vote for someone, finally have someone I believed was good for the community and the country. We stayed up until five in the morning just to make sure it was real," she recalls. "And you know what, I felt honored. I was able to exercise one of our greatest gifts in this country finally," she says, before taking a deep breath. To watch her recount her story is to know that this moment really meant something for her.

"For as long as I remember, I thought of professional politicians as *the* problem," she says.

"You know, when Trump says 'drain the swamp,' well, that is the other big part of why I like him. Still do. It's going to take time, the swamp has been filling for decades and decades.

"And the press and the politicians and the lobbyists, well, they have all been part of it; that is why they don't like him. That is why they are trying to destroy him," she says.

Zuba is well-read to the point of distraction. "I just cannot read one more negative thing about the president, since Day One it has been an avalanche of disruption towards him. First they questioned his legitimacy, then they made sure that they said he lost the popular vote every time they mentioned his new presidency."

Does she regret her first vote? Hardly.

"This time I had this deep feeling, this deep commitment that I just had to do it. I just had to vote for Trump. And I'm not sorry I did. I'm behind him one hundred percent," she says.

"We have a neighbor next door to us. And she is very religious, and from the time that Trump was going to run and during the election night and all, she has been saying the rosary every night, she's a nurse, and she's been saying the rosary every night when she comes home from work, for Trump. To protect our country and him and for everything to go all right for him," she explains.

"Going out there to vote for him really meant something to me," she says. "I don't know how to explain it except I felt compelled not for me, but for my country. For my town, my family. This election wasn't about politics, it was about you, me, us, and everyone, that's why I had to vote. I just had to."

Gloria Devos

Armada, Macomb County, Michigan

When you meet people like Gloria Devos your immediate impression is this is a person you wish you had known all of your life. Not because she is perfect, but because she is perfectly wonderful.

She's warm, funny, full of boundless energy. It is clear she loves to interact with all people and they in turn enjoy the interaction—mainly because of her infectious love of life. At seventy-seven, she has still not retired from work. "I have worked at J. C. Penney's for twenty-six years," she says, explaining that for most of those years it was as a second job to supplement her full-time job as a union bus driver for the Utica school district.

"I started out in Penney's picking up the trash and picking up hangers and vacuuming and doing all that stuff when I was still driving the school bus. So at five p.m. after my first job ended I'd go and do that, then Saturdays I'd go there and we were cleaning up and all that stuff. And I enjoyed that. Ray calls me a workaholic, because I love to work," she says of her third husband.

"It keeps you busy. But now with me getting older, it's kind of hard sitting around, so I work. Now I am an associate there. And you know what, I love working with the people. I mean that's why I'm still there. I have so much fun with them, I joke with them. Just so much fun," she says of her job at the Lakeside Mall in suburban Sterling Heights.

Devos grew up in the city of Detroit and sounds like a Detroiter, with her local shorthand. "I grew up near Conner's Airport," she says, a reference to the Detroit city airport that locals called 'Conner's' when it was relocated near Conner's Creek on the city's east side back in the '30s. Major commercial carriers stopped flying into the facility in the mid-1990s, preferring the more modern hub terminal built farther out in Wayne County.

Devos is a Michigander by every definition but birth—she was technically born in Chicago, Illinois, to her two German-born parents. Her father was a chef at the Belmont Hotel, a luxurious residential hotel on Chicago's North Side that was designed by the premier architectural firm of Fugard & Knapp in 1924. Postcards from the era showcase an exquisite dining area, with well-appointed chandeliers, elegant white tablecloths, and a bountiful smorgasbord in the center of the dining room.

Six weeks after Devos was born, her parents moved to Detroit to realize her father's dream—owning a restaurant of his own.

"The first one he owned was on Jefferson Avenue in Detroit, then he had one on Mack Avenue, I remember living on Mack Avenue. I think we lived upstairs and I think I was young, five years old or something, when he had that bar. I worked there as a kid; then, when I got pregnant, I got married and everything," she explains.

Devos did everything at the bar; she waitressed, cleaned, helped with the cooking, and she loved it. What she loved most was the pride her father and mother took in their small business. German was spoken freely during family discussions and sometimes at the bar—to this day, Devos has retained her ability to speak the language.

"My dad was this wonderful pastry chef. He made these delightful soups and he baked bread. Oh, did he make bread. In the restaurant, he made food so good. It was corned beef and cabbage, and he had it always fixed so nice. The plate wasn't even smeared or anything, he always wiped it off with a towel and everything. I remember that. My mother worked there also and my brother did the dishes," she says of her only sibling, who was six years younger.

Devos describes in detail the ethnic delicacies her father would prepare every day with pride at his bar—called the Paragon. Her memories are so vivid and rich, you can almost imagine a plate of tenderly cooked veal sausage, crusty breads, and tangy sauerkraut sitting on a platter before you.

At the old Mack Avenue address for the Paragon now stands a shuttered building; the structure shows signs of faded charm despite the boarded-up windows in the former upstairs living quarters for her family.

Graffiti covers the entranceways on the front and side of the building—an all-too-common description of buildings that carried out the good times during the golden years of the city that was the cradle of America's proudest product, its cars.

Politics was rarely discussed at the family dinner table growing up, "All I know is that they were Republicans," she says.

Devos never went to college—she just loved to work. She worked at the Paragon until she was twenty-three and became pregnant with her first child, her son Richard. "I married when I was twenty-three, then I got divorced. I had my son first, then I got divorced, then I got married again, so I've been married three times."

Her current husband, Ray, has been her husband for thirty years. "So the first one I was married to was only for a couple of years, then the second one I was married to was for fifteen years. And this one here, quite a while. We live on a farm in Armada," she says of the village in the northernmost corner of Macomb County, the burly suburban neighbor just to the northeast of Detroit.

Armada is a picturesque agricultural area with an assortment of residential homes and smaller farms like hers, which sits on the lazy curves of Coon Creek.

She has two goats, two mini horses, one full-size horse, two collies, too many cats, and one donkey. And she loves cowboy boots. "Wear them all of the time." The pair of boots she has on during the interview is fur-lined. "They are very comfortable," she states.

The first time Devos ever registered to vote was when she was seventy-two years old in 2012; until that time she had never voted in a presidential election—and she didn't make a choice between Mitt Romney and Barack Obama in that year either. "Didn't [vote] that year either, it was for a local race," she explains. "Pretty sure it was a Democrat."

The first time she ever voted for president was in 2016, "for Donald J. Trump," she proudly proclaims.

There is no hesitation in her voice, no pause in her pride. Her support for Trump, she says, has only grown since she voted for him, "despite everyone telling anyone who will listen that our support for him has waned. Heh. Well, it hasn't."

Devos is not very ideological; she has her core beliefs, but they are a smorgasbord of individual values that don't belong to a party. "They belong to me," she states flatly.

As far as politicians go, she has little use for them. "Honestly, they are all of the same."

"I only voted one time here in Armada for something before this election. I told the lady, I said, 'This is the first time I'm signing up to vote' and everything, and they were so happy I was doing it. But I can't remember what I was there for the first time," she says, making no apology for her political indifference.

"But I did know that I was going to vote for Trump," she says, and it had nothing to do with his policies or his party.

"He was not a politician. He was not part of the system, a system that has been failing a lot of people. He was his own person, with his own style. And honestly, for the first time in the fifty years I was able to vote, I was excited to vote. Because this guy, this guy will make a difference. And the only people who will try to get in the way are the people who operate the swamp," she says, using the jargon insult for Washington, DC's political establishment that Trump has used himself, in an era when the newsy social media platform has made shorthand essential.

She likes Trump for what he's not. "It is really that simple."

Devos spent thirty-three years driving a school bus after her parents' restaurant closed down. "I went to work at Big Boy's at 21 Mile Road and Vandyke, and I worked there for a year and a group of women I knew came in one night and said, 'Hey, Gloria, come on, why don't you come over here and drive the school bus, because you can make six thousand dollars.' Now mind you, that was forty years ago. So I went over there and the man checked me out and he says, 'Well, you're going to stall this, you're going to do this and this and that.' But I didn't stall anything because my dad taught me how to drive a clutch, and this was a stick-shift bus, and I drove smooth. Everything was fine, and they hired me. I was there thirty-three years. I loved it."

What she loved about it was refreshing: "Just to get up early in the morning, and knowing I was doing something meaningful. Heck, I even enjoyed the twenty-seven-mile drive to the school from my home. There was a purpose, a sense of belonging and contributing. It is hard to describe, but it meant something to me. And I don't know, I just enjoyed the children. I drove the big bus first, then I drove the small bus, the handicapped children and stuff. But I loved the kids. I loved doing things with them, taking them places. I got to watch them grow up, I got to be part of getting them to school every day safely, and I tried to make sure I helped their day start out with a smile," she explains.

Devos met her first husband when he was working at Hudson's Department Store. "He was working in the luggage department," she says. For generations, Hudson's Department Store was synonymous with style, fashion, and traditional Christmas shopping in booming Detroit. The building, which occupied the corner of Woodward and Gratiot Avenues, was shopping on the grandest scale possible, with thirty-two floors serviced by fifty-one passenger elevators.[8]

But like the heyday of Detroit's union-powered automobile economy, Hudson's crashed—literally. On October 24, 1998—symbolically at 5:45 p.m., the store's traditional closing hour in its vital years—the building was imploded in just over thirty seconds—leaving yet another vacant hole for Detroit to fill, not just physically but emotionally.

"Really was a shame," she says, uncharacteristically abrupt, about the store. Detroit's political clout has shrunk with its economic decline. In 1980, Wayne County, which includes the city proper, cast 23 percent of the state's vote for president; by 2016, its share was down to 16 percent.

Clinton lost Michigan and its 16 electoral votes by only 10,704 ballots—a loss entirely attributable to her failure to carry Macomb County; she lost it to Trump by 48,348 votes, while Barack Obama had beaten Michigan native Mitt Romney in Macomb by 16,103. Perhaps more important for Trump, Macomb County surged to produce more votes in 2016 than it had in all but one previous presidential election, thanks in part to the mobilization of first-time voters like Devos. Macomb yielded 13,797 more voters in 2016 than it had in 2012, and just a scant amount fewer than in the nationally record-breaking year of 2008. Meanwhile, the Democratic bastion of Detroit proper, Wayne County, saw its turnout in 2016 sag a bit—down 35,417 from 2012.

The inability of Clinton to motivate her party's most marginal voters—and the perpendicular ability of Trump to energize irregular voters on the right end of the spectrum, like Devos—was one of the least told stories of the 2016 campaign postmortems.

Devos is a good example of a critical, perhaps decisive, part of the Trump coalition—the missing link in what otherwise could have been a Romney victory in 2012, when Barack Obama's popularity was on the wane. She's an infrequent, right-of-center voter who'd rather tune out of politics than tune in. Like many Perot-istas, it takes something well out of the ordinary in politics to get Devos's attention. For others, nearly a generation ago, that something out of the ordinary was independent presidential candidate Ross Perot. For many of them, and for people like Devos, the emergence of another enigmatic billionaire candidate, Donald Trump, is what was needed to jolt them to action.

Devos's ticket for the Trump Train came through her husband, Ray.

"He liked Trump from the beginning, but he always votes. I don't know, just all the things Trump was saying and what he represented in terms of independence from political games and his business dealing and I thought, 'Well, I will give him a chance, you know? He must know something, he certainly has been down in the trenches, and he knows how to survive. He knows how to stay being his own man.' Well, I liked that."

Like many swing voters, Devos made her decision in a manner that seems to have been more guttural than logical.

"And you know what else that really appealed to me was the idea that I could be part of changing something that I thought was going terribly wrong," she says of the direction of the country. "People always say 'change,' and I didn't know what that felt like until this election. I felt it, I wanted to be part of change," she explains of the fever that captures the imagination of many ideological people.

But that's the difference with Devos and other Trump enthusiasts; their passion, like his, isn't especially ideological. "I was really about moving things. Making a difference. Like when I am working and you help someone and you make a difference, and no one is paying attention and you don't get credit for it, you know, when it means something. That was what this felt like. Doing something good and important and significant while no one was watching. It was not for credit.

"When he said 'drain the swamp,' you know, clean up Washington if you will, well, I really liked that. And I still like that. It is a shame that nobody in the press has given him a chance," Devos says, writing off criticism of the president's first months in office.

"No one in Congress is bending just an inch to get things passed—it really makes you feel as though everybody's against him. It's awful. Like my husband and I were talking about it, we just throw up our hands and quit when we turn on the news or pick up the newspapers," she says, clearly frustrated.

Such impatience, and a history of nonengagement in the often incremental political process, highlights perhaps the greatest danger to the GOP as the populist-tinged Trump coalition becomes its most logical formula for future Republican victories. Voters such as Devos, who were unmotivated to vote for the GOP—or anyone— before Trump, may not have the political stamina to slog through a series of legislative disappointments. And it remains to be seen whether Trump can motivate this most important group of his loyalists to show up on behalf of other Republican candidates who are now his allies, or whether they will remain engaged once he leaves the political scene.

Eighty-nine percent of Trump voters represented in the Great Revolt Survey agree with the statement "Republicans and Democrats in Washington are both guilty of leading the country down the wrong path"—a stunning rebuke for congressional Republicans from their own voting coalition, and a cudgel that Trump will be tempted to wield when he reaches an impasse with his party in Congress.

The Great Revolt Survey in August 2017 asked Trump voters to rank five institutions in order of their trust in them to "do the right thing to benefit the country": Trump, Republicans in Congress, big businesses, Democrats in Congress, and national media outlets. Trump was rated most trusted by 60 percent of respondents, congressional Republicans by 25 percent, big business by 6 percent, congressional Democrats by 4 percent, and national media outlets by just 2 percent. Congressional Republicans fared better in the larger urban and suburban jurisdictions where Trump was the softest in the 2016 elections, and among college graduates, but he was still given sizable margin advantages on trust even in those sub-cells eight months into his tumultuous presidency.

For marginal voters drawn to Trump's nonideological, antipolitical message more than to the GOP's conservative orthodoxy, it may not be enough for Republicans merely to be the alternative to Democrats in subsequent elections. Earning the votes of this slice of the Trump coalition may depend foremost on their perception of a candidate's loyalty to Trump as an individual. It is through this lens that Devos sees congressional inaction—and she contrasts it with her belief that congressional Republicans were feckless in opposing Obama.

"I just wish they would let that health care go through," Devos says of the failed GOP attempt to repeal the Affordable Health Care Act in 2017. "I mean, with Obama, they went and let him do everything he wanted. I mean, they didn't stop him doing anything, and poor Trump is trying to do everything good, and everybody's trying to stop him," Devos says.

She claims there isn't much that would make her not like Trump anymore. "I mean, I guess if he became part of the swamp, but honestly there may be plenty of disruptive things he does, surprises and so forth, but that isn't one of them."

It is not hard to imagine Devos deciding that congressional Republicans have not done enough to support Trump to earn her confidence in the 2018 midterm elections, in which he will not technically be on the ballot himself—or that voting for president again in 2020 will not make a difference. The physics of that equation—going from the drive of a traditional left-right tension to the unpredictability of an inside-outside conflict—is a part of the 2016 election's payoff that many GOP leaders have yet to accept or, in some cases, grasp. In the age of Trump, the toppling of institutions may be a larger and more important measure of progress for Republicans than the advancement of any political philosophy. But the toppling of institutions is hard to accomplish from the institutional perch of the three branches of government.

Devos, and many like her, simply do not need the outlet of politics.

After a lifetime, she checked in and can just as easily check back out. It's not central to her identity and she likely won't miss it if she does. With five grandchildren, three from her son, two from her daughter (and her husband has grandchildren and a great-grandchild from his first marriage), a job at J. C. Penney, and a healthy commute, she enjoyed her life plenty before she got on board the Trump Train.

Devos reaches back in her memory bank to discuss food and family cooking again, and her descriptions really make you hungry. "My mother just made pork chops and stuffing and dumplings, but my dad, oh, my dad he used to make these pancakes. I think they are really crepes that he made, because I remember they were thin pancakes and light and fluffy, but back then you wanted to fit in, so I think we just called them pancakes."

She goes on to create an image of a delicate dough, almost like lace, artfully rolled on a plate. "They were wonderful with orange peel gently grated on the top." Somewhere, she says, her brother has her father's recipes preserved from the Belmont Hotel; she'll have to make them sometime.

One gets the feeling her family dinners will be just as filling even if politics gets taken off the menu.

4

Rough Rebounders

Unconventional candidates attract voters for unconventional reasons. And the way Americans choose between presidential candidates is as emotional as any consumer behavior. The old axiom among political pros is the "beer test"—which of two candidates would most voters prefer to share a beer with. The consensus answer to that question rarely loses on Election Day.

In 2016, one group uniquely attracted to Donald Trump, regardless of their politics, was voters who had experienced a setback in life and saw the same kind of vulnerability and recovery in Trump as they had experienced.

A billionaire who regularly bragged about working back from debt and broken real-estate deals, Trump was also a twice-divorced playboy whose personal life was far from unimpeachable. Unlike the perfectly coiffed, family-portrait, groomed-from-childhood-to-be-president Mitt Romney or the image-conscious, guarded, lifetime political calculator Hillary Clinton, Trump was perfectly imperfect to a wide swath of the electorate. For all his braggadocio, he was vulnerable in a way neither Romney nor Clinton could be. His coarseness and profanity on the campaign trail reinforced his authenticity to them—and made him a candidate worth walking through the fire of media ridicule to support. With every fact check done by the media on his outlandish, technically false boasts, typical of a condo salesman, he ironically proved he was exactly what they were looking for—the opposite of the stereotypical politician.

To this group, the Americans who had overcome adversity and imperfection in their own lives, Trump's appeal was inextricable from his foibles, be it bankruptcies or family ruptures or tragic mistakes. Even in the primary season, focus groups found that this type of voter, the Rough Rebounder, was the earliest, and often most enthusiastic, adopter of Trump.

The Great Revolt Survey reveals that the Rough Rebounders in the Great Lakes states are decidedly more secular than the rest of the Trump coalition. Only 24 percent self-report weekly church attendance, compared to nearly 40 percent of overall Trump voters in those states. Barely more than half of this group call themselves conservative, compared to almost two-thirds of Trump voters overall. One in three Rough Rebounders are not Republicans, and fully 30 percent say they voted for Obama in either 2008 or 2012. Correspondingly, they put more trust in Trump to do the right thing for the country than other Trump voters do, relative to their trust in business, the media, or congressional Republicans and Democrats; a full two-thirds of Rough Rebounders rank their trust in Trump ahead of those other institutions, and an additional 16 percent rank him second.

Rough Rebounders were the most forgiving of Trump's lewd comments to *Access Hollywood* host Billy Bush—the only archetypical group of Trump voters surveyed in which fewer than 4 in 10 were offended by his comments. Given the fact that so many have experienced economic tragedy in their lives, it's no surprise that Rough Rebounders have the highest level of anti-corporate sentiment among Trump voters, with 85 percent saying corporations do not care if their decisions hurt working people.

When Republicans lose elections, donors and media pundits routinely admonish party leaders that they must become less ideologically rigid, and less conservative, to win. It's unlikely that the Rough Rebounders—a more pragmatic group than the normal GOP base—is the bloc those critics had in mind to broaden the Republican coalition into a winning one in 2016, but with Donald Trump at the top of the ticket that's exactly what happened. A less glamorous target than elite upscale social moderates, hip millennials, or racial minorities, Rough Rebounders nonetheless helped add votes to the GOP coalition that neither John McCain nor Mitt Romney got—and Trump's ability to keep them active and supporting his legislative allies will help shape Republican prospects in the 2018 midterms.

Cindy Hutchins

Baldwin, Lake County, Michigan

Take one step inside Cindy Hutchins's variety store on Michigan Avenue and you know that if you want it, it's here, somewhere, if you can find it.

Northern Treasures is a throwback to the old five-and-dime department stores that once flooded America's Main Streets and cities—with wide aisles, lunch counters, hardwood floors, and stock that included sewing items, soaps, canned goods, fishing gear, gadgets, and wooden yo-yos.

While there is no lunch counter in Northern Treasures, there is pretty much everything else.

Outside, the sign welcoming shoppers reads, NORTHERN TREASURES, A VARIETY STORE AND A WHOLE LOT MORE. Not only is the sign not false advertising, this scrappy little store in a town of 1,500 serves as a portrait of Hutchins herself: compact, punching back against the odds, and achieving the American dream one dollar at a time.

Hutchins's approach to retail is a complete rejection of the overflowing, fluorescent-lit multitude of bargain dollar emporiums that now serve as anchors in strip malls across the country. Dollar Tree, Dollar General, Family Dollar, and the Dollar Store are places where the shopping adventure goes to die, with seasonal items in the front to lure you in; no name brands; cleaning products and plastic items made from China and India flooding the shelves in back.

Northern Treasures is like a walk into your grandmother's pantry and attic simultaneously; there are cubbies filled with colorful balls of yarn, antiques on sturdy bookcases sold by consignment, bolts of calico fabric, T-shirts celebrating the town's biggest event of the year—the "Blessing of the Bikes" motorcycle rally—canned goods, locally made crafts, fishing gear, sewing kits, spinners, makeup, and purses. So many purses.

"That is how this whole thing started," says Hutchins of her purses, then gesturing toward the entire contents of the variety store, which is larger than your average chain dollar store.

"I was always one of those people that was an entrepreneur-y type of a person. I started out selling purses after my husband went and got hurt in an accident. I thought, 'I got to do something. I can't just sit here,'" she says.

Hutchins's husband, Norm, went to one of the local flea markets and opened a booth selling a variety of things when he could no longer work construction after getting hit by a beer truck. For a while things were tough for her family. "That didn't work out, because the overhead was too much. In the meantime, I set up somewhere selling my own thing," she says of selling the item every woman needs, to carry all of her stuff—and wants, because they are either stylish or practical: purses.

"I worked in a hospital. I'd set up in the break room after my shift, and I'd sell a thousand dollars of purses in three or four hours. I'd start doing different spots 'round the hospital, I'd just set up and sell. It helped pay the bills," she says.

Cindy and Norm began coming up to bucolic Lake County, Michigan, from their home in Elkhart, Indiana, years before her husband's accident, camping and fishing up here so often that they eventually bought a small home. After Norm got hurt, she soon started dragging her purse inventory up to Baldwin, eighty-five miles north of Grand Rapids. "We'd set up down at the corner there," she says, pointing to an empty lot kitty-corner from their present store.

"The owner would rent us the lot for a holiday weekend, and we would clean up. We thought we wanted to live up here because of the situation down there [in Elkhart] and the circumstances. My husband didn't know if he'd be able to work again in construction, and we thought, 'Well, let's move up here. The house is paid for,'" she says of their second home.

Every day, Cindy and Norm grow out of the shadow of a life-altering tragic event, thanks to a new start in a new place. They see themselves as underdogs who are beating the odds the system gave them. And in 2016, Cindy Hutchins found an unlikely presidential candidate who was the biggest political underdog in recent memory—a billionaire who loved to tell a story about how he bounced back from being nearly a billion dollars in debt in the early 1990s:

> I was walking down Fifth Avenue with a very beautiful woman . . . and I said, isn't that amazing, right now that man is richer than I am. And this beautiful woman said, "What do you mean? He's not richer than you." I said yeah, he's worth $900 million more. I said, right now, that man is richer than me. She said why? Because let's assume he's worth nothing. But I'm worth minus $900 million.
>
> —Donald Trump, Washington Post interview[1]

One of the unique archetypes in the Trump coalition in 2016 was a group of voters who did not come to him via a shared political affinity, but from an unlikely connection of perspective. The Rough Rebounders saw in Trump not only someone who had beaten the odds, but someone who might give a damn about other people trying to beat the odds, and shake up the political system as he went.

Rough Rebounders could be found in the front rows of every one of Trump's signature packed-house arena rallies. They were his enthusiastic defenders in even the roughest days of his up-and-down primary and general election campaigns. Unfazed by his scandals, galvanized by the knowledge that it seemed the political establishment and the press were adversarial to him, they projected their own uphill climb onto his.

Whether they were bouncing back from foreclosure, bankruptcy, multiple family breakups, or business calamity, Rough Rebounders saw in Trump something they wanted to believe about themselves—a resilient and unconventional survivor who seemed tougher than his critics and his obstacles. Trump's missteps and gaffes and penchant for saying the impolitic, the inappropriate, or just the inaccurate, endeared him even more to many of these voters. Where journalists and political elites in both parties saw someone unready or uninformed, they saw someone winning in an arena totally foreign to the rest of his career. In that, Rough Rebounders saw another parallel to their own lives—making things work in an unlikely and unexpected new phase of life where the rules aren't always easy to follow.

Politics might have been the last place to expect Donald Trump to succeed. And Lake County might be the last place you'd expect for a rebound like Hutchins's.

With 11,539 residents, according to the last census, tiny Lake County is known primarily for three things: an abundance of pristine lakes and rivers, superb all-terrain-vehicle trails, and the fact that you are never legally required to stop at a red light. Why? Because there aren't any. Literally, there is not one traffic light in this entire northern Michigan county.

Baldwin, where Hutchins's shop, Northern Treasures, is located, is the largest town in the county, but it isn't even a town in the legal sense; it's a village, and also the county seat. It has to be; there are no larger populated places in Lake County.

Baldwin relies on tourism of the active variety: fishing, canoeing, hunting, and camping, which attract city dwellers in the summer and fall.

The foot traffic from locals and some snow sports help keep the lights on at Hutchins's store in the winter, as well as in the two bars located on Michigan Street.

Life in Lake County is for the hardy. It will never be easy, there will never be an abundance of jobs, but the pace is good and so are its people. It is also known for deep economic deficiencies; a study done by 24/7 Wall Street shows that the county's poverty rate of 30.5 percent, coupled with an 11 percent unemployment rate, makes Lake the poorest county in the state. The results also show that a typical household in Lake County earns $20,000 less than the typical household in any other county in Michigan.[2]

Just east of Baldwin is a small town called Idlewild, once one of the few resorts in the country where blacks vacationed in high style and owned property. When racial discrimination became illegal in 1964, it faded in popularity and eventually slipped into oblivion.

The county has endured a complicated relationship with its largest employer, the North Lake Correctional Facility, for a decade. State budget cuts closed the facility in 2005. It briefly reopened in 2011, then closed again until June 2015, when inmates arrived from Vermont.

In 2017, the privately owned and operated facility—which has housed only inmates from outside the state during its roller-coaster existence—again faced uncertainty when it closed again, costing a community of 1,500 more than a hundred full-time jobs.

Lake County's voters are traditional blue-collar Democrats, and the jobs that matched their skills and work ethic were once abundant here. But that has not been the case for a very long time.

Still, Lake County stuck with the Democrats. In presidential elections, it gave local majorities to Barack Obama, John Kerry, Al Gore, Bill Clinton, Michael Dukakis, Walter Mondale, Jimmy Carter, Hubert Humphrey, and Lyndon Johnson. It even voted for landslide loser George McGovern—one of fewer than two hundred U.S. counties to do so.

For U.S. Senate, Lake County has voted for only one Republican nominee in more than half a century, and that was only by forty-one votes in 1994, the same year the GOP routed the Democrats. During election-night television coverage, Lake was consistently a blue Democratic dot surrounded by a sea of rural Republican red in northern Michigan.[3]

Obama won this county by over 12 percentage points in 2008, and by 5 points in 2012.

Then the dam broke.

In 2016, Donald Trump pummeled Hillary Clinton in Lake County by a whopping 23-percentage-point gap, the fourth-widest swing from Democrat to Republican among Michigan's eighty-three counties.[4]

Hutchins is one of those voters who broke the dam—voting for Obama twice, only to flip to Trump.

The petite brunette with sun-streaked hair is fiercely determined and independent. Twenty years ago, before political correctness had taken over our vocabulary, Hutchins would have been called a "firecracker." Ironically, she has no self-awareness of her unflappable persona, maybe because for her, life has never been easy.

Hutchins was born in Marcellus, a village along the Michigan-Indiana border, with work the only constant.

"Grew up on a farm. Dad worked in a factory. Mom worked part-time sometimes in some restaurants," she rattles off. "I worked cleaning houses and in the high school cafeteria, to help so I could pay for my school clothes."

She calls her upbringing blue-collar, middle-class, and staunchly Democrat. "My dad was a union factory worker, at the dinner table politics was always discussed; back in the day, the Democrats represented the working people. They actually represented them and their interests . . ." Her voice trails off. "Yeah, well, that's just a thing of the past."

A customer comes in looking for a certain kind of thread. Hutchins is out, but gives her cell phone number to the woman to call when she knows she is heading back to the store.

"And if I don't pick up, just leave a message, sometimes when I am on call doing home care there is no cell service," she tells her. Home care nursing is her other job—Lake County is the kind of place where people who get by do it with more than one occupation.

Democrats *were* the voice of the people, and they protected the working class, Hutchins says as the customer, turning to leave, chimes in even though no one asked: "Yep, and that's the way it was. A lot of older people don't realize that's not the same anymore," she says.

Straight out of high school, Hutchins registered as a Democrat and joined the army.

"I was at Fort Jackson, South Carolina, then Fort Hood, Texas," she says, explaining that she left the army with an honorable discharge soon after she got married and moved to Elkhart, Indiana.

"I just did waitressing jobs, and then I saw the economy in the country collapse right in my backyard. Elkhart, Indiana, is the recreational vehicle and manufactured housing capital of the world, it essentially sets the tone for a lot of the economic climate in the country because of the RV industry."

RVs, a luxury product consumed almost exclusively by the middle class, sell well when those customers are comfortable with their economic prospects—and the market dips when they are uneasy.

"It was the 1990s and the recreational vehicle and factory housing bubble had just exploded," she says, and while she did not work in the industry directly, her bottom line was impacted along with that of the factory workers.

"I was a waitress at Bob Evans, and I remember it. I started making maybe seven dollars a day in tips and I usually made at least a hundred a day in tips. I'd owe the babysitter six dollars, which wasn't much back then. And I thought, 'I have to do something different.'"

Her first marriage ended in the downturn, leaving her a single mom with two sons.

With nowhere to go but up and out, she headed to the local welfare office and took a test to see how her skills could match up with available careers or classes.

"I think I finished the test in half the time and only got one question wrong, so they said, 'Whatever you want to do, you can pretty much do.' So with the help of some grants because I was a veteran, I went to school to be a registered nurse." After graduation she started working in long-term care, remarried, and moved north to Lake County after her husband's accident.

"Somebody in a beer company truck slid into his van and messed him all up so he couldn't work," Hutchins explains. "We had wage replacement from the insurance company, but after a while, they sent him to a doctor and the doctor said there was nothing wrong with him, which was totally not correct," she says.

"I could no longer pay our mortgage and the mortgage company won't work with me. Ten years, never been late, never missed a day, and the mortgage company was like, 'If you send us ten thousand dollars . . .' I said, 'Yeah, at the end of the day, you can kiss my ass is what I say,'" she says, laughing.

She essentially handed the mortgage company the keys to her home and moved the family to their modest Lake County weekend home. Eventually her husband was able to go back to work, her two sons made it out on their own, and she found a job doing home care.

Her union-member father's affiliation with the Democratic Party rubbed off; her first vote for president was for Walter Mondale in 1984, and she stuck with the party through the next seven presidential elections, with particular enthusiasm for Barack Obama.

"Obama had this incredible presence. It was just like, 'Wow, fresh, and he seems like a good Christian man and he has values and his family seems not all scandalous and all that.' Yeah, I did. I voted for him twice. I thought, 'Well, the first year he's just getting his feet wet, or first term. Getting his feet wet. He didn't do a whole lot of harm,'" she explains. But midway through Obama's second term, Hutchins was tired of his policies and tired of the Democratic Party she had spent an entire lifetime supporting.

"The second term, I think it was almost like he just did whatever, whenever. I don't know that it was by his own doing or that he was influenced that way that he should do that, or coerced or anything like that. He was actually to the point of I think dangerous as a president to our country. He ran our country into the ground.

"It was very much a part of who I was and part of my identity, it was not an easy break to make, but now that I have made it there is no going back," she says.

"Towards the middle of the second [Obama] term I was like, 'Oh my god, the end of this can't come soon enough.' He keeps doing damage. He keeps doing irreparable damage to our country, financially. Financially, we were just out of control and everybody started expecting everything can be free. Free cell phones, free college, free health care, it was just like people were just excited about anything they got free. The entitlement was crazy.

"One lady that worked for me at the store who gets some government assistance said to me during the election, 'If Trump wins, I'll lose all my free stuff.' That was exactly her thoughts. That's why they all liked Bernie Sanders, because he said everything could be free. Well, everything can't be free, and that's what these young kids were thinking that are all in college that voted for him. Give them free stuff and a hug. We cannot sustain ourselves as a country with nothing but hugs and handouts. And that was what my party became, it is ridiculous. It pains me to say this, it really does, but my party used to value hard work, used to value climbing up the ladder. Now everyone wants to just sit at the bottom of the ladder and expect someone else to climb it for them and then hand over the prize."

Hutchins had for years resisted even the notion of voting for Republicans. "I used to think that the Republican Party stood for country club folks in nice suburban homes who talked about bottom lines and stock prices. Not anymore; they are for the blue-collar worker, they are for me, and the irony is not lost on me."

Hutchins knew the moment Donald Trump came down the escalator at Trump Tower in 2015 that he was her candidate. "I knew because I knew he was a businessman and I knew as a businessman that I liked his ideas. I liked his honesty. I liked the way he didn't take crap from anybody, and he didn't let anybody run his opinion," she says.

"I knew it was only going to get worse. I knew if Hillary Clinton got elected, oh my god. Socialism. I don't know if we'd be able to sit here right now, if Hillary got elected, and speak," she explains.

Obamacare was certainly one of the tipping points of her fracture with Obama, the Democrats, and Clinton; her monthly health insurance costs are more than 50 percent higher than they were before Obamacare. "And my deductible went from $1,000 to $2,500 a year."

"You know, one of the things I really don't get about the Democratic Party or the news media is the lack of respect they give to people who work hard all of their lives to get themselves out of the hole. It is as though they want to punish us for the very things we hold dear: hard work, no dependence on the government, no debt, and so on," she says.

"Don't even get me started on how they feel about gun ownership. I was raised in a home with guns. A card-carrying union Democrat home with guns, and yet someone says there is something wrong with me for being comfortable around a gun or using one.

"A lot of people probably think, 'Oh, you're a woman with a gun. You're probably a bitch.' That's probably what they think . . . It doesn't make you a bad person. It makes you a protected person. I got my concealed pistol license when we first moved up here. I had a .22, [and] a long gun," she says.

A bad experience in her store led her to that decision. "We had somebody walk in our store and walk out with merchandise, which I would never shoot anybody for that. I would just call the police, which is what I did," she says.

It's the backstory about that person that changed her. When they took him to court, the shoplifter claimed on the witness stand to have multiple personalities, and that he hadn't taken his medicine for a month.

Describing the robbery, she says, "At first I confronted the person, but then I just backed off because I could tell with my nursing background something wasn't right there. And I thought, 'You know what? I'm just going to call the police and they can handle it.' And they did. They caught them and they were prosecuted, but it was just like I thought. You never know when this could go a different direction. I need to be protected, plus I'm out here and I'm by myself at home sometimes.

"Where I live is very isolated. I've had a van pull up one time and this young kid comes towards my door with a roll of paper towels in his hand. Before he got too close I came to the door and said, 'First of all, I just need to let you know that I do have a gun and you need to leave my property.' I had it holstered. He left. I walked back inside the house and went to check out the back door and the van had driven back there . . ." She called the police. "This is why I need protection. And I have the right to that protection."

Today she has four guns. "They are all pink in some way. One's dipped in muddy girl camo, my little .22 that I carry. The other one, I just got it Christmas, is a nine millimeter. I got a Taurus .380 and a .38 Special—a .38 Special's a revolver."

Hutchins's independent streak extends beyond her desire for physical self-protection.

"I don't charge anything. I have no credit cards. If I can't pay for it, I am not buying it," she says of her personal spending habits.

"A lot of people don't understand what the 2016 election was about. It really wasn't about Trump, I mean not really. It's about this town and this county, and this state and this country, and that is all very hard for the news media to boil down because it does not make sense to them and their worlds," she says.

Another customer walks in looking for fidget spinners—the latest widget toy for distracted kids—and Hutchins points her toward a basketful, to the young mother's delight. Hutchins again gives out her cell number in case the mom is looking for something different next time.

"You can't get that kind of service at the dollar store," says the woman.

"Heck, you can't get that kind of service from your doctor," Hutchins says. "But you can from a nurse." She beams about her other full-time job.

"That election was about this store. Everyone in this country has some version of this store, something they achieved either by accident or determination or both. And we had been missing that for years. We kinda didn't know we were missing it, but we all finally pulled together and did it.

"But because it is larger than Trump, at least I think so, that thread between all of these various types and kinds of people has begun to stitch together. Yes, we were angry, but we were and are hopeful, aspiring for a better life, a better town, a better country."

David Millet

Erie, Erie County, Pennsylvania

David Millet tucks his half-eaten sandwich back into the black-and-white checkered parchment paper inside the basket in front of him. He stands, carefully wipes his hands and face, steps away from the picnic table, and begins to sing.

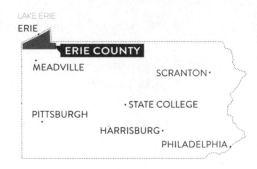

"On a warm summer's evening / On a train bound for nowhere / I met up with a gambler"

His raspy baritone voice croaks and croons, pitch-perfect. His snow-white hair—a little on the longish side—enhanced with a neatly trimmed goatee and sparkling blue eyes, could convince you that you're listening to Kenny Rogers freestyle singing without a band in the parking lot of the Ugly Tuna Tavern on Peninsula Drive on Erie's west side.

For an instant, you are convinced you are looking right at him. Except, of course, you are not. Nonetheless, a handful of young people walking into the popular bar cheer him on and coax him for more.

He obliges; he can't help himself.

Then he smiles shyly and sits down to finish his dinner. At sixty-eight, Millet has seen it all and then some. But for now on Tuesdays and Thursdays, he does Kenny Rogers impersonations.

"Years ago, when I was working in Connecticut, karaoke first came out. That was, like, 1990. I was with a bunch of managers at dinner to kind of get to know everybody, you know what I mean kind of a deal? This is who this person is, that one runs that department, that kind of stuff. We're sitting at a restaurant, and we got out of work late 'cause we're managers. We don't get out of work on time. We get out late. It was like seven before we started eating, nine by the time we're done. Just bullshittin' there. This guy sets up this machine there. He brings books around. Nobody else is in the place."

Millet recalls asking him what he was doing. "The guy explained it's like the old days of the bouncing ball, you just follow the words on the screen and you sing along. As the department heads were getting to know each other, one of them says, 'Well, I'd do it, but I gotta have somebody sing with me.'"

"'Shit. I'll sing with you,' I told him, and I got up and I sang with him. I was in love. It was so much fun. Wow."

Since then Millet has also cultivated an uncanny physical resemblance to Kenny Rogers. He has won contests, and done the "impersonator circuit" at small clubs and casinos around the Great Lakes cities and towns.

"I never bought tapes, CDs weren't out yet. But my daughter had Kenny Rogers's *Greatest Hits* in the car. I had an eight-hour trip every weekend back one way from my job in Connecticut to my home in Erie. Eight hours, eight hours, eight hours, eight hours. To keep myself awake, I'd listen to that Kenny Rogers tape and that's how I got good."

Millet was born and raised in Wesleyville, a working-class Erie County town and suburb of the city of Erie. The township literally sits in the shadow of the massive General Electric locomotive plant to its north. U.S. Route 20, the longest U.S. route in the country, spanning 3,365 miles coast-to-coast, runs straight through the middle of town.

Downtown Erie is only a few miles away, across more than a few sets of railroad tracks. Over Millet's adult lifetime, Erie County has fought to just hold its own. Just over halfway between New York and Chicago and situated on a Great Lake, a major highway, and trunk railroad lines, Erie boomed in the period following World War II, adding 100,000 people to reach a population of 275,572 by 1980. It's hardly ever been larger since. Now aging and in economic transition, Erie's trying to rebound itself—a situation that runs in David Millet's family.

When he was young, Millet's father managed a car dealership. "And then eventually that dealership closed. So, he got into insurance. He was into insurance for a long time. Became a claims supervisor. Then my brother got out of the navy and wanted to start a body shop, and that was where my dad's heart was, so they opened a body shop," he says. It is the job from which his father eventually retired.

After high school, Millet served an apprenticeship to be a tool and die maker.

"During my apprenticeship, you had to take at least two nights a week for classes. I went four. I took engineering instead, because I figured I might as well do something with, you know, my time and my abilities. So, I got an associate's degree in engineering. I got into management later. I was a unique kind of a guy, where I understood the whole mechanics of tools and the process. I got to learn the process at a place that I worked, so I became valuable that way," he says.

Despite his tenacity, he has never worked at the same place for a very long time. "The longest I worked anywhere was eight years. But, five years, you know, six years, here and there. I moved around a little. I got a job in Connecticut for a year, and just stuff like that. I managed Tetra Tool over here in Erie, then Emsco Plastics."

And then he got sick. Very sick.

"I was forty-nine years old and I couldn't even write my name. My body was just done for six years like that. I couldn't even get off the couch," he says.

Everything on his body hurt, nothing worked, even his eyelashes hurt. For a long time, no one could figure out what was wrong.

"Chronic fatigue syndrome is what they called it, but I found out what it really was. It was a yeast infection. It's called Epstein-Barr Candida Albicans yeast, and I stumbled onto it later," he says.

While he was sick his wife, Evelyn—"Evie"—was stricken with cancer. "My wife passed away. She got cancer. I couldn't work. Things really were bad, you know?"

Tears fill his eyes, his ruddy complexion flushes red, and he stares off for a very long time. He struggles to maintain his composure.

Millet's is a very masculine presence; it is clear that he takes pride in his role as a man in control, but for the moment he is not.

"I could take her pain pills. I finally got the doctor to prescribe them for me. I said, 'Hey. I'm just telling you, with the Vicodin, I can do something for, like, four hours. I can't do it any other way.'"

He needed a couple of hours a day of pain relief so he could care for his dying wife. "I had to take care of her, so I did," he says.

She died in 2002 at the age of fifty.

A couple of years later he met a woman who had teenage children. "I was helping her kids with the Internet, because I build computers for a hobby. They didn't have Internet access. Nowadays, it's like you got it on your phone, but back then it was different," he explains.

Millet eventually connected the old computer to the Internet and the kid was able to use it to do research for the project. It was a biology report on different funguses and how they impact the human body. The research revealed what Epstein-Barr Candida Albicans yeast is and what it does to your body.

"I started reading down through it, and I was like, 'That's me. Oh, shit,'" he says. "So that was it. I changed my diet, and [in] three months, I was like a new man again.

"I lost my career out of the whole thing, but I've started back bartending with my friend. She worked down here at the Clifton Manor. One night, two nights. They were only open three nights. Did that. Then a guy one night comes in and after we talk for a while he offers me a job at FedEx. And I am back in the game."

Politically, Millet has never been a Democrat, but he's also not exactly the most loyal card-carrying Republican.

"I was attracted to the Republican Party at a young age. Let me rephrase that: I was attracted to the ideas and values the Republican Party is supposed to stand for; a respect and admiration of the Constitution and the virtue in working for a living," he says. "I'm very skeptical of organizations, though, including the establishment part of the Republican Party, so in that way I am not one of those ideologues."

Millet is skeptical about Republicans, but he's not skeptical about Donald Trump, a take-charge guy after Millet's own heart—and someone with the black-and-white approach a Rough Rebounder can rally behind.

"My dad always worked. He worked two jobs. We had seven kids, so he was a smart man. Smart, smart man. He did bodywork on the weekends to supplement working for an insurance company as an adjuster. He built his own house, you know what I mean?"

At the beginning of the 2016 primary season, Millet liked the outsiders such as Ben Carson and Trump and Ted Cruz ("because of how Cruz was always sticking it to the establishment in Washington").

"I never liked Jeb Bush. Not even the least little bit did I like Jeb Bush. Chris Christie, nope. John Kasich turned me right off at the end there when he tried that crap political stuff, manipulating stuff with his delegate argument for a brokered convention. Oh man, that just froze him for me," he says.

In the past, Millet has voted for candidates he didn't particularly like, such as George W. Bush. "You gotta vote for one or the other. That's what America's about. We got only a couple parties worth voting for. I didn't want to throw my vote away. This whole swamp shit that's down there is so corrupt on both sides that I felt he was the lesser of the two corrupts. He was for pro-life. When it gets down to it, I gotta go pro-life. I can't monkey around killing babies, okay. Can't do it. If you have that choice, I gotta go that way.

"George Bush never impressed me. Never impressed me. I wasn't fond of his dad. Okay with him, but not fond. [Not like] 'God, I want to follow this guy anywhere,'" he says of Bush senior.

Ronald Reagan, on the other hand, was Millet's hero. "I've got every time he was ever on TV on VHS," he explains of the old analog videotape recordings popular from the 1980s until the turn of this century. "I got racks and racks of tapes of everything he ever did."

Millet started taping him because he could not believe what he was hearing, "This guy's not gonna do this stuff. None of them do. They can say anything they want to get in office. What they do after they're in office generally doesn't match up. They get swayed, whatever, whatever.

"I was interested in holding his feet to the fire, just like I am Trump," he says of another man that has really impressed him. "I just love the guy. I mean, I have to say, I just love him."

Millet isn't the only person in Erie with an outsized affinity for Reagan and Trump. The latter's plurality victory in Erie County, with 48 percent of the vote, was the highest total for a Republican here since Reagan's 51 percent in 1984, and the only other time a Republican has carried the county since Richard Nixon did it in 1972.[5]

"As I got to listen a little closer and realize the gist of what [Trump] was saying. What would you say as a nonpolitician? You'd say, 'Let's bomb the bastards.' Right? It's not like he's going to, but he says it to let people know he means business," Millet explains.

"The press takes him too literally," he says, echoing a refrain that became popular during the campaign by those trying to explain Trump's appeal.

Trump has to rely on the people he picks to be good at their jobs. If they aren't, he will find a not-too-subtle way to get rid of them, Millet says.

"When I managed Tetra Tool, my boss relied on me. When a customer called in and asked for something, he would say to me, 'Dave. When's that mold gonna be done?' I'd say, 'Thursday at two.' If I was wrong more than once, I would be in a different position real quick. I had to have my shit together because he relied on me. He was running the big show. He relied on me to run the whole shop, and to be into the nitty-gritty of what was going on. So, I can understand Trump, totally, being that way," he says of Comey's firing and Trump's displeasure with Attorney General Jeff Sessions.

"You know, being a toolmaker, you don't know what you're gonna make tomorrow. It could be making a case that looks like this with those cutouts like that. Could be that glass. It could be that cup. It could be the front of that," he says, pointing to a garden boundary stake. "You don't know. They throw this at you. What are you gonna tell them?

"Well yeah, I am going to tell them I can do it. You're gonna do it. You're gonna figure out a way to do it, and you have a certain logic that you follow and you say, 'Okay, okay, okay, okay.' There's nothing that stops, no doors, you know what I mean? At that point, you gotta have a can-do attitude, and that's what Trump has," Millet says.

He becomes animated explaining the Trump way. "I just love his moves with North Korea. When to hold 'em, when to fold 'em. He's like, 'Okay. I can go toe-to-toe with this young punk with a little-ass country like that. I'm big America. I can go toe-to-toe with 'em. I gotta show 'em a little lesson first. Okay. China, come on over here. You and I haven't gotten along. We haven't dealt with this. You don't like to buy our products. Whatever the reason, let's talk about it. But,

I'm gonna tell you, you're in missile range of North Korea. We're not, yet. Okay? They don't like you. Just sayin'. We'll help protect you. We're gonna do that. We're somewhat trading partners, but it's for your benefit.' He told everybody on the news, 'That son of a bitch. They're taking advantage of us.'

"It's a true statement, but you don't talk to 'em face-to-face that way either," Millet says, talking a mile a minute now.

"He knows what you said. He knows coming into that meeting what you think about him. Now you say, 'Okay. Here's the deal. You've been buying that coal from them. We gotta put a hurtin' on 'em. We don't want to bomb 'em. They're crazy. But we're crazier. We'll bomb 'em back. Their missiles ain't even gonna get off the ground and we're gonna knock 'em out. If need be, but we don't want to go that route. Cut their money off first. Now, you need coal. We have coal. All you gotta do is loosen up that trading so that it's a little more fair. And we're gonna make sure that, with that money we make, we'll put missiles, we'll line the whole 38th parallel with missiles, if you want, to help protect you.' 'Cause it protects us, it protects them. It's a win-win," Millet says, finally stopping to breathe.

Millet admired Trump when he met with the premier of China. "Their system is completely different than ours. I've worked with a lot of guys that have a completely different system of building a mold, building whatever, dealing with life. You find common ground, you get along. Doesn't mean you like him. Just means you're not gonna fight with him," he says.

His son, one of five children he had with his late wife, Evie, worked at the General Electric plant in the background. "He just got laid off from GE, so I know a little bit about GE . . ."

General Electric recently opened a new high-tech plant in Fort Worth, Texas, that Millet—and many locals interviewed in the spring of 2017—believes will eventually upend the plant in their city. "They're chasing the ball out of here. Drive down the street and see. All the regulations and all of the new technology chased everybody out," he says. (Their concerns would prove not off-base; in late July 2017, GE Transportation announced plans to end most locomotive production at the hundred-year-old plant, eliminating nearly 600 jobs. The work done in Erie will now be done in Fort Worth, Texas, beginning in late 2018.)

The last bastion of Erie's massive midcentury industrial base, GE Transportation had only recently lost its long-held status as the county's largest employer to the local hospital branch of the University of Pittsburgh's medical arm. In a graying city, the job of attending to the retired locomotive makers is becoming more lucrative than being a working one.

Millet's son, like his father, is remaking himself and trying to rebound. "Going to college right now. Forty-two years old, going to college."

His son also loves Trump. "Yeah. Absolutely. Absolutely. He [my son] is very much like me in that what gives you satisfaction in this life is the work, not the handout, not any of that stuff. Work. Not to get rich. That's why I'm still working at sixty-eight. I just love working. I want to have a job where I feel like I'm doing something. I only work part-time, so it's like I get the best of both worlds," he says.

Millet is not a fan of anything big. "Big banks, big media, big corporations, I want nothing to do with them." For him, it is personal.

"When I worked at Emsco, we made our own products. Snowboards, you name it, we made a lot of products. Walmart handled a lot of those products. Emsco liked to get into Walmart because, of course, you got nine thousand stores, and whatever, whatever. It makes sense, right?

"Okay. Here's what they did. We [Emsco] came out with some lawn edging," he says of the common pound-in landscape edging found on lawns across America.

"Walmart was like, 'Whoa. We'll take fifty thousand of them.' That's a lot of edges. Boxes of 'em, hundred to a box. Walmart says, 'We'll see how they go,' " Millet explains.

"Well, they sold like hotcakes. Emsco got about twelve to thirteen dollars per one hundred. Next year, Walmart orders 250,000 of 'em. We ended up having to build eleven molds altogether to produce like this. Hired people. Got machinery. We're banging these things out," he explains.

Millet says in the third year Walmart tells the company, " 'We weighed them. There's only an ounce of material in each one of those. We figure the cycle time on this should be thirty seconds. You should be able to make this many in a day for your machine. We're gonna give you eight dollars a hundred.'

" 'Wait a minute. It's our product. It's our product, and you're telling us how much? Now that we got eleven molds based on what you projected for the following year and you are essentially cutting our price nearly in half?' They went to China, had 'em built, knocked us off totally."

As a consumer, they're good for you, says Millet. "As a business thing in this country, they weren't so good. That is essentially the core of why I don't like big businesses or big political parties. It's kind of why I love Trump. He's not part of the ideological crowd, he is part of the 'let's do something' crowd."

Despite losing six years of his life to Epstein-Barr, Millet keeps going. "You can't give up. You reinvent yourself, you make bank, you find a way. You fall down, you get back up. I've lost plenty of jobs and I've earned plenty of jobs," he says.

Millet says he will "absolutely" vote for Trump again. "Well, here again, like Reagan, I'm gonna keep his feet to the fire. Long as he's trying, as long as he makes sure he has our back, well then he has my support."

Renee Dibble

Ashtabula, Ashtabula County, Ohio

Renee Dibble has eleven children, fifteen chickens, several roosters, a couple of rabbits, a goat, several ducks, three dogs, four kittens, and a lovely, modest home in Ashtabula, Ohio.

"The cows and the pigs are in the freezer," she jokes as she slowly makes her way through the kitchen into the living room.

The menagerie of animals is outside on this brisk spring day without a cloud in the sky. Her home is immaculate and charming, with a steep ceiling and rustic fireplace enhancing the living room.

Three separate photos of young men in Marine dress blues are at the center of the mantel. "Those are my Oreo cookie," she says of her three sons, two black, one white, all three smiling broadly.

The daughter of workhorse small-business-owning parents, Dibble has been a waitress, a caterer, a school bus driver, and a lifelong Democrat in a lifelong Democratic town that has seen better days.

She has soft, wavy blond hair that just reaches her clavicle, and her eyes are blue; she is built sturdily, but is struggling slightly. She is recovering from breast cancer.

She is in remission, but has had some recovery complications. She's on the rebound, and like a lot of people on the rebound, her tenacity has made her both pragmatic and impatient with politics—factors that drove her vote in 2016.

Outside the home, her husband is mowing the lawn. He is a detective with the city of Ashtabula's police force; she first laid eyes on him when he was a beat cop at a traffic stop. At the time both were divorced; she had two children, he had three.

"I was driving the catering truck for my parents' business and he had these older people who could barely see over the dashboard pulled over for some traffic violation. And he was smiling and he had these big teeth. I'm telling you, I could see these white teeth and I kept staring at him as I drove by and was wondering who the heck the little dude with all the teeth is," she says, smiling broadly, then blushing at the memory.

Her accent is classic eastern Ohio, where the sentences end in a preposition and the ends of words are bluntly clipped—as if the speaker is trying get to the point faster, using the fewest vowels and consonants possible.

It is a legacy of the early Scots-Irish settlers who migrated here centuries ago.

"I just kept thinking about him. That smile. And then a week later there was a riot at one of the bars that me and my sister were at. We go there and dance and shoot pool and darts and stuff. There happened to be a riot that night, and I happened to be there, and he was one of the cops that came. And I told my sister, I said, 'I think I'm going to go out with that guy.'"

They still had never met. It wasn't until months later at her son's Little League baseball game that she realized his son played on the same team. "I wasn't sure if he was married, he wasn't sure I was married. Then his daughter asked my daughter to play Barbies in the car while the boys were playing baseball that I found out he was divorced.

"Then I just kind of knew it was destiny," she says.

Renee Dibble grew up in the heart of the city of Ashtabula to working-class parents who were driven to succeed. "Sometimes I'd say too much," she says, explaining her childhood. "I spent most of my time with babysitters. My parents owned their own business, a catering business, and I was raised as an only child for ten years with workaholic parents."

Ten years later, her parents decided to adopt, and during the adoption process her mom got pregnant. "Yeah, when I was ten years old. I got two sisters," she says.

As a child, Dibble went to a Catholic elementary school. "It was church like every day, and then it was church with my dad, because Mom was Protestant, Dad was Catholic. So Mom didn't go, just Daddy. It was Dad and I. And then she would stay home with the little ones after we got them, and so it was just Dad and I," she says, smiling at the memory of the special time she spent alone with him.

"When I was ten we moved out into the country, got horses and a goat, you know, stuff like that."

In junior and senior high, she attended public schools. Both of her parents were staunch Democrats.

After high school she worked for her parents. "By then, in addition to their catering business, they bought a bar. Mom also had a craft shop," she explains, and sighs. Her body language is evident; her parents' prolonged absences impacted her.

"We had three businesses at one time, and it made it hard. So as a child, I was raised by babysitters. Mainly my grandmother. And then when the two little ones came, either one or the other would be home, just a little bit, but they were workaholics. They really were, it was constant," she says.

"It was hard," she repeats.

She spent a dozen years after high school working for her parents, and then decided to go back to school, "Only 'cause my baby sister talked me into it," she says of her biological sister.

"She graduated that year from high school and she asked me if I would take the test, 'cause I took her to go take her test down in Youngstown, and it's like, ugh, I really don't want to do this, but I'm going to take it for shits and giggles, basically."

Both she and her sister attended ITT Technical Institute and got secretarial certificates. But neither sister used her associate's degree.

The blended Dibble family eventually expanded to six, but that did not last long.

"We ended up building our own house out here in Jefferson when the kids started getting older, and just bursting and stuff. But my adopted sister, the one that's in the middle, gets into some trouble. She ended up getting pregnant and having a little girl. When the baby was born, the baby wasn't in good shape and needed a stable home. So she signed her over to me. So that's how we ended up with number seven," she explains dispassionately, as if reciting her mailing address or Social Security number. But she does not stop there.

"I was a bus aide for Ashtabula city school systems. There was two little boys, two little black boys," she says as she points to their military photos on the mantel. "My pictures are up there, a couple of them," she says, and smiles. Tears form; she brushes them away.

"They were living in a Home Safe shelter with their mom and younger brother and sister, and they were in kindergarten and the first grade. They came on the bus every day with these oversized ill-fitting clothes, their shoes were falling off their feet, because the clothing that they had and the shoes that they had were what was given to the home for spare clothes for the kids who were there with a parent," she explains.

"I told my husband, one day I am going to end up bringing these two little boys home to play with Nick, who was four—that's our biological son. I told him I couldn't handle this. These poor little guys are just . . . They just make my heart bleed. Their clothes are always dirty, they wear the same thing for weeks at a time. I can't handle it."

Her husband's response was that of a devoted husband used to his wife's big heart. "Yeah, yeah, okay, okay," he told her.

The two brothers, Matthew and Devon, were a bit older than Nick at five and six years old. But the boys became fast friends and Renee had fallen in love; the playdates soon became sleepovers, which soon became the boys living with them full-time.

"They had been with us for a few months—but then the mother ended up taking them back. Then one day she called and said she was moving with the kids to Cleveland," Dibble explains.

"My heart was broken, they were like my kids now."

After they moved to Cleveland, between Thanksgiving and Christmas, Dibble would call them every other night. "I called New Year's. We just pulled into my friend's driveway, and I had called to wish them a Happy New Year's and all that. Shortly later, the mom called me back, and it's to ask if we would take them for a couple of weeks. She had decided to leave Cleveland and move back to Ashtabula in a few weeks, and she wanted them to not have to keep changing schools until she got back."

The Dibbles picked up the boys on the second day of January, and when March rolled around they still had them. "It is 1998 and I get a phone call from Children's Services in Cleveland. They said, 'Do you have these two kids?' And I said, 'Yeah.' And they said, 'We'll be there to interview you, and possibly pick them up.' I said, 'You're not taking them anywhere.'

"Their mom had had another child at home that was born crack-addicted, and then found out that the youngest one that we had was also born crack-addicted, and there had been three others from him on down, that was three kids that were born crack-addicted. She's had, oh my god, ten kids and never raised any of them," she explains.

"So here they are . . ." she says, pointing to Matthew's and Devon's photos bookending her biological son, Nick, in the middle, "still our kids. I guess they're both in the Marines, and doing pretty well."

She beams.

Over the next ten years, the Dibbles became foster parents and eventually adopted two more children. "So our youngest is ten. We got him and his brother. They're ten and thirteen . . . so we decided to stop now."

With eleven kids, she is exhausted. "I don't like kids anymore," she deadpans. Then smiles.

Just then James, her youngest, walks in. He is put in charge of bringing the dogs—two Yorkies, Sophie and Lexi—in from the backyard. He politely balks.

"Oh my gosh. I said go get Lex, honey. Oh, that's Lexi rolling in the chicken coop. That's the thing to do! Go get her please, honey. He doesn't like bugs," she says, rolling her eyes at her son, explaining his aversion to going outdoors.

James relents and goes outside. He loves his mom and is silently willing to let a stranger know it.

The breast cancer hit Dibble in the middle of the night in 2015. "It was in March, sometime after midnight, and the blond Yorkie, the older one, had to go outside. And I let her out that door. And when I did so, and it's really weird the way it happened, because why did I not feel this sooner? Because already, it was a good size across the top of my breast. Anyway, I leaned, I crossed my arms and put my head against the door. And when I did that, it felt just right on the top of my hand. And I said, 'Something ain't right. That doesn't feel right.' Well, then I felt it, and it's like, 'I've got a lump.'"

The next day she visited the doctor, who told her to skip the mammogram and go straight for a biopsy, and asked sternly and urgently if she had a surgeon she preferred. She was shocked at the suddenness of everything. But it's one year later as she replays the story, and she is in remission. She had complications with the incisions and wasn't healing properly. She has been off from work for the longest stretch of her life. "I'm a full-time bus driver, yeah. But I had to take this whole year off. It has sidelined me a bit."

The cancer has stagnated the family's income for the present, and for the near future.

She says she feels pretty good, and then she says this: "Well, except they're watching a spot on my right breast that's got a bit of lump. Yes, I've got a lump, almost at the same exact spot that I had the lump the first time. Going to keep an eye on it. It's about two centimeters. And if it decides to get any bigger, if it does grow at all, they're going to go ahead and they'll do a biopsy and just take it from there. That's fine with me, 'cause you know, *pfff.* I'm not nursing kids anymore these days, and my bikini days were over thirty years ago. You can take both them girls," she says, pointing to her breasts, "I don't care."

She is clearly the kind of woman who does not dwell on things she cannot control. "Like I always say, I am the kind of person who doesn't let any grass grow under my feet."

Both Dibble and her husband were raised Democrats, and have always voted Democratic. She says they did not care for Barack Obama, but they also didn't care for John McCain or Mitt Romney.

But then came Donald Trump; for her, the attraction to him as a candidate was instant. She even switched her registration so that she could vote for Trump in the Ohio Republican primary—helping Trump rack up a 7-point win in Ashtabula over home state governor John Kasich, even as Kasich was carrying the state as a whole by 11 points.

"What [Trump] had to say was as if he had been part of my community all of my life; he understood the economic problems, the decay of our society, and that drain of our treasure, our children, out of our communities because there are no jobs or future in Ashtabula for a young person," she says, articulating a common concern among Midwest voters who have watched their communities bleed young people for three decades. That pull is very real for people who have lived here for generations—the sons and daughters of the sons and daughters who carved out a decent life here cannot do the same for their own sons and daughters.

"It makes you feel weak and powerless," says Dibble. "Like you have no control to hold your family and your community together, because you have no future to offer them."

The sentiment is expressed in census statistics. Ashtabula County's population peaked in 1980 at 104,215—it's 98,231 today and sliding by 0.5 percent every year, exemplifying the entire state of Ohio's population flatline while the Sunbelt grows. The county, which was once an economic engine, with chemical and power plants and bustling wharves on Lake Erie, now has an unemployment rate of 5.8 percent, which ranks it as just 60th best out of Ohio's 88 counties.[6]

Dibble's feeling of powerlessness led her to do something in October 2016 that she had never done before in her life. She went online and signed up, along with her husband and one of her sons, to attend a political rally.

"I was like, 'Oh hell, I'll try it.' So I went ahead and I did it, and I got tickets. Well, then I got a hold of my husband and I'm like, 'You're not going to believe what I just did.' He's like, 'What?' And I said, 'We're going to go see Trump.' He said, 'I am not going to go see Trump.' I said, 'Yeah you are, I got three tickets.' And he's like, 'How did you get three?' I said, 'This is what I did,' and he's like, 'Okay.' So I called my son Nick and I said, 'Listen, this is what's going on. I got tickets to go see Trump. Do you want to go?' And he's like, 'You got to be kidding me, I've always wanted to do something like this.' But when do you ever get the chance? You know?"

And off they went.

Trump's rally in Geneva was local history in the making—the last time a presidential candidate had come to Ashtabula County was 1960, when John F. Kennedy stopped there during a cross-country train tour.

The local paper reported that many in the crowd of thousands "had been lined up for hours to witness Trump's speech." He railed on Clinton in his rally—not for her liberalism, as most other Republican presidential aspirants would have done, but for her elitism.[7]

"The elites in government like Hillary Clinton believe they are entitled to do whatever they want," Trump said. "She lives the high life off the rigged system."[8]

Before they went to the event at the SPIRE Institute, an Olympic sports training facility, the Dibbles were a little apprehensive, due to what they'd seen of previous rallies on cable newscasts.

"Well you know, a lot of the portrayal was these rallies were negative, the people there are terrible. Then you go there, and now trying to explain what the atmosphere was like is difficult, it was so positive. And my expectation was that it wouldn't be," Dibble says.

"To me, it was really exciting. We had our banners, we still have them. The Trump banners, I got like one in every color. And I couldn't believe how even my husband, who is on the quiet side, was enjoying it and raising the banners with everyone else.

"It gives me goose bumps just thinking about it. You have to understand, we've never done anything like this before, we are not those people," she says, echoing another characteristic of otherwise hard-boiled Rough Rebounders—their own surprise at the level of enthusiasm they had for a candidate for public office.

Twelve percent of the Trump-voting respondents in the Great Revolt Survey report either attending, or having an immediate family member attend, a Trump campaign rally like the one in Ashtabula County—a key element of his campaign strategy.

Trump was never expected to do well in this northeasternmost county of Ohio—President Barack Obama had bested Republican presidential nominee Mitt Romney here by 13 percentage points, and neither President Bush ever carried the place for the GOP.

But win Trump did—carrying Ashtabula by a shocking 19 percent, and washing in a slate of local Republican candidates with him. It's a story repeated in hundreds of Midwestern communities where most every other Republican since Reagan had failed. In Ashtabula, Trump got 23,318 votes, which was 4,000 more than Mitt Romney had earned in 2012. Two local GOP candidates for county commission, the local legislature, rode his coattails with similar vote totals— wildly exceeding the GOP commission candidate totals from four years ago. A Republican candidate for an open state senate seat also carried Ashtabula. The unbroken row of local Democrats in the courthouse offices, such as sheriff and prosecutor, likely only survived because they ran unopposed.

Ashtabula is a portrait of Rust Belt America. The county hugs the shore of Lake Erie where the Port of Ashtabula was once one of the most important shipping and commercial hubs in the region; coal and iron and the other hard physical products of five states passed through here on their way to the world. Its votes and voters have almost always been reliably blue. The Democratic New Deal imprint on its election returns has been as indelible and as evident as the New England influence of its earliest settlers was on the county's famed wooden covered bridges.

Political experts and reporters have diagnosed Trump's disruption of Democratic streaks in places like this as the consequence of voters who are either uninformed, stupid, angry, or racist—and that rankles Renee Dibble.

" 'Racist.' Every time someone throws that at me I spit right back out: 'Let's see, our daughter that we've adopted is biracial. I got two hundred-percent black sons. I've got a half-Japanese grandson, a biracial daughter-in-law, and a daughter-in-law that is half Puerto Rican and half Mexican. I'm racist?' I love it when people say, especially if they're black or something and they say, 'You don't know about me, you don't know about . . . ,' well you know what, buddy? You have no idea who you're talking to. My family is, well, we are like a rainbow family. We're all mixed. It does not matter what color you are.

"And we voted for Trump because it's . . . Obviously, you are not too intelligent, either. Oh my god. That's a bad subject," she says, clearly agitated.

Voting for Trump has changed Dibble. "I don't see politics the same way anymore. Before, I saw it as this other thing, this thing I wasn't part of, this club where I didn't belong. And now I see it as a moral obligation, not just for myself and my family but for my community."

If Hillary Clinton had won, and a woman with Renee's background had said she was the mother of a rainbow family and that is why she cast her vote for Clinton, she'd be cast as the billboard for a public-service ad campaign about empowerment.

But "empowered" is not the kind of word most observers use about Trump voters.

"So to ask what would extricate me from Trump would be like asking me to remove me from myself, from my family, and from my community," she explains.

Her displeasure with traditional politicians in both parties has been twofold: job creation and direction.

"They have taken this country on the wrong track and ignored the economic conditions that were deteriorating right before their eyes. Ashtabula has been deteriorating since 1990, not since July of 2016. This is every politician's fault for the past thirty years; they have managed the decline while getting reelected off of our empty promises," she says.

Dibble outlines the contours of a third political movement, one that checks the other two while keeping its eyes wide open to the faults of its standard bearer.

"It's not that I think he is perfect, but we didn't want perfect. The reason, I think, and my husband will tell you the same darn thing too, it's because he tells it like it is.

"But see, that's why we would really get along really good, him and I," she says of Trump, as if he might walk up the sidewalk at any minute. "Because I'll tell it like it is, and if you don't like it, I don't really give a shit."

The implied intimate and personal connection Dibble projects between herself and Trump is not uncommon among voters who fit the Rough Rebounder archetype. They watched Trump on prime-time television and in entertainment rags for twenty years before he ran for office. They have seen him mocked and derided and isolated by people who they believe sit comfortably inside the economic and cultural balconies of America. They identify with his separation and see him, flawed as he is in his policy experience and personal character, as an authentically separate force that might serve as a counterbalance to things they no longer trust—a proxy for them in a battle they see themselves fighting in their own lives.

"I look at the world of politics totally different now than what I have in the past. You know, it's like you're trying to weigh things out when it comes to politicians. You're trying to weigh, you know, the good and the bad, this and the other. But from the beginning with Trump, it was different for me. That will never leave me. Not because I am blind to his faults, but because the other politicians' faults are so worse. Because their failures were our lives, and that is unforgivable," she says.

Outside, the lawn mower switches off, and her two Yorkies are ready for attention. Her son is ready to come in and play video games; she has other things for him to do. "Homework first," she says.

He smiles. He knows this isn't a battle he will win.

5

Girl Gun Power

In modern national campaigns, there's no such thing as a secret strategy and therefore almost no such thing as a tactic that goes ignored. During 2016's race, one of the most influential advertisers in the campaign spent over $35 million on a strategy that was largely unanswered by the other side. The National Rifle Association sought to persuade women that their self-defense rights would be at risk if Hillary Clinton got the opportunity to replace deceased pro-gun Supreme Court justice Antonin Scalia. The NRA's commitment to help Donald Trump was notable for several reasons—it was twice the size of any of its previous presidential efforts; it came in an impact-magnifying vacuum, with much of it airing before Trump himself had committed advertising dollars to his effort; and its video component targeted women almost exclusively, instead of focusing on the NRA's more traditional male membership base, associated with hunting and shooting sports.

The NRA's contributions to Trump were noted immediately after the election, if not before. When it became clear in the wee hours of November 9 that Trump's electoral college lead was unassailable, NBC News host Chuck Todd said, "Donald Trump did not get a lot of help from a lot of Republican institutions, but he did from the NRA and they came through big, and this is a big night for the NRA, and they just bought a Supreme Court seat."[1]

While the NRA, one of the most established brands in American politics, spent tens of millions on this one issue, targeting true swing voters, Hillary Clinton and her supporters largely ignored it. Previous Democratic contenders had made a play for gun rights supporters— John Kerry went goose hunting with cameras in tow just before the 2004 election, and even President Barack Obama had assured voters that he regularly participated in skeet shooting at Camp David. Clinton took the opposite tack in 2016, and made a play to win the election partly on the strength of her pro–gun control stance. The Democratic National Convention prominently featured gun control advocates.[2] Clinton's campaign website had an entire section devoted to her gun control positions, including a pledge to "take on the gun lobby"—a position in keeping with the principal wedge she drove in her nomination fight with Senator Bernie Sanders, a past NRA ally. Clinton's web page on gun issues made no mention of the Second Amendment, and offered none of the homage her predecessors had paid to the right to bear arms.[3] Even Clinton herself had run to the right of Obama on guns in 2008.[4]

Post-election surveys indicate that the NRA accomplished its goal, and found a vein of swing voters overlooked by most pundits and the Clinton campaign. The Great Revolt Survey found that the one demographic group among Rust Belt Trump voters most likely to agree with the notion that "every American has a fundamental right to self-defense and a right to choose the home defense firearm that is best for them" is women under age forty-five.

During the Obama years, the number of concealed handgun permits tripled, to more than sixteen million. Over 6 percent of all American adults now have carry permits. In Pennsylvania, a key state that Trump flipped from Obama's column, there are now more than a million permit holders, and in some counties more than one-third of the adult population is licensed to carry.[5]

The NRA's own post-election survey of eight battleground states showed that women under forty-five are more likely to be interested in the gun rights issue based on self-defense grounds than for other reasons.

The saliency of the issue of self-defense among women in that younger demographic was critical, because they were exactly the group most likely to bail on Trump in the wake of the revelation in October 2016 of the lewd comments he had made to *Access Holly-wood* host Billy Bush. The Great Revolt Survey results indicate that female Trump voters under age forty-five were the most likely group to admit that, before the presidential election, they'd felt "uncom-fortable telling friends" they supported Trump because they "knew that they would disapprove." Thirty-four percent of Rust Belt Trump voters identified with that sentiment in the survey; but a majority, 51 percent, of women under age forty-five did so—the same voters who were most likely to take a strong self-defense position on gun rights.

The success of Trump and the NRA in coalescing a key niche of younger women, in an election in which every one of those votes mattered, is the story of a voter archetype few saw coming—Girl Gun Power.

Amy Giles-Maurer and Christine Baker Borglin

Kenosha, Kenosha County, Wisconsin

Amy Giles-Maurer sits in the conference room of TG3 Electronics—the company where she works along with other members of her family.

She is the CFO.

There are keyboards everywhere. Not in a haphazard, sloppy way, but on display. Old ones, new ones, colorful ones, high-tech ones; if you can imagine a keyboard to suit your businesses needs or your personal flair, it is here.

The company, which started in her family's cellar after Maurer's father lost his job, makes both standard and custom keyboards for ambulances, hospitals, aircrafts, drive-through restaurants, and police cars. They also make bump bars, control panels, and custom display devices.

"My father started this company when I was in the fourth grade. It was started on the pool table in our basement, with a piece of plywood put over it. That was our assembly line and my brother and I came home from school and we would key-cap. You know, you would grab the bag of W's and you went around the table and you put all the W's on the keyboards. And then you grabbed the bag of E's. You know, the next person in line and so on. So that we were the assembly line. I learned how to solder at a young age," she says of the process of fusing low-melting-point alloys with less fusible metals—one of the most fundamental skills needed in the field of electronics manufacturing.

"Although I didn't have to solder quite as much. And I've actually been doing payroll since I was twelve. That was out of necessity, because they didn't have anybody else to do it," she says.

Maurer is a very striking woman, her blond hair cut short in the kind of dramatic fashion you would see in the pages of *Vogue* or on a Paris fashion runway. Her green eyes are large, her makeup is elegant, and at forty-three, she looks ten years younger, with the obvious drive of a woman twenty years younger.

She reels off the story of her life in a series of categories: successful businesswoman, suburban mother of two, wife, civically engaged member of her community, and a feminist. And as she and her best friend, Christine Baker Borglin, discuss the merits of going to a Dixie Chicks concert, given the group's outspoken liberal political stances, she casually tells her interviewer that she is carrying.

"To me, being a feminist means being in control at all times of your destiny. That includes not just carrying a gun, but knowing how to use it," she states matter-of-factly.

"Got a couple in my office," she says of her firearms, pointing toward her office suite just outside the conference room. "It's smart, it's empowering, it reminds me I am in charge of taking care of myself and my family at all times."

"This one here," she continues, pointing to Borglin, "she carries now too. She just got her concealed carry permit."

The statuesque brunette smiles. Borglin is equally attractive— she in no uncertain terms looks less than her age of forty-nine, and she bears an uncanny resemblance to the Ralph Lauren model whose classic brunette looks were the face of his women's clothing line during the 1970s.

"I have buildings up in the ghetto in Milwaukee and it's a dangerous area," says Borglin, who has an MBA and does contract work for the government.

"We've had people, actually we just had our security guard shot a couple weeks ago. We are sportsmen anyways, we like the right to have guns, but now I actually conceal carry because, where I work, well, it's a dangerous area," she says.

"One of the things I think that Democrats did not understand about women and guns is that empowerment that a gun gives you," stresses Maurer. "That you are the ultimate person in charge of yourself. And all aspects. Not just to carry.

"I was a single mom for a while. I've mowed the lawn with a child on my back in one of the backpack things. Don't tell me that I can't carry. Don't tell me that I can't do it on my own," says Maurer.

"And don't tell me I am not a feminist because I carry a gun; the right is the ultimate freedom, the ultimate empowerment," explains Borglin.

TG3 is located in a sprawling industrial park in Kenosha County, Wisconsin, in a belt of similar light manufacturers and distribution centers running up the center of the county on either side of Interstate 94. The building is modern, the campus is well kept with trim lawns. It's a good example of the new economic face of a county that was once known for the cars that rolled off the American Motors Corporation—and subsequently Chrysler—assembly line in the older part of town. That car factory, built in 1902, was closed in 2010, and had its last remnants flattened by bulldozers in 2017.

Outside, a storm is rolling in—the midafternoon sky, seen through the wall of glass, goes from flat gray to black in a startling fashion. Rain starts to pelt the glass wall as lightning streaks across the horizon.

Maurer and Borglin are the kind of civically minded professional suburban women who had any number of reasons to take their practical, moderate votes away from the Republican nominee, Donald J. Trump, and give them to Hillary Clinton.

The Clinton campaign tried hard to win over women like them—with ads highlighting Trump's crudest misogynistic remarks, his sexist tropes from tabloid talk shows past, framing a picture of an unhinged troglodyte that no self-respecting woman could support—or let her friends support, for that matter.

"They believed, I think, that the social pressure from either our friends or professional peers would be too much. That we would cave because of his behavior," says Maurer. "Well, they misunderstood where the emphasis of our vote was. They thought, 'Feminist, right? Successful, kids in the home, married, college educated, oh, they cannot vote for Trump. They just cannot not.'"

She smiles broadly. She turns to Borglin. "They thought wrong."

Clinton's campaign strategy succeeded to a point—Trump underperformed 2012 Republican nominee Mitt Romney's vote tallies with women in general, white women in particular, and with suburban women. A large survey of voters in eight presidential target states—taken by Republican pollster Wes Anderson of OnMessage Inc. days after the election—found that 16 percent of Clinton's total voters said the reason they voted for her was Trump's inappropriate language and behavior regarding women.

But Trump held on to just enough of those women to win: Wisconsin by 22,748 votes, Michigan by 10,704, and Pennsylvania by 44,292. Those three states had all voted Democratic in the six previous presidential contests, but switched sides to deny Hillary Clinton's bid to become the first woman president. With a combined decisive margin of merely 77,744 people out of 13.97 million votes cast in those states, the few narrow slices of votes that defied the larger political trends and resisted the full thrust of the losing campaign's appeals merit the most study.

As the campaign progressed, few pundits focused on the prospect that there might be a credible cluster of women who would reluctantly stick with Trump based on the issue of gun rights—but the evidence was there in the form of a seat on the U.S. Supreme Court left vacant by the death of Antonin Scalia. That vacancy would loom large in voters' minds, and the Democratic nominee willingly made it loom larger still. As Clinton navigated her way through a tougher-than-expected nomination fight against Senator Bernie Sanders, she created a general election vulnerability that no recent Democratic nominee had—she ran hard in support of gun control. Political strategists on both sides of the aisle know it's a truism of politics that gun rights supporters are more likely to vote on the issue than gun rights opponents.

In the first Democratic debate in October 2015, Clinton was asked by moderator Anderson Cooper which enemy she was most proud of, and the first one out of her mouth was the NRA.

Two of the general election debates dwelled extensively on gun rights and the 2008 Supreme Court decision in *District of Columbia v. Heller,* in which a 5-4 majority ruled for the first time in history that the right to self-defense is fundamental, individual, and protected by the Second Amendment to the Constitution—a Scalia-written opinion on a case that Clinton said was wrongly decided.

For its part, the NRA responded to Hillary's challenge, endorsed Trump earlier than it had ever endorsed a presidential candidate, and spent tens of millions independently on his behalf. The NRA's advertising in this race wasn't just different from its efforts in previous races in scope and timing; it was different in tone and target—focused squarely on persuading women in the suburbs and exurbs of a Supreme Court pick's ramifications for self-defense rights.

While women in general are less supportive of gun rights than men are, by pushing herself to the extremes of anti-gun policy, Clinton created a soft spot with just enough women in the political middle, and the NRA capitalized on it.

Trump repaid the favor, speaking of his support for Second Amendment—and of his NRA endorsement—more frequently and more explicitly than his predecessors had. For a candidate who eschewed connections with most of the constellation of ideologically conservative organizations, Trump's embrace of the NRA was striking. By Election Day, two-thirds of voters in Pennsylvania and Ohio told pollster Anderson that they were aware of Trump's position on gun rights—and, by wide margins, voters in that group who lived in suburbs, exurbs, small towns, and rural areas said Trump's support made them more likely to vote for him.

A full 88 percent of all voters Anderson surveyed in eight target states said the Supreme Court issue was important to deciding their vote—with Trump voters more likely to say the issue was "extremely" important.

For Maurer and Borglin and others in their cohort, it took the course of the campaign to convince them, and Trump's peccadilloes got in the way.

Neither Maurer nor Borglin had Trump on the top of her personal list when the seventeen Republican candidates walked out on the stage for the first GOP debate in Cleveland in August 2015. And at times, long after the election, Trump still rubs them the wrong way.

"But the vote was larger than him, it was about us, our families and our community and the preservation of our rights," says Maurer.

Maurer grew up in Kenosha in a two-parent family with one sibling. "They're still married, although they bicker a lot," she says of her parents—and business partners. "They get on each other's nerves," she says, smiling as if remembering an incident earlier in the day.

"I have one older brother who is four years older and he has the office right next to mine." Is that good? "Sometimes," she says, laughing.

"So, my dad was raised by his grandparents after his parents had to get married when they were young. When he was born they divorced, and neither of them really wanted him. So he lived with his maternal grandparents.

"He went into the Marines, right out of high school. Just volunteered and he was sent to Vietnam where he fixed F-4 Phantoms," she says, referring to the tandem two-seat, twin-engine, all-weather, long-range supersonic jet interceptor and fighter-bomber used extensively during the southeast Asian conflict.

"He picked up electronics there in the Marines. As a kid, he was always kind of naturally technical and they utilized his skills," she explains. After Vietnam, her father got a job at Delco in Milwaukee, where the company was helping to design navigational systems for the Boeing 747, and for the space program.

From there, he went to Cherry Electronics in Waukegan, a family-run business where he stayed for quite a while. She explains, "He was downsized in the mid-eighties. They were cutting out their keyboard division, which he was the head of. And so, with the president of Cherry's blessing, he started his business, TG3, which is derived from his name, Thomas Giles III."

Maurer's upbringing was pretty middle-class, she says. Her mother, who was born in Mississippi but moved north with her parents as an infant, came from a Democratic family whose father worked construction. "Grandpa also owned some of his own excavating equipment, and so he would do side jobs, you know, for extra money," she explains.

Politics at home, for her, was centered on who was best for a family struggling to make a small business work. "Growing up with the business," she says, "I always knew every year at a certain date when my parents met with the accountant when I was little.

"I mean, a lot of times my mom would come home crying, with

what they owed in taxes. Because when it's half of what you've made for the year, things are tough.

"As a kid in junior high school I can remember my mother telling me, 'If [your father and I] ever get hit by a car, don't call Nanny and Grandpa, don't call your aunts, your uncles; call the attorney and the accountant, because you know things have to get set into motion because of the death tax," Maurer recalls of the ramifications of the federal estate tax.

Her parents most certainly were Republicans when she was growing up. "We started talking politics a little bit in high school. I wouldn't say they were Republicans to the point where we do today. But sure, my senior year I was eighteen and I voted for Ross Perot on my own. My parents didn't, you know, tell me one way or the other. But he was for a flat tax. And that made sense to me," she says.

Maurer did not go into the family business right after she graduated from Marquette, a Jesuit university thirty-nine miles north of Kenosha, in Milwaukee.

"I actually dabbled in speech pathology for a while. And then every summer the business seemed to need a receptionist, so I was the receptionist for the summer. All the while I still was doing payroll. So, I was doing accounts payable, payroll, that kind of stuff for the summers. And then just kind of got a little bit more immersed. My mother was always the financial person and my dad was the technical person. So, it was sort of natural that I kind of took over for her."

For her older brother it was easy—he always knew he wanted to work in the family business, she says, while her transition was more gradual. "I guess part of it was a sense of loyalty. There's a sense of who else is going to run it and care about it as much as somebody in the family."

Many of her employees have been there for what she says seems like forever. "We've got employees here that are . . . I mean, quite honestly, most of the people here are like family," Maurer says. "We've got a large engineering department. We have an assembly line. People run machinery. Quality, purchasing, accounting, and sales and marketing. Thirty-five employees in total."

Her father is technically still the CEO. Her uncle, who is closer to her age than her parents' age, is the president.

"There is also my mom's brother. Sometimes it can get heated," she explains of the complexities of integrating family and business life. "But there is a lot of satisfaction of having something like this in my hometown."

"I think we fly under the radar a little bit because we're not a retail store. We don't make things like Case tractors, which is a household name. You know, if you're using our product you probably have no idea that it's our product," she says of the keyboards under many of our fingers every day.

"Most of our employees, I would say over ninety percent of them, have been here for ten years. Finding new employees is difficult now, though. We don't have young people coming in wanting to do assembly work, even if you do pay the magical fifteen dollars an hour and you offer benefits that nobody else offers," she says, explaining how they provide unconventional perks for employees, including trips to sporting events such as Green Bay Packers games.

"We've flown them to Dallas for Packers games, playoff games. So, you know, we try to treat everybody really well," she says, noting how hard it is to attract and retain skilled workers. "I think you find young people don't want to do this type of assembly work and be machine operators. Quite honestly, I think when the government got involved in making school loans their business so that everybody could go to college, and they promoted the notion that everybody should go to college, I think they're doing a huge disservice to the trades. I think you could make a very good living in the trades. I don't think there's anything wrong with that," she says, echoing a common theme of employers and economic development recruiters interviewed across Trump Country.

Maurer says that in ten to fifteen years, tradespeople are going to be able to write their own ticket, because there are going to be so few of them. "We're always going to need a plumber. We're always going to need an electrician, somebody to work on your car. And as much as automation does come into our lives, there's still going to be people who need to repair the machines. The machine operators and repair and setup. We would pay well for that," she says.

Maurer's prediction of talent demand may prove right sooner than she thinks. In the summer of 2017, Wisconsin officials inked a deal with Taiwanese electronics giant Foxconn—contract manufacturer of the Apple iPhone in its Asian factories—to open a new 3,000-employee plant in southeast Wisconsin, just north of Kenosha in Racine. The deal, announced by Trump and House Speaker Paul Ryan in a White House event, will create "a new generation of advanced manufacturing jobs, requiring high levels of engineering skills—skills sorely lacking in the American workforce," according to *Wired* magazine.[6]

Wisconsin governor Scott Walker was Maurer's candidate when the process started in the Republican primary in 2015. "I still like him," she says of the governor, who is now seeking his third term in office.

Walker lost Kenosha County in a 2012 recall election, but he won it in 2014. He generally gets high marks from businesspeople in the county, who feel the positive effect of the state's tax and regulatory framework. Situated directly on the border between the two states, on a major interstate highway, Kenosha County has been a natural landing spot for Illinois companies looking for a lower-cost location that lets them remain in outer Chicagoland.

"The last five to seven years it's been a pretty steady stream of new investments," says Todd Battle, president of the Kenosha Area Business Alliance. "You could probably tie the timeline to the election of Governor Walker, as far as Wisconsin having a fairly strong emphasis on its business climate and its tax policy," he says, echoing a sentiment heard frequently in the county.

For Maurer, Walker's aw-shucks Midwestern temperament was a more comfortable fit than Trump's New York bad-boy bawdiness.

"Sometimes Trump, oh, I mean he just causes his own problems," she says.

When the *Access Hollywood* tape came out in the fall of 2016, she was not thrilled. "It was not his proudest moment and President Trump was not my first choice, but when it came down to Hillary Clinton or him, well, I was more concerned with what she was hiding. I always knew what he stood for, because he always puts it out there. Yes, it's not always put out there in the most elegant ways, but it's there."

She made the transition to Trump much more quickly than Borglin, who was stalled by his unorthodox behavior.

"So Walker was my first choice too, and then Ted Cruz," Borglin says. "I didn't like that Trump tweeted. I didn't like that he just wouldn't take his turn at the debates. I mean, I went to the debate in Milwaukee and I rolled my eyes. I still do. There were plenty of times where I was like, all right, you don't need to tweet. I get now, though, that he's kind of bypassed the media to get his own message out."

Borglin's life was not too different from that of a military brat. "We moved a lot. My dad worked in retail, so he started off being like an assistant manager, then general manager, then buyer, then regional manager," she says. "In total, we moved about twelve different times.

"My parents had me when they first started college. And my mom dropped out then to have me. And then had two sisters after that. And my dad, it was during that time where middle managers were all different ranks, just kept progressing through and getting moved. So, we lived everywhere in Iowa," she explains.

"My mom stayed home and she babysat kids out of the house for a while. And my dad worked two jobs at times. So we were definitely middle-class." Both parents were very conservative. "Dad has always been very vocal about it. And even now, with retiring, they get together their little politics group and they complain and everything else."

Borglin's mom struggled with Trump's antics too. "I think this election took a big toll on my mother; she is so conservative, but very quiet," she says.

After college, she went to work for publisher McGraw-Hill on *Aerospace Daily*. "And that was right when the Persian Gulf War came out. So, I was an editorial assistant. We covered a lot of the procurement and the deployment during that time. And I was still very conservative-minded." She was in Chicago when she met her husband. "Then we moved to London, lived there a couple years, and I worked in government relations," she says, explaining that her job there was for Nortel, looking at emerging markets for the then telecommunications giant.

When their first child was about to arrive, they moved back

home to the American heartland. "I wanted my children to grow up around family," she says. "We tried the suburbs of Chicago, which was very impersonal. So, since his family is up here, we moved up to Wisconsin."

That was fifteen years ago. Amy and Christine first met when their children were attending the same Montessori school. "We both had volunteered to do fund-raising activities," Borglin says.

"All of my female friends are successful in their own right; one runs a division of a company where she works, another holds office, another runs a large company, and another is the main breadwinner in the family. I guess I gravitate towards strong women. I just do. My father raised me to be a feminist," says Borglin.

She believes that the women's political movement has lost its way. "I saw the footage from the women's rally they had the day after Trump's inauguration, and you saw women there and their daughters, dressed like vaginas, and I wonder how they think that makes us feel stronger about our accomplishments?"

Maurer says that while she remains a more traditional Republican, she accepts that motivations are changing and we might be seeing something new after the 2016 election. She places the responsibility for what she calls "this new alignment of voters" back on the political class in Washington. "It is not our fault that they stopped listening to our concerns. And that they stopped being connected to the places they come from. Not only do they not hold any of those values anymore, they look down at you for that. That goes not just for politicians, it's cultural, it's in how we purchase our clothes and necessities, it is how we shop, how we consume our music and our entertainment.

"There has been sort of this seismic shift. People stop and they react. Not only in what their choices are in politics but just in other choices, period. I think that part of the Trump election was not that it was not just about Trump. I think this was about something much bigger. It was about . . . things changing, and trying to get more control of it. Because things are getting out of hand," Borglin says.

"The one thing that this election did for me is just dissolve trust in . . . like the media, for instance. I know that is now a cliché, but hear me out. I took journalism courses as part of my English and political science degree. And it was always 'you follow the truth and you follow the story.' And I started to realize that historically, when you judge what revolutions or what countries go through, I realized that our media had become propagandist. And that was frightening to me. Especially with social media."

Borglin says the news can be so biased that it provides a slanted filter instead of delivering just straight news. "My kids are very susceptible to that," she says, explaining that they don't understand they are only seeing one point of view instead of the whole story.

"Even though I think my kids are intelligent enough, it's what's coming at them all the time. And a lot of what portrayed itself as news, isn't really news, it was propaganda. And they saw it as, sometimes there was truth, but a lot of times there wasn't. And then all of the things you taught them start coming apart," she says.

Both Borglin's daughters, a high school student and a college sophomore, despise Trump. She gets that, but she's uncomfortable with the thought process behind it. "It was based on things they saw online, which turned out not to be factual. That process bothers me, that process of not digging in to make sure you have all of the facts.

"I'll tell you, I did not feel good voting for Trump at all," says Borglin flatly. "Because I didn't like him. I just didn't like him. But I knew things that were important to me were at stake, like the direction of the Supreme Court and the protection of gun rights."

Like many voters who had questions about his temperament and character but voted for him anyway based on their concerns about the Supreme Court, Borglin feels like the calculated political bargain paid off.

"I will say this, he's impressed me much more since then. I like him more now. The one thing that I like about Trump now is at least he says what he's going to do, and he doesn't try to pander to the audience. And the problem I had with Hillary Clinton, because I really disliked her—and I know people are like, 'But you're a woman.' And I am like, 'I'm not voting gender'—I disliked all of her lies."

For Borglin, Clinton's mishandling of classified information—with her home-brewed e-mail server that circumvented the security process at the State Department while she served in Obama's cabinet—could not be dismissed.

"So, I work at a defense contractor. We deal with classified information. Everyone understands how to handle information at that company. There are five hundred people that work there and that's one site; there's multiple sites. There's no way that in her position she didn't know what she was doing with the information. I mean, I have to tell you the amount of checks and security that we go through . . . And it's insulting for people who understand that for her to sit there and lie," she says.

Many Democratic operatives are convinced Clinton's e-mail scandal only became politically lethal because FBI director James Comey released a letter to Congress in the last two weeks of the campaign indicating that while he had exonerated Clinton of a crime in the act, he had struggled with the decision. Democrats say they saw a measurable dip in Clinton's poll numbers as soon as the letter became public and brought the scandal back to the forefront. Even the National Rifle Association featured her lying about her handling of classified information in its late campaign advertising, paired with her position on gun control, in pricey prime-time ads aimed at Rust Belt voters during the World Series between the Chicago Cubs and Cleveland Indians.[7]

Borglin shifts back to culture and how the media looks at women like herself and Amy—who check the box on everything you are supposed to achieve as a feminist—and are befuddled. "We're in flyover land. So, we're not New York, we're not L.A., we aren't women who feel as though we have to do what pop culture and politics dictate, so we have a brain."

Seeing the derision of Trump voters by talking heads on national television irks her.

"We're not crazy, how people try to describe Trump supporters, especially the female ones. So many of the celebrities, and the women on *The View,* say rather indignantly, 'How could any woman vote for him?' Did I like that he said what he said in the *Access Hollywood* tape? No. Do I like everything that my husband says? No."

Amy would just like to enjoy sports or entertainment without an actor or actress or singer or quarterback preaching politics to her. "You know, I am just tired. It's like, come on, just sing for us. But at the same time they're Americans too, and they have every right to voice their opinion. But sometimes I just want to watch *Real House-wives* and just veg out without Andy Cohen calling me 'a Trump supporter, stupid.' I can deal with if they have an opinion that's different from mine. Just stop being so damn rude about it," she says.

The all-out assault on Trump by leading figures in entertainment and media is a contributing factor to the galvanizing of his support in places like Kenosha, even as his administration struggles to find legislative success. In many ways, Trump voters like Amy see themselves behind the siege walls with him, even if he is more conservative than she is on issues such as abortion.

"And also it was insulting to have them pick out things and attack Donald Trump for it, when I'm like, wait a minute, Clinton did the same thing. I don't like that at all. I don't like how he debated. I don't like how he handled himself at all. I just took a look at what he said as far as policies go. I'm pro-choice. He said he's pro-life, but he thinks the states should decide. That's what I want in my conservative government. I want to be able to live where I can vote and make that decision. I want to live in a place that's pro-choice. And I know that's different than how my friends feel. But I don't want government telling me that the whole country is going to be that," says Borglin.

These Trump-backing women who dislike many of the crude things he says or his impulsiveness on Twitter find a silver lining in his communication style—authenticity and pugnaciousness.

"I also like that if they ask him, he'll say something even if it's very unpopular. He's not judging how people are going to take it or trying to find the ways to make everyone happy. You didn't feel like he was trying to pander. I didn't like everything that he had to say, but I felt like that he owned it. And I wanted straight ownership," says Borglin.

For her, the Clintons' opposite style of speaking in measured sound bites is part of what's wrong with politics.

"Every word out of Hillary's mouth was so artfully crafted; everything Trump said was inelegantly delivered. You knew what was going on in his head," says Maurer.

Trump's candor, and even his fabrications and verbal gaffes, reinforced his authenticity as a nonpolitician. When the press picked Trump's words apart for strict fact analysis, voters assumed he spoke directionally; the press took him literally, but voters like Borglin took him merely seriously.

Borglin believes Trump's win realigns politics in the same way that Bill Clinton's did. "Yeah, I think yeah, it has changed things. I mean similar to when Clinton first went on *The Tonight Show . . .*"

"With the saxophone," Maurer interrupts.

In Wisconsin, that sense of a new movement, one that pushes back against big government elitism, predates Trump. It can be traced to soon after Walker was elected governor in 2010 and immediately passed a law known as the Wisconsin Budget Repair Bill, sparking months of protests led by liberal groups and state employee unions that culminated in a divisive statewide recall election in 2012. Walker and the Republicans prevailed in that recall and have lost only one statewide election since—after decades of Democratic dominance.

"For us it started with the recall election for Scott Walker, and he won with more margin than he did the first time. I think it was sort of this collective 'Oh, we don't have to be quiet now.' You know, conservative people are conservative. Most people are not the marchers. We're not the in-your-face people. But we voted with our feet, we turned out. And this didn't start with Trump and it doesn't end with him," says Borglin.

The local realignment in Wisconsin politics that benefitted Trump seems to have cleaved in two the old New Deal Democratic coalition here—separating the blue-collar trade unionists from the white-collar government unions.

That schism is rooted in a fear of what Maurer articulates as a decline in the American work ethic, and one she says worries her about the culture at large. "We are struggling hard to find people in the pipeline to come in and do assembly, testing, and engineering. We're running the well dry. And we're fighting for the same resources as the Rockwells," she says, referencing larger companies moving into Kenosha, against whom she must compete for talent. "We want the business to come here; the problem is we don't have the workers. And when we are finding people to come in for assembly, their skill level is so much less than it used to be. I mean, they're struggling taking an exam that gets them to like an eighth-grade level."

And getting people to show up on time—or consistently, or at all—is exasperating, she says. "It is those kinds of intangibles in politics and culture that fed into my vote."

"Mine too," interrupts Borglin, drawing a straight line from that fear to angst over Democratic politicians such as Hillary Clinton and Bernie Sanders focusing their rhetoric on government safety-net programs instead of job creation.

"That fed into people voting for Trump. That the direction of the country, politics, government, and culture is really going in the wrong direction," Maurer concludes.

Nine months after Trump's election, Democratic pollsters Pete Brodnitz and Jill Normington, working for a group closely tied to Nancy Pelosi, delivered that message of tough love to state Democratic leaders. "Democrats have a small advantage on health care but Republicans have more credibility on valuing hard work and the economy," blared a PowerPoint slide show to House Democratic leaders, analyzing a large survey of white working-class voters in the summer of 2017.[8]

Pride in country also played a role for both women. "I'm a huge patriot. I always have been. That was something that I really didn't like about the previous administration. I'm a descendant of Betsy Ross, put it that way, through my dad's family," Borglin says proudly. "And my dad, well he was a Marine. So 'Make America Great Again,' it speaks to a lot of people. It really does. Because I think people are tired of feeling like they're getting beaten up. But also to have an administration basically apologize for your country all the time—it's just hard. It was disheartening."

Outside, the rain is still pelting the ground relentlessly. Both women have to leave to take children to different activities, Maurer in her SUV, Borglin in her pickup truck—not the kind you see on the backroads of Appalachia, mind you, the kind you see in suburbia, four doors, shiny and new.

Dawn Martin

Pleasant Plains Township, Lake County, Michigan

The majority of the time Dawn Martin spends with other women, a gun is usually involved.

Breakfast on a chilly summer morning with two Lake County, Michigan, friends is no different; she is not only carrying, but the conversation between the three women she is with centers on a firearm one of her students brought to a class she taught just the day before.

"She brought a gun out that I'd never seen before and it was huge! I shot it, and it hurt my hands so bad. I was like, 'Oh my god, this is so much fun,'" she explains to her friends.

Martin is picking at her breakfast burrito inside Northern Exposure, a no-frills Lake County diner along Michigan Avenue in Plains Township. The eatery is cheery with buttercup-yellow walls, wood paneling, large bay windows, and photos of local wildlife and scenery added for ambiance.

At fifty, Martin shows no signs of losing her fresh-faced, girl-next-door looks or cheerful smile as she goes into detail about the previous day's gun safety class, which she taught. The woman to her left owns three guns, all with pink on them somewhere; the woman to her right just purchased her first gun two years earlier.

Sitting in the Plains Township diner, all three look remarkably unremarkable, just three regular middle-class mothers having an early-morning breakfast before heading off to work. Martin's blond hair is bobbed stylishly, her navy blue Swiss-dot blouse is tailored, and her makeup is simple but elegant: red lips, some mascara, and blush.

All three women were raised to be Democrats, all three are college-educated, and all three point to protecting the Second Amendment as their main reason for supporting Donald Trump in the 2016 presidential election.

"No one saw my vote coming, or at least the reason for my vote," explains Martin. She has three children from her first marriage; the youngest, who is biracial, was adopted as her first marriage was ending. "It was all about protecting the Second Amendment. I'm a huge advocate. Everything else, I guess if I was honest with myself I could negotiate a little bit on, because I am willing to see both sides and listen to both sides," she says of her independent-leaning tendencies.

Martin is an NRA Certified Firearms Instructor, a certified Glock armorer, a certified NRA instructor on personal protection outside the home, an NRA Chief Range Safety Officer, and a Michigan ORV and snowmobile safety instructor. She also owns, along with her husband, Rich, Bob's Country Kitchen, a log cabin breakfast-buffet-style restaurant that is open only on weekends, spring through fall, to serve the folks who come from "downstate" to enjoy the abundant trails, lakes, and rivers of Lake County.

"We are only open weekends because of where they are located," she explains. "I'm on the main trail system for the RVs and stuff. My customers are primarily people who come from Indiana, Ohio, places like that, for the weekend. Financially, it doesn't make any sense for me to be open during the week."

Her gun safety classes, mostly filled with women, are held in the back of the restaurant during the week, where targets are set up for the students.

"When I was growing up, feminism was about empowering women to have choices, choices outside of what society was then dictating. Well, self-protection is the ultimate empowerment a woman can have. I have been a gun owner since 2001, when the law changed here in Michigan, making it easier to obtain a concealed pistol license."

Now, she shoots every chance she can get. "I'm not a hunter. I don't kill things, but I get out as much as I can, put up targets, just keep myself proficient. I believe in the ability to defend myself and protect myself from any threat, whether it's government or somebody coming meaning to do me harm."

Martin gets more than just the confidence of self-defense from her practice. "Actually shooting a gun for me is relaxing. It's a huge stress-reliever."

Martin says she became an instructor because she sees the importance of being able to bring others in and have them understand that having a gun, being a gun owner, isn't the stereotype they know from popular culture.

"People have a preconceived notion that we're all like a bunch of . . . I want to use this word carefully, oh, what the heck, they think we are a bunch of 'rednecks.' A bunch of hillbillies, gun-toting hillbillies," she says, and sighs. The last thing Martin looks like is a hillbilly; Talbots yes, hillbilly no.

"I want people to understand that there are many reasons to own a gun, and just because you've got one doesn't mean that you're any different than anybody else. It just means that you just have a different level of expectation for yourself. You have to carry yourself in a different manner. You can't walk around with this chip on your shoulder," she says.

"If you're a typical road-rage person, like I am, you have to remember that when you have to go in the car. You have to hold yourself to a higher standard, and that's important. Being able to separate your personal feelings sometimes and keep yourself, it's a checks-and-balances system."

Three men in county sheriff uniforms walk in and take a seat in the restaurant, wave, and smile. She returns the greeting as the waitress pours her coffee. "You know your husband was here earlier, just before you got here," the waitress tells Martin.

She smiles, and replies, "Of course he was." Everyone in the township knows Rich Martin—not just because of the restaurant or the tactical outfit he runs with his wife; he is the newly elected county sheriff, the first Republican to win the office in decades. He won by 80 votes out of 5,233 cast, swept in with the man at the top of his ticket, Donald J. Trump.

The waitress, overhearing the conversation, says she can't ever remember a Republican winning anything in her county. "Her husband won me over, he came to my door and listened and listened. He probably wished he didn't knock on my door," she says, laughing. "But he won my vote."

Before moving north to Irons, Michigan, where Trailside Adventures and Bob's County Kitchen are located, Martin and her husband lived in Kalamazoo, where she was a TSA supervisor for seventeen years; he was in law enforcement and also owned a security company that he began at the age of nineteen.

"In fact he was the youngest person ever to own a licensed security guard and investigation agency in Michigan," she explains. Now, as an elected official, her husband has no time to devote to the Kalamazoo company, so she makes the trip downstate several times a month to make sure everything is running smoothly.

As with her gun safety classes in Lake County, the Kalamazoo operation has a large number of women as clients. "You see, I think that these are the women that the national press does not understand. They don't get the importance of not just owning a gun for a woman, but how to properly use it and how that knowledge and expertise has given them a different perspective when they walk into the voting booth.

"They are younger, they are single, and many of them have young children. I think they will have a bigger impact, a growing impact, for a generation or two," Martin speculates. "The amount of young women, educated young women who want to protect themselves and ultimately want to protect their right to do that, is a hidden movement."

Survey research shows that this slice of female voters played a pivotal role in the election of Donald Trump. Republican pollster Wes Anderson of OnMessage Inc. conducted a comprehensive survey immediately following the election in November 2016 in eight presidential swing states, and found that gun rights were a key motivator for the group of women Trump had the hardest time keeping in his camp—women who were not across-the-board conservatives.

"Eighteen percent of those who voted for Trump told us that before Election Day they were 'uncomfortable telling people they supported Trump.' That's the shy Trump voter and it's almost one in ten people in the entire electorate," Anderson says. "Who were these voters? They were a little more female than all voters, they were a little more educated than all voters, and a very strong eighty percent of them said they support the goals and objectives of the National Rifle Association."[9]

Anderson's research found that the issue of gun rights cut broadly in Trump's favor, with 47 percent of all voters saying the potential for the next president to choose up to three Supreme Court justices was an "extremely important" factor in deciding their votes, and 59 percent saying they had seen, read, or heard about Trump's and Clinton's positions on gun rights. Of that clear majority informed on gun positions, 54 percent report voting for Trump while 42 percent voted for Clinton. And of the voters driven by the potential for Supreme Court nominations, Trump held a 14-point margin, 56-42.

The Supreme Court issue was slightly more important to voters further up the economic ladder than those lower down, with 91 percent of those making over $75,000 in household income saying it was important and only 9 percent rating it unimportant, compared to 85 percent and 14 percent among the similar-sized group of voters who make $40,000 or less in annual income.

Perhaps most significant for Trump, the gun issue held Clinton back in the suburban and exurban counties where she otherwise ran stronger than most Democrats have. On this issue, according to Anderson's research, suburban voters' attitudes toward Clinton more closely mirrored those of rural voters. Strikingly, Clinton's gun position did not even clearly help her in urban areas, with 44 percent of those voters saying her gun position made them less likely to vote for her and only 41 percent saying it made them more likely to support her.

Martin believes that women who get interested in self-defense become as instinctually protective of the right as they would of any gender equality.

"It is hard to take that right away . . . once they have felt that personal empowerment of protection within their own hands," Martin says. "They don't have to depend on anyone but themselves, and isn't that honestly the entire core of what the women's movement was all about? It is not some slogan, it's not some hashtag, and it is a real feeling."

For Martin personally, the issue of Second Amendment rights

drove her vote in 2016. "I will always vote for someone who is pledged to protect that: he did that and I was in," she says.

The NRA's ad campaign, which was targeted at the Great Lakes states, was the earliest and most consistent outside allied effort supporting Trump, and it prominently featured women who advocated for the right to self-defense. An early-October national television ad, which aired while Trump was reeling from the *Access Hollywood* tape, featured an Indianapolis lawyer named Kristi McMains who used her gun to fend off an attacker. "A man attacked me in a parking garage, tried to stab me with an eight-inch knife. But I carry a pistol. I fight back. That's why I am still here," McMains said in the ad. "Every woman has a right to defend herself with a gun if she chooses . . . Donald Trump supports my right to own a gun. Defend your rights. Vote Donald Trump for president."

Longtime political analyst Fred Barnes of *The Weekly Standard* credited that ad, and the NRA's efforts in general, with Trump's margin of victory. "There are many claimants to the honor of having nudged Donald Trump over the top," Barnes wrote. "But the folks with the best case are the National Rifle Association."[10] Barnes gave particular credit to the ad featuring McMains and another featuring a young Colorado rape survivor named Kim Corban, who said, "My fear of firearms disappeared when I got my second chance at life." In Barnes's view, "Absent the NRA, I think we know how Trump would have fared. He'd have lost."

For Martin, the gun range owner in Michigan, her decision to place the Second Amendment issue prominently in her own decision matrix fits with her overall view of individualism.

"A big part of the problem in our culture is our dependence on things we should not be dependent on," Martin says. "We are Americans. That means something. That means figuring it out without the government giving us free stuff, without the big banks and big companies making us need them so much, and not feeling as though we are entitled to something once we get it once."

Martin says the overexpansion of our country's social safety net has created such a negative sentiment about it that even those who use it resent it.

"I think history has shown, when you are dependent on something, at first you're grateful, especially depending on what kind of a dire situation you're in. Then, that gratefulness soon becomes resentment because there's so much unsaid obligation that they expect from you. They feel as though, 'Okay, we own your vote. This is why you're voting for us, because you're in that house or you have that car or you have that free phone because of me.' Eventually, you start to resent that," she says.

Martin is no fan of big government, and she puts big news organizations in the same category. "The big media and the Democrats have not shook off that understanding that we are not beholden to them anymore. We are not dependent on them anymore. We did this thing and we are not going back.

"Empowerment, when you are responsible, is a heady thing," she adds, then says her goodbyes—she has target practice in an hour.

Kim Dull

Franklin, Vernon County, Wisconsin

Kim Dull grew up in a traditional family setting; she and her mom did all of the work around the home, while her three brothers and father did most of the heavy lifting on the farm where they raised cattle and grew crops.

"One of my biggest chores was helping Mom clean house and do laundry. Unfortunately. We didn't have a fancy washer. We had the old ringer washer. It was done once a week, so I remember many times sitting down on the basement steps with my radio and I would take care of washing clothes and it would be an all-day thing," she says.

"We actually got a dryer given to us by my dad's sister-in-law or something, and that was something else, because we had never had anything like that. We had always hung everything out so when we got that, we thought we were pretty special."

Dull is the opposite of her married last name; her laugh is infectious, her wit is sharp, and her love of life and family is her center. Like many folks of Norwegian descent, she likes to keep her private life, well, private.

At fifty-seven, her hair is sandy blond with striking silver streaks running through it, making a stunning contrast between her rich peach-toned skin and penetrating blue eyes. She is built Midwestern-sturdy.

She and her husband live several miles off of U.S. Route 61, the infamous highway that connects New Orleans with Minnesota, built well before interstates bypassed America's Main Streets.

Long nicknamed the Great River Road by travelers because all of its 1,400 miles hug the winding Mississippi River, it is also now officially designated as such for most of the route.

It's the kind of road that passes great big patches of rural geography, tiny towns, hollowed-out industry, and soaring views of the rich soils of our country.

These vistas inspired many musicians to sing about the land and its people, including folk singer and poet Bob Dylan, who named his sixth album *Highway 61 Revisited.*

In his memoir, Dylan calls Highway 61 "the same road, full of the same contradictions, the same one-horse towns, the same spiritual ancestors. . . . It was my place in the universe, always felt like it was in my blood."[11]

The counties like Vernon on either side of the Mississippi River, from St. Louis all the way up to Minnesota, have long been Democratic—the rare solid stretch of blue counties on post-election maps in the rural center of the country. But they weren't blue in 2016—and the swing from Obama to Trump in these counties helped flip Iowa and Wisconsin from Democrat to Republican, and they nearly flipped Minnesota too.

Trump carried Vernon County by 4.4 percent—just four years after Mitt Romney had lost it by 15 percent. President George W. Bush lost the county by 7 points both times he ran—and Republican senator Ron Johnson lost it in both of his successful statewide races too.

The people of Vernon County work hard and make independent decisions at the ballot box. They don't fit easily into today's Democratic strategy of targeting high margins among the cosmopolitan and the diverse—but the people here and in counties like them, far outside the orbit of metropolitan Milwaukee and academic Madison, have always been a critical component of Democratic victories in the Badger State. There just aren't enough urbanites to muster a majority in this slow-growth, native-heavy state; any winning coalition will be built with a fair share of people who live out of the way.

Twenty-three counties in Wisconsin switched from supporting Obama in 2012 to Trump in 2016—all but four were rural counties with fewer than 50,000 residents. Trump's margins in rural areas of swing states even beyond Wisconsin blew away all previous norms for a competitive presidential contest. Trump lost just 197 of the nation's counties of fewer than 50,000 people—and won more than 1,900 of those counties.

The area where Dull lives is the town of Franklin in Vernon County, Wisconsin; it's not exactly a one-horse town, but it is close. Just over 900 people live here, and it has the three unincorporated communities of Fargo, Folsom, and Liberty Pole located within the town's lines—all of which qualify as one-horse towns by themselves, connected by that famous ribbon of asphalt.

Franklin is at the same time pristine, beautiful, and isolated.

As a girl, Dull felt protected from that isolation, and the unexpected dangers that accompany it, by her brothers and father. In fact, she says she never thought of it. All the men carried guns, they all knew how to use guns. She wasn't afraid to use them herself—she just never had to because her father and brothers were always there to protect her and her mother.

"I grew up in a two-parent family. We were pretty close. We farmed all our life. [We] rented when we were younger; I remember it was hard getting by, we didn't have much to go on, but there was always food on the table and we always made do with what we had. We didn't have all these things like kids have now. We did outside things. We made up our own things, our own games.

"My dad very much made sure, whether we had stuff or not, he kind of joined right in with us. He was like a big kid. Most of the cousins would know that because they liked my dad a lot," she says, her voice rising as she remembers moments with her father.

"Family was central, we didn't have much, but you really didn't notice that because we felt happy, secure," she says. "On my mom's side it was a Sunday dinner every weekend with cousins, grandparents, aunts, uncles."

The family raised cattle and some crops, including tobacco—most Americans may not think of Wisconsin as tobacco country, but much of the nation's loose-leaf chewing tobacco, such as the Red Man brand, historically came from here. As a child of the late '60s and early '70s in rural America, Dull and her brothers went to a two-room schoolhouse.

"My dad taught all the boys how to hunt and everything, but I kind of got left behind on that. Remember, that was the age I grew up in."

Her parents stopped renting farms after a while and purchased one when she was in junior high. She married shortly after graduating from high school.

"We actually lived right in Readstown for three years in a small trailer house, and then we purchased, with the help of my father. You see, my dad found this place where we're living actually still now. It was like three miles from where I grew up. It's just a small farmette, is kind of what you would call it," she explains.

When they were first married, Dull and her husband raised a few head of cattle. "We raised them and then we'd sell them, and we raised tobacco. Then the rest of the acreage, my dad farmed," she says.

When her first child, her daughter Jessie, arrived she stayed home and took care of the tobacco crop. After her second child arrived and they got older, she started working outside of the home, first at a nursing home for seven years and then in local government as the township clerk.

"My dad talked me into it because the township was having some issues with their previous clerk and the books were really bad. So my dad asked me if I'd be interested. Not knowing what I was getting into, so I took it and, boy, did I get into a mess, but after about two or three years, I got the books turned around and I did that job, the town clerk, for twenty years," she says.

Today she is the department head at the Nelson Agri-Center, which takes up an entire block in downtown Viroqua, the county seat of this agricultural county that is home to the largest organic dairy cooperative in the country.[12]

Occupying the corner of East Decker Street and North Center Avenue, the Agri-Center is a stark contrast to the hip storefronts of nearby places like the Driftless Café, the Driftless Angler, and Kickapoo Coffee Roasters on North Main Street—a visual juxtaposition showcasing Vernon County's current marriage between the generational agriculture of its heritage and the groovy, semi-hippie culture that may be its future.

Here, downtown, is where the working farmer, mechanic, and homeowner find exactly what they need to make their lives and livelihoods run smoothly. Nelson also manages a deer registration station during buck season—where hunters bring their bucks to register their harvest, and purchase ice to preserve them until they reach home.

Vernon County is located in the region of Wisconsin called "Driftless," a formation of deglaciated topography. It is filled with fertile valleys, plentiful trout streams, herds of deer, and ancient cliffs.

Dull says that apart from her BB gun, she really did not use guns as a young girl; but after she married her husband, an avid hunter, the sport caught her attention.

"I started shooting with him once in a while. And I kind of found out how fun it was to target shoot. That feeling as though I am protecting myself. No one else but me. That was very different from when I grew up. My father and brothers fit that role. Then my husband did. But it was him who encouraged me to do it for myself. First because he wanted me to go deer hunting with him, but then for protection," she says.

"I had tried deer hunting one year and I had practiced and practiced, and a lot of things kept going through my head, and my husband kept telling me, 'Know your target. Know your target.' So I got out there and I see a deer, but then I heard voices, and I did not know where those voices were. I told my husband when I got back, I couldn't shoot. I did not know where those people were. And he goes, 'Well, did you see anybody?' And I go, 'No, that's the problem. How do I know they weren't standing on the other side of that deer? I couldn't shoot.' He goes, 'Well, you're not . . .' I don't know how he put it. He didn't feel I was confident enough, and I said, 'I guess not.' "

Then she overcame her anxieties and got confident. "I think by the next year I carried." That next step, to carry a gun on her person, came only after a lot of instruction.

Now she has that knowledge and skill to feel more comfortable home alone, in a home that is isolated. "It's a whole-mile driveway so it's kind of back in there. My husband has showed me many times what I have to do to use the pistol."

In its campaign to support Trump in 2016, the National Rifle Association aimed its advertising and grassroots activities squarely at women like Dull. One of the NRA's most-seen television ads, which ran heavily in the Midwestern Rust Belt states on the Big Ten Network that is home to college football in this area, featured a woman in her thirties jumping out of bed after hearing a window break downstairs. By the time the woman grabs the phone to call 911 and rushes to her gun safe across the room, her firearm disappears as the announcer warns that Hillary Clinton would appoint Supreme Court justices who would take away the right to self-defense.

The Supreme Court case that drove those ads was *District of Columbia v. Heller,* a case decided in 2008 that struck down a municipal ordinance requiring any handgun in the home to be kept disassembled in four or more pieces. The court, led by now-deceased justice Antonin Scalia, ruled that such a restriction eviscerated any practical chance that a handgun could be deployed in self-defense.

The premise of the NRA's campaign was that women voters, particularly those in the upper Midwest, would be motivated not just by Clinton's ability to replace the deceased Scalia if elected, but also by the empowerment they get from their own right to self-defense.

"Women are the fastest-growing group of gun owners and concealed carry permit holders in the country," explains Chris Cox, executive director of the NRA's Institute for Legislative Action and its top political strategist, citing data from the Crime Prevention Research Center showing that women now account for 36 percent of permit holders, and a study showing they are obtaining them 326 percent faster than men.[13] "The national media wanted to portray Donald Trump as anti-woman and the fact is that he fully respects the right of women and all law-abiding Americans to defend themselves and their families. We wanted to use the facts to counter the false narrative."

Dull likes being in charge of her own destiny: "It does make you feel better. I hope to God I never have to, but it does help that, you know . . . It is like you said, the way things are going now, though, you may have no choice. This area is becoming thieving and everything else, so you just don't know," she says.

Dull has been a conservative all her life, but not a Republican, "Well, I don't want to say fully Republican because I have done on elections, I don't always vote straight party. It depends because I do read up on the candidates and I kind of go from there, so I do veer off once in a while."

Her top issue in the last election was the protection of the Second Amendment, which is why she found Bernie Sanders interesting, initially, in the Democratic primary. "He was very pro–Second Amendment," she says of her initial impression of Sanders.

But she was also strongly driven by national security. "As a mother and grandmother and wife, I wanted someone strong, someone who would protect our treasure, our people."

What she remembers distinctly is an early Democratic debate between Hillary Clinton, Lincoln Chafee, Martin O'Malley, Jim Webb, and Sanders during which Clinton said that the National Rifle Association was the enemy she was most proud of. "What was that all about?" Dull says. "I felt as though people in my community were, you know, being attacked."

She was by then turned off by all of the Democrats. "I could have gone with Webb, but he didn't stand a chance," she says of the former Virginia U.S. senator who had been both a Democrat and a Republican, served in Vietnam, was secretary of the navy, and had stronger positions on national security than any other Democrat running.

When the general election came along, the same things Dull liked about Webb, she liked about Donald Trump. She liked his strength on national security, his forthright position on guns and the Second Amendment, and plans for changing the direction of the country. But with Trump, she found something else she liked that was unusual for a Republican.

"It was larger than politics, I think. I believe this election was a rejection of how big corporations, all kinds, have treated people over the years. We've become disposable and so we've lost faith in them. And that was what I wanted to be part of," she says.

"We've finally said we don't want to be part of that, we want something better. It is not a look backward, it's a look forward."

For Dull, the larger business and entertainment culture has made a turn for the worse. "Think about how the government has treated our military men and women after they came home from serving all of us. Now think about the scandals with the Veterans Administration. Then think about companies that don't hire people who have served. Or think about how people are portrayed on the news who aren't living in a big metropolitan city? All of these things add up over the years."

Dull still likes Trump, a lot, well into his tumultuous presidency. But she wearies of his tweeting. "I wish he'd keep his mouth shut. I think he would do so much better if he would just quit tweeting everything or whatever. Just some of the things he had to say and how he was looking forward as trying to better this country I love, but the tweeting?"

Dull does not want to leave Trump's team, but the chaos he generates with his social media account on an ad hoc, but regular, basis is starting to wear on her. "It won't cause me not to vote for him, but it does bother me," she says.

Both of her grown children live nearby, with her first grandchild heading off to college in the fall of 2017—and she is thrilled by his support for the president.

She watches his posts on Facebook in support of Trump, and says she refrains from responding because of who she is connected to on her own account on the social media platform. "I'm Facebook friends with some family that just absolutely hates Trump, so I have to kind of watch letting people know my point of view."

That's hard, she explains. "You know, to keep my opinions to myself but you just have to around certain people because you just don't want it to affect your job. So you really have to watch. Some of the coworkers are anti-Trump, so it's just easier to not get into a discussion with them. My dad always said there's a few things you just don't discuss—politics and religion—except with family or friends."

Dull shares a picture of herself that she is not sure even some of her family members would believe was her. "So last fall I went bear hunting—with my husband. We know a friend up north and he baits," she says of the legal practice in bear hunting whereby hunters set up a bait stand of food in one specific spot to lure the bear.

"We don't do dogs, we bait, and I went with my husband and my husband has already gotten a bear, so he told me from the time he got his, 'You need to go start getting your kill tag,' because you have to apply so many years to get a kill tag in Wisconsin. So he wanted me to do it because he thought it was such a big deal.

"Now mind you, I've never gotten a deer, or anything, but what the heck," she says. "So I went. It was fun and it was kind of thrilling. An accomplishment. Plus I really wanted the bear meat. The bear meat is actually very good.

"I'm now tempted to try turkey hunting, because I seem like I have more patience nowadays and I think I could sit and do that," she explains. Avid hunters consider turkey hunting a refined skill because the birds have such keen senses that they prove elusive to hunters.

As far as having a gun in the home to protect herself, Dull is satisfied. "Things have changed in the world, they always do. Each generation there are new dangers, the world gets smaller, different kinds of problems happen with each generation. You have to be aware of those dangers, of crime, and how to stay safe, and you have to be able to protect yourself."

Protecting those rights, she says, clinched her vote for Trump. "There really was no other choice. Remember, this vote was for us. How can you not continue to vote for yourself, your family, your community to move forward? I think many of us did in the past and we finally looked up and said, "What is happening in this is more than politics, this is culture and values, and it is everything." Politics was just the thing making the most noise, and while it is hard to remember every detail of that election, one thing not hard to remember is this was like . . ."

Dull struggles with the description, as if there isn't an adequate word to describe it.

Awakening?

"Yes, an awakening," she says. "There were so many emotions during that election and they still continue, hard to remember all of them, but yes, like an awakening."

6

Rotary Reliables

Donald Trump's general election gamble, whether he made it deliberately or not, was that he could be the kind of disruptive force needed to widen the Republican coalition that had fallen short in 2012, while not bleeding too many typical GOP voters who crave stability and are wary of disruption.

Journalist Jim Tankersley wrote on the morning after the election, "Trump's challenge was inspiring the blue collar whites without alienating the college-educated ones."[1]

Trump slashed and burned his way through the Republican primary field, mocking and taunting his well-credentialed opponents all along the way with derisive nicknames such as "Little Marco" for Senator Marco Rubio, "Lyin' Ted" for Senator Ted Cruz, and "Low Energy" for former governor Jeb Bush. He threatened to bolt the Republican Party entirely several times, even as he sought its nomination. He bailed out on prime-time debates, if only to demonstrate that they got better ratings when he was there. He referred to "the Republicans" as if he wasn't one, poking and testing the resolve of the rock-ribbed denizens of the very coalition he would seek to coalesce in the general election.

Trump's gambit worked, but, to be sure, he lost plenty of card-carrying Republican voters in the suburbs, running 5 to 10 points behind even Romney's losing total in bedroom counties surrounding almost every major city in the country. It nearly cost him

Pennsylvania's electoral votes—he ran 9 points behind Clinton in suburban Chester County, just west of Philadelphia, even though Romney had carried the Republican bastion in 2012, and even as GOP senator Pat Toomey was carrying it in 2016, piling up 133,662 votes to Trump's 116,114. Toomey ran up a similar 16,000-vote headroom above Trump in next-door Delaware County, and did 27,000 votes better in Montgomery County just north of the city.

Those defections by suburban Republicans were seen nationwide. Trump, for example, ran 5 points weaker than Mitt Romney had in the Milwaukee suburb of Waukesha County, Wisconsin; 10 points behind Romney's number in Johnson County, Kansas, the affluent bedroom county of Kansas City; and even 8 to 9 points behind him in the signature ruby-red suburbs of Texas's metropolises—Collin County, Fort Bend County, and Williamson County.

Of the forty-four mega counties in the nation with populations over one million, Trump carried only three—Tarrant County, Texas, which includes Fort Worth; Maricopa County, Arizona, which includes Phoenix; and Suffolk County on Long Island, New York. Trump's net margin of votes in mega counties was worse than Romney's in thirty-two of the forty-four.

Press analysis of the election returns and exit poll data highlighted Trump's softness among college-educated voters, but it left out a critical exception to that trend. Trump did very well among the college-educated in counties farther away from major cities—a vital component of the record margins he assembled in those nonmetropolitan counties.

Part of this schism can be explained by social pressure that might be unique to the 2016 election. In counties with far more than the national average of 29.8 percent of adults with bachelor's degrees, Trump fared poorly. Of America's one hundred most educated counties, he carried only nineteen—Romney had carried twenty-six in defeat and outpolled Trump in almost all of them by significant margins. Simply put, Americans who live their lives among a group of friends and neighbors with varied educational backgrounds preferred Trump more than Clinton or Romney, while college-educated Americans who live exclusively among other degree holders were less likely to support Trump, even if they were otherwise Republican.

Trump's performance among college-educated voters who live in counties below the national average in education levels was right on the Republican par—particularly in midsized and smaller counties in the Great Lakes swing states that determined the outcome of the election.

These voters did not face the kind of social pressure to oppose the lewd and coarse Trump that their college-educated peers did in the suburbs. These people—whom we dub "Rotary Reliables"—are at the top of the pyramid in their communities, the kind of people who run the factories, banks, and civic organizations. But unlike the upper class congregating in the nation's most elite zip codes, these voters spend much of their lives intersecting not with fellow college-educated professionals, but with working-class voters. They hunt and fish with them, they share PTA duty at school with them, they sit on the same church pews. Unlike the corporate manager who lives in a cul-de-sac outside Dallas or Philadelphia, these college-educated voters in less-educated communities knew plenty of people who were not only voting for Trump, but were enthusiastic about him.

Among the Trump-voter archetypes identified in the Great Revolt Survey, these voters are the most likely to have a college degree, and the most likely to have served in the military. They're the least populist among Trump's Rust Belt voters, less likely than other Trump-voter archetypes to say corporations don't care if they hurt working people or not. They are mostly conservative, more likely to cite the Supreme Court as a motivating factor in their vote, and less likely to have voted for Obama in a prior election than any other archetype except the King Cyrus Christians.

Rotary Reliable voters will be the easiest for the next Republican nominee after Trump to retain in this voting coalition—but, as they are opinion leaders in their communities, that nominee needs to keep their enthusiasm in order to sustain the intensity of his or her non-urban support overall. As Democratic campaigns make a hard push to capitalize on anti-Trump sentiment among educated suburban voters, it bears watching to see if this group sticks with its geographic peers or can be swayed along with the national narrative.

Joe Steil

Keokuk, Lee County, Iowa

Donald Trump struggled mightily in the 2016 election to win over the two-college-degree, two-car-garage, two-income families that fill up America's subdivisions—a group that has been the core of the modern Republican coalition.

But you wouldn't know that from talking to people like Joe Steil in Keokuk, Iowa, a Mississippi River town whose faded Gilded Age glory is still visible in its residential neighborhoods and on the wide streets of its downtown district.

Steil is the chief executive officer of the Lee County Economic Development Group, and it's his job to help solve the unemployment problem in the locality, which has the second-highest jobless rate in Iowa.[2] The county today has 34,615 people, fewer than were recorded in its post–Civil War census of 1870, taken soon after the city's most famous onetime resident, Mark Twain, called Lee County his home.[3]

A holder of bachelor's and graduate degrees in banking, a civic leader, and a political centrist, Steil fits the profile of the exact kind of right-of-center voter most likely to have defected from Trump. But he didn't. Unlike his demographic peers in the suburbs of Houston, Dallas, Denver, and countless other metro areas, Steil and the people like him who populate the civic service clubs in the small and midsize communities of the Great Lakes region—the Rotary Reliables—voted with their neighbors and not their economic or educational class.

Much has been written about Trump's large gains among working-class whites, but barely noticed has been the resilience of his support among the upper-class whites who live among the Red-Blooded and Blue-Collared.

"If you're in larger cities and things like this, you flock with people much more like yourself," Steil says. "Where in rural America there's a huge cross section and you're a part of that cross section."

Sitting in the conference room of a spec building in an industrial park now home to the economic development agency, Steil projects the thoughtful calm you'd want from your accountant, relaxed in a dark-checked button-down shirt, large glasses sliding slightly down the bridge of his nose.

"I think that we're more diverse, is a good way of putting it," Steil says of the social circles in places like Keokuk, where blue and white collars worship together, fish and hunt together, and, in 2016, vote together.

Steil is literally a Rotary Reliable—a member of the local Rotary Club, a business leaders' group founded in Chicago in 1905—but he just as easily could be a member of the Lions Club, Sertoma Club, Optimist Club, National Exchange Club, or Kiwanis—all groups that have international footprints today but strong histories in the Midwest. Members meet weekly or biweekly, usually for a Dutch-treat lunch, to hear program speeches about other professions and to plan local charitable service projects.[4] Even as the institutions of formal connectedness decline in America as a whole with the rise of the casual links of social media, these groups still form a backbone of the leadership class in many small and mid-sized communities, particularly in the Midwest. The emblems of these groups still adorn the city limits welcome signs in towns across the region, and if you want to find out who the movers and shakers are in a heartland community, you can probably find all of them at noon on Tuesday or Thursday in the banquet room of the town's oldest restaurant.

In addition to his Rotary membership, Steil has volunteered for the local chapters of the American Heart Association and United Way, been president of the YMCA, and helped develop Bentley's Playground, a specialized playground for physically challenged children.

Aware of Trump's obstacles among white-collar voters in larger areas, Steil believes the economic crisis in much of the Midwest enabled Trump to succeed with the same kind of voters in places like Keokuk.

"Rotarians, or just call them leaders within rural communities, they know what makes their community tick, and they saw that high unemployment," Steil says.

He is reluctant to talk politics at all—and he deftly pivots questions about Lee County's role in the election through the prism of the county's economy. "Looking at it from a Lee County point of view, high unemployment was not good for our area so therefore there needed to be a change. As much as you can help guide that change . . . you want to be a part of it."

And that's part of the reason Trump carried this southeastern-most county in Iowa when no other Republican had in recent times. Trump won Lee County by 16 points—the same margin by which Romney had lost it four years before. Eight consecutive Republican nominees for president, including two Bushes and a Reagan, had lost the local vote here before Trump took it in a runaway. Even beloved former Republican governor Terry Branstad only carried the county once in his six successful gubernatorial campaigns. Lee County was the buckle on the Democratic belt in eastern Iowa that kept the state one of the most elusive prizes in the Midwest for the GOP.

"Lee County wanted to see change," Steil says. "We were the poster child for unemployment. There were orders leaving the country for, let's just say, product that wasn't as good as the product that could be manufactured here. Things went overseas and they were into high volume, low dollar, whereas here it was lower volume, higher quality."

Even though it has higher unemployment than most other Iowa counties, Lee County still holds on to a diverse manufacturing base, albeit over a smaller footprint than at many points in its past. Steil, the economic recruiter, reels off the list of survivors like a man who makes this pitch often.

All the staples of the historic Iowa economy are represented: agribusiness giant ADM has a local plant, as does canned meat mega-producer Pinnacle Foods. Anyone who's ever opened a can of Vienna sausages out of his or her school lunchbox has tasted Lee County. "It's a mainstay," Steil says of the plant, formerly known by the Armour Foods moniker. "They've been continually reinvesting in the plant."

The Mississippi River hits a natural fall line near Keokuk, and railroad giant BNSF has long had one of its major transcontinental river crossings here, along with the footprint that comes with the smaller railroads running the switching operation involved. French food-additive maker Roquette owns a large industrial presence making corn-based sweeteners in a riverfront facility that has traded hands over decades. Agrochemical company Scotts Miracle-Gro has its second-largest American factory here, and DuPont has a paint plant, a legacy of the Upper Mississippi River Valley's once dominant position in the international chemical sector.

Outside the traditional Iowa industrial base is a plant on U.S. Highway 218 midway between Keokuk and its co–county seat, Fort Madison, that at first glance looks like the exterior of an airplane hangar—with massive winglike structures, longer than any vehicle, lined up on the asphalt outside. They're wind turbine blades made from fiberglass by Fortune Global 500 company Siemens in what used to be a tractor-trailer factory.[5]

And the shining anchor of the county's most recent economic development efforts is a gleaming new $3 billion fertilizer plant that has just risen out of cornfields in rural Wever. With a projected annual payroll of $25 million, lured by more than $108 million in state tax credits, the Dutch-based, Egyptian-controlled corporate parent of the Iowa Fertilizer Company offers hope that southeastern Iowa is doing more than just nursing its historical industrial base through hospice.[6] The list of corporate nationalities of the surviving job providers in this county reads like the roster of a U.N. subcommittee—demonstrating that even the counties in Trump Country are now intertwined with the global economy, even as their voters push back on the excesses of globalism, a complexity that often went uncovered by journalists who chose only to paint Trump voters as "nationalists" in the ugliest sense of the term.

In the years after 2008, when the Sheaffer Pen Corporation closed up in Fort Madison, after a century of making writing implements here, many feared that the county's future was irreparably bleak.

According to Steil, the reality is that places like Lee County have to focus on workforce development as much as recruitment in order to regrow their job base in the age of automation. "Our plants are in desperate need of good, solid, skilled workforce. That's the number one thing they're all telling us," he says; he is aiming for an education system that doesn't channel every student into a four-year college, where they might fail or get skills unsuited to the economic opportunities of the technical-industrial jobs of today.

"Some people are better off to graduate from high school and go learn the trade," he says. "They can learn that, they can go to work in a plant, and perform a function and make very good money. Others can go on and get that associate's [two-year] degree . . . and then there's going to be a smaller percentage that will go on to four-year colleges but finish."

Steil has four grown children, and the youngest still lives in Keokuk and works in the supply chain of a local factory, using his associate's degree. In his spare time, when he's not doing community work or playing with grandkids, Steil likes to hunt, and his hunting buddies are mostly plant managers or factory accountants—people with white-collar jobs in blue-collar environments.

Like Steil, the son of a truck driver, they all feel equally comfortable at the Rotary Club lunch or talking taxidermy with guys on the factory floors. Unlike the bankers and economic developers in suburban cul-de-sacs of larger cities, Steil and his crowd were not subject to the social pressure to oppose Trump. Quite the opposite, they were surrounded by people voting for Trump, even breaking party allegiances to do so.

But that commitment to Trump may not last; at least in Steil's view, places like Lee County could flip back to their Democratic political roots just as quickly as they shifted to Trump: "I think this area here always does a wait-and-see and they're gonna want to see progress, and they're going to judge that progress when the next election cycle comes around."

Michael Martin

Erie, Erie County, Pennsylvania

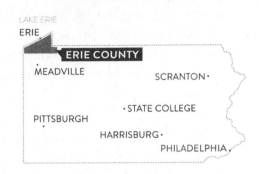

In the summer of 1972, the remnants of Hurricane Agnes spread destruction across the mid-Atlantic for three days; the onslaught of heavy rain was so severe it washed out foundations from homes, destroyed entire business districts, and tore up highways and bridges in its wake.

The ruin spread from the Hudson Valley in New York all the way here to Lake Erie; it took lives, livelihoods, changed the shopping habits of locals for a generation, and hastened the looming economic recession of the 1970s.

The storm also did its best to derail Michael Martin's ambition to go to college. The middle child of seven children, Martin had just graduated from high school and was about to enter Edinboro University in Pennsylvania to become a teacher.

"That is what I would call an interesting time in my life. An organization had come to me, they had asked me if I would go into a program for them, and they would pay for my college education. Two weeks before school is supposed to start, Hurricane Agnes came through, the sponsoring organization didn't make any money in their summer bazaar, and they said, 'Hey, we don't have any money to send you to school.' And life just tripped me along to where I'm at today," Martin explains.

The son of a schoolteacher and a nurse, and one of seven, he had no way to pay for his education, so Martin got a job driving a delivery truck for a company that sold paper and packaging materials to industries and businesses in this region.

"After being in that position for about a year, the general manager of that operation offered me an inside sales position, and then a year later he offered me a sales position, and I've never looked back," he says.

Today, Martin sits in the conference room of his own paper and printing company, thanks in large part to a storm that changed the fortunes of an aspiring schoolteacher to those of an entrepreneur who employs thirty people and finds a way to give back to his community in every spare second he has.

The community involvement comes naturally to Martin as the grandson of the late Joseph C. Martin, a former Democratic mayor of Erie, its first port commissioner, and a sports editor of the *Erie Daily Times*.[7] "I grew up here in Erie, Pennsylvania. I'm a fifth-generation person here in this community from my family. We must've been horse thieves, they wouldn't let us leave," he jokes.

For most of the country, the enduring image of Erie is that of a third-tier Rust Belt city down on its knees, filled with ghosts of its industrial past haunting the remains of the hollowed-out factories and manufacturing facilities.

But if you grew up in western Pennsylvania, eastern Ohio, or along the western panhandle of West Virginia, the Erie you know features different imagery. It's likely where your family spent a summer vacation, thanks to the miles of beaches along Presque Isle Bay, on a peninsula jutting into Lake Erie and protecting the city's harbor on the back side. The large park has long been used by landlocked working-class families who can pretend it's a reasonable facsimile of the ocean within a two-hour drive from home. The Waldameer Water World, an amusement park lovingly maintained by a local family, sits at the gates of the state park and offers a throwback to the prototypical beach scene of half a century ago.

For the local people of Erie County, this spot is a combination of a lakefront place to raise a family, a place steeped in religiosity, and a place to wager you can carve out a successful life if you are willing to reinvent yourself as the manufacturing world changes underneath your feet. It is also a place filled in the summertime with tourists in clapboard cottages, campgrounds, and old-fashioned mom-and-pop motels that dot the city's shoreline along with a kaleidoscope of sleek sailboats, small yachts, and modest fishing boats.

Across the bay, the remnants of industry anchor the city proper: a General Electric train engine plant that is the last giant remaining from Erie's industrial peak. It recently lost its standing as the largest employer in town. Fewer than 3,000 people now work at the union facility—in its heyday it employed 15,000 people. In the lead-up to the 2016 election, 1,500 workers lost their jobs; in 2017, an additional 200 were furloughed. Since then, GE's transportation division has moved its headquarters to Chicago and opened up a new plant in largely nonunion Texas.[8]

"GE just announced a sale of a hundred locomotives to Egypt, but that may not yet be good for our town because, again, a lot of those jobs have disappeared around the world, and they've built a new plant in Texas," Martin says. "For each one job that is lost, an additional five others are as well, waitresses, small businesses, mechanics; every single job lost costs another one in the community."

Like many Rust Belt counties, Erie has seen a great departure of manufacturing jobs in many sectors in the past decades, headed offshore or points south. When jobs move, people move next, and Erie County's population of 276,207 is lower today than it was in 1980, even as the state's population has grown by 8 percent and the nation's by 43 percent over those two and a half decades.[9]

The quickest replacement for lost manufacturing jobs has been a focus on tourism, both the existing base of regional lake tourists and those drawn to newer attractions, such as the twenty-two area wineries. "We're trying to resurrect it as a tourist town, but tourism jobs don't pay what manufacturing jobs pay," Martin cautions.

After years of decay, the private sector and volunteer leaders of city and county are partway through the pains of reinvention. Martin—who has been a committee member of the chamber of commerce, vice chair of the transit authority, chair of his township zoning hearing board, and on both the board of governors of the philharmonic and the board of the governors of University of Pittsburgh Medical Center (UPMC)—knows a little something about reinventing to survive.

"It all began for me with Agnes, I had to change course. Did I think I was going to drive a truck forever? Of course not, but I was willing to find out where it would lead me," he says.

He came from a family of Catholic Democrats who were thrilled when John F. Kennedy won the presidency in 1960. "I don't think Kennedy would get elected in today's world on either side. He wouldn't be far enough left for the D's and he wouldn't be far enough right for the R's," Martin theorizes.

Since local politics ran in the family, Martin recalls some political discussions around the family table. "Global issues were kicked around concerning where the country was at and what should we be doing, what we shouldn't be doing. My family believed in the [Vietnam] war. My family believed in that we needed correct civil rights. I believe then, and I believe today, the vast majority of Americans are moderate."

Martin voted for Donald Trump, and in him he saw a politician who did not fit the frozen ideological grid. "We're not Far Left, we're not Far Right. I think that's one of the things that was borne out in this last election."

Martin is charismatic, confident, and direct, qualities that likely guided him along the way from the cab of a paper-company delivery truck to eventually owning a printing company. His conference room is wide and welcoming, and filled with natural light thanks to a broad skylight overhead, a large picture window that looks out onto a freshly cut lawn in front of his business, and a glass wall that separates the room from the reception area.

Dressed in a green-and-white-checkered short-sleeved shirt and khakis, he wears glasses that frame a face topped with closely cropped sandy blond hair; he has the build of a former linebacker or maybe a Marine.

Martin's printing company is surviving, thanks in part to a solid market share. "In my industry, virtually all of our competition is gone too. It doesn't have as much to do with technology as it has to do with what was here. We used to have four banks headquartered here. There's no bank that's headquartered in Erie now because of all the acquisition of things that came along. This used to be known as the paper capital of the world, with Hammermill Paper Company here. That company's gone," he says. As the customers for printing decline locally, so does the competition for Martin, who took over his own company when it faced desperate choices.

"During the turndown in the economy in the early nineties, I was a straight-commission salesman," Martin says. "Many of my customers were either being acquired or they were going broke. The company I presently own was one of my customers who we had to shut off because he couldn't pay his bills, and about a year later he and I chatted because my customer base was falling apart, and we constructed a deal that I should come to work as a minority owner with the opportunity to buy the rest of the stock out over a period of time.

"I pretty much bought a company that was technically bankrupt." He credits one thing for its recovery: building a solid reputation. "For quality, for on-time delivery, and for affordability. Before I bought it, the company had a great reputation for quality, great reputation for on-time delivery. Price affordability was something it did not. So I started negotiating with customers . . ."

All around Martin in his conference room is evidence of his success and his philosophy at the sheetfed commercial printing company; cheery direct-mail pieces, college admission packets, and business portfolios for the medical industry, hospital programs, and private schools; and nonprofit mailers of different sizes and approaches are pinned to a board on one wall. Several framed testimonials are on a long shelf on another.

Other Erie companies were not so lucky. "The town has had a lot of changes," Martin says. "We've lost a lot of manufacturing jobs. We used to make steam shovels here, a company called Bucyrus-Erie, gone. We used to make kids' toys here, Louis Marx toy company, gone. We used to make boilers and things, Skinner Engine Company, gone. Zurn Industries, which makes that little apparatus that automatically flushes toilets, was headquartered here and it's virtually gone from our landscape now."

Martin has seen the consequences of Erie's economic struggles beyond the numbers as well. They aren't just felt structurally, they don't just impact tax bases; they mean neighborhoods deteriorate, as homes and small businesses shutter when no one is moving in to replace the exodus, or to buy their groceries or widgets in the local stores.

Churches close too, including the one the Martin family had been a member of for generations. He partly blames the population loss, but also the emergence of a less religious society. "Is that tough? Yes, but I do understand, nothing's the same forever. Things change. Because our country has changed and I unfortunately believe we've become less faith-based. Faith requires accountability and responsibility, and nobody wants to be accountable for the actions and nobody wants to be responsible," he says.

Martin agrees with the professional staff of Erie's Regional Chamber and Growth Partnership—the long-term path forward for this city likely centers not around manufacturing or tourism, but around the Eds and Meds imprint: the anchor assets of universities and hospitals.

"The universities and colleges in the region literally connect their communities to our community and connect all of them to the world; that kind of innovation can serve as a building block to a stable foundation economically," says Rick Novotny, executive director of the Erie County Redevelopment Authority.

"What we strive for in success is a balance in our economic landscape; yes, manufacturing will still be part of that, but so will growth in education, medical, and medical technology, hospitality, and professional services sectors like the insurance industry," Novotny said in a recent meeting with several members of the Erie Regional Chamber and Growth Partnership and redevelopment authority.

The director is also a bit of a maverick himself. "I voted for both Ross Perot and Donald J. Trump," he says proudly. The other members of the authority staff at the meeting did not share his enthusiasm for Trump, but they are all in agreement about Erie's path forward. They must be making progress investing the community's leaders in the strategy, because Martin, plugged in as a community volunteer, can recite it when interviewed separately.

"Erie does have the potential to attract professionals like professors, doctors, scientists to the region," Martin says. "Eds and Meds is a base that allows you to do other things; we're fortunate we have Gannon University, Mercyhurst University, Penn State Behrend, Edinboro in our backyard. The real interesting little school we have here is LECOM medical school. LECOM is the largest osteopathic medical school in the country. Started here about twenty-five years ago."

What Eds and Meds doesn't do well is employ, with a family-sustaining wage, the unskilled person who did not do well in school and isn't able to get a job sweeping a floor in a factory. "Many of those workers are still here. If you take a look at the city of Erie, there's a lot of blight in the city, lot of homes that basically are uninhabitable or close to being uninhabitable," Martin says. "Once the manufacturing jobs are gone, what's left? People lose hope. They've lost hope.

"We used to be a place that made stuff. And I don't think people in Erie have figured out that we're no longer a manufacturing town. They still hang on the fact that because we still have, percentage-wise, a decent number of manufacturing jobs."

Psychologically, the transition hasn't happened yet.

"We have not yet reinvented ourselves. We're talking about it, we're finally doing some things," Martin says. "I think as a community we're still struggling. I think our best years are ahead of us once we figure out what it is we want to be, but we haven't figured it out completely yet."

Martin's own three adult daughters could not wait.

After five generations making their way in the same town, this next generation of Martins has left Erie County for better opportunities.

They would have liked to stay, but there are no jobs for them, Martin says. "One's in Cleveland, one's in upstate New York outside of Rochester, and one's down around Meadville. So they're close, but they're not here for Sunday dinner.

"They are the kind of people Erie needs to stay. They all have advanced degrees and deep family ties, the kind of things that strengthen the community and the economy," Martin says, worrying not just about the numbers of people Erie is losing, but also about the county's ability to rebuild itself without them.

"If you take a look at the statistics of Erie, and I don't know the exact numbers, but they say the vast majority of people in Erie never even went to college, let alone have advanced degrees. So, the brain drain only makes the community worse."

Martin lost his wife, Sandra, at the age of fifty-six to breast cancer in 2011. She, a registered nurse who worked in the local hospital's critical care unit for twenty-six years, was a dedicated volunteer to the Erie community, just like her husband.

Martin is the definition of a civic-minded businessman; he does not just talk the talk, he walks it. "All of my family lessons have been examples of giving back to the community," he says. "I have been blessed with disasters turning into gifts; to give back to my community is a gift we should all be willing to do."

Martin's activism is more service than political, but he did inherit a strong interest in national politics. The last Democrat Martin voted for was Bill Clinton; Barack Obama's policies were too progressive for his liking. He did not care for John McCain or Mitt Romney, but voted for them anyway. And the first person who caught his eye during the 2016 primary election was John Kasich, the Ohio governor.

"He was my guy. I also liked Carly Fiorina. Trump was not my guy," Martin says, but quickly his voice becomes elevated. "And then he came to my state. He came to my city. And I saw that he could connect with the very people who were being left behind, and that impacted me."

Martin was not the only voter Trump converted during the candidate's landmark visit to the city on August 12, 2016, for a rally attended by 10,000 people at the local hockey arena.[10] The reliably Democratic city is not a normal stop for candidates, much less a Republican, as the local paper noted the day before the rally. "By stopping in Erie . . . Trump has signaled that he intends to continue bucking the trends of more traditional campaigns," the *Erie Times-News* wrote. "But in most respects, there is little evidence to suggest Trump can turn the county red, or at least sway enough undecided voters to make a meaningful difference in Pennsylvania."[11]

But that's exactly what Trump did. The same county Romney had lost by 16 points, McCain lost by 20 points, and even Bush lost to John Kerry by 8, Trump won by 2 points and almost 2,000 votes. Erie's Democratic track record had been so unblemished that even Walter Mondale carried it in 1984, despite losing forty-nine states to President Ronald Reagan.

"Part of the difference as to why Trump won Erie and no other Republican has in recent history is that Trump actually came here. He showed interest. He told a different story. I believe Romney and McCain both just basically felt, 'Hey, I'm the Republican candidate.

Statistics show I can't win Pennsylvania, so I'm not gonna spend any time there,'" Martin says.

"Trump did what nobody else did. He paid attention to the states that he shouldn't have won and when he did that, that was one of the things that really brought people to his attention. People were craving someone to pay attention to what was going on in their community."

Martin, like so many other civic leaders in towns like Erie all over the Midwest, did not initially prefer Trump, had misgivings about Trump, but had no problem voting for him in November.

"Did I like Trump better than Hillary? Absolutely," Martin says. "But I do wish he would throw his Twitter account away and . . . Yeah, I do. He doesn't have to fight his own battles. The more he fights a battle, the more the flame grows."

Martin also states he feels a part of something that is bigger than Trump. "So I think whatever happened in 2016 goes beyond him. It wasn't about a person, it was about the community around you, even communities that are not geographically attached to you."

The sense that Trump was looking at the overlooked, and fighting for the forgotten in Middle America, enabled him to succeed with the upper-middle-class voters in places like Erie who are scarcely different demographically from the suburbanites who were the weakest part of the Trump coalition.

Martin, despite his religiosity and active Catholicism, was able to compartmentalize the jarring parts of Trump's demeanor that showed up throughout the campaign—including the sexism on the *Access Hollywood* tape.

"I knew what we were getting when he ran for president. That's his personality. You show me a person, or you show me a group of people at a country club, and I'm going to tell you five out of ten of them, maybe more, have said everything he's said. Do I think that some of the things he said are offensive? Absolutely. But go across the spectrum of our country. It's there."

In the end, for Martin, Trump's consistent praise of Americans who work, and his pledge to defend them, won out. "In my world it just came down to being . . . I work hard. I've been fortunate to get to where I'm at in life, but it wasn't handed to me."

Martin says he also likes the direction of the third-way movement of the Trump coalition. "When the American public voted, the halls of Washington hadn't quite figured out what happened. They're still fighting the party lines and even within the Republican Party, the right wing of the Right doesn't want to try to move any agenda forward," Martin complains, echoing a sentiment often heard among Trump voters, who have come to trust him more than the GOP he ostensibly leads.

The Great Revolt Survey asked Trump voters to rank the institution they most trusted to do what was right for the country; Trump was chosen by 60 percent of the survey takers, compared to only 25 percent who chose congressional Republicans. The fact that people like Martin, a Rotary Reliable voter who by all rights should be a loyal Republican, share this sentiment is a wake-up call for the congressional wing of the GOP.

"So we're back in gridlock, which as far as I'm concerned is only going to make Trump stronger moving forward," Martin says. "Because the guy who doesn't have a job, or the guy who's struggling to make ends meet, is tired of the politician who's a career politician."

Martin, a late convert to Trump, well after he was the Republican nominee, sees in him a potential check-and-balance on traditional Washington. "In other words, there are the two parties and then there's him. He's not an R completely, he's not a D completely. Both parties at times have turned their back on him."

Jonathan Kochie

Freeland, Luzerne County, Pennsylvania

Freeland, Pennsylvania, population 3,500, wears its weary heart on its sleeve.

When a sudden snowstorm plowed through here in late spring of 2017, Centre Street—the main business district of this Luzerne County town outside of Wilkes-Barre—was impassable. So were the sidewalks. Which meant the handful of businesses—which try to keep what little commerce is left here humming—were facing the prospect of days without customers. Jonathan Kochie had little choice but to take matters into his own hands.

The slight thirty-nine-year-old with bright blue eyes, neatly trimmed dark blond hair and beard, and an engaging smile got his shovel and began digging. And digging. For several blocks and several hours.

"I shoveled Centre Street. And the sidewalks," he says matter-of-factly. "If I didn't, no one would get around; if the neighbors don't get out, then no one does any business that day, do they?"

Kochie owns the Other Side, a bar and restaurant establishment that has been in his family for years. "My parents bought it in 1989, back then it was Eddie's Bar and Grill. They had another restaurant across the street called Northside Pizzeria. For years we operated both," he says. They closed the pizzeria after thirty-nine years.

"The Other Side got its name because when we were over there"—Kochie points across the street—"we said, 'We're coming to the other side of the street for the bar,' and the name stuck," he explains.

Centre Street in Freeland is complicated. On one end of the main artery is MMI Prep, a private college-preparatory day school that was funded by a nineteenth-century coal baron who understood the need for technical schools in America that would provide education to students who would otherwise lack the opportunity to receive one.

In 1879, the Industrial School for Miners and Mechanics opened its doors to fewer than a dozen young men who worked the mines during the day and attended school at night, giving them the technical abilities necessary to elevate themselves in the chain of command.

The number of students grew and so did the school, evolving from a night school to a day school to a sweeping campus with a college-preparatory curriculum. It went from all-male to coed, all along changing the lives of the sons and daughters of hardscrabble miners in the heart of this northeast Pennsylvania region that still produces 4.6 million tons of hard, hot-burning anthracite coal every year.[12]

MMI has an impeccable, near-perfect success rate of its graduating students heading off to college, but it has also undergone an alarming decline in its admissions; in 2017, the school graduated forty students, but its incoming sixth-grade class has only twenty-seven.

That decline is reflected—or perhaps related to—the decline of the stretch of Centre Street's business district between MMI Prep and South Street.

It is hard not to wonder how this entire Luzerne County town is holding it together: storefront after storefront has shuttered along Centre Street, and the flat gray skies of the late-spring afternoon add to the impression that things aren't just stagnant here; they are in a death spiral.

"People feel stuck. They do, they just feel stuck," says lifelong resident Jason Volciak, a deputy at the Luzerne County sheriff department, standing in front of a vacant business across from the Garden Chen takeout Chinese food restaurant. A red-and-blue OPEN sign, the kind you'd see at Sam's Club, was flashing as cars slogged by to jump on Interstate 80, presumably to get out of town.

"Yeah, no one really works here in Freemont anymore. You have to get on the interstate to get to your job anymore," he says, as he walked toward the Other Side for dinner.

Every other car honked or waved at Volciak as he made his way for all-you-can-eat-spaghetti night at Kochie's tavern. "I am sort of like the unofficial mayor," he says. Any observer would conclude he is the mayor: "Hey, Jason!" was repeated five times in one block, as the neighborhood deputy tipped his ball cap to men and women alike who shouted hello.

Freemont is a town of used-to-be—it used to be a thriving coal town, it used to be a thriving manufacturing town, people didn't make bank, but they were able to keep a modest home, provide for their family, maybe buy a fishing camp in the Poconos and carve out a decent middle-class life. Their jobs were mostly underground and mostly dangerous.

Those days are gone. But Freeland could be a town of rebirth. Its location along the two interstates could be its saving grace, attracting folks working along those corridors looking for affordable housing, a place to call home.

One sign of possibility is a brand-new CVS store on Centre—it replaced the locally owned Nocchi's Pharmacy. The brand-new fancy building stands out as the other buildings decay under the weight of neglect.

Freeland is partly a suburb of Wilkes-Barre, the much larger but not healthier city of 40,000 nearby; and partly a town of its own.

The decline started here in the 1940s with a 7 percent population drop; twenty years later, that loss dramatically doubled to 14 percent. It has never stopped bleeding souls since, although the declining percentages are now in the single digits per decade.

The town's biggest employers are the Citterio meat-packing plant and the hospital. "The plant employs around a hundred people, used to be a lot more; the hospital is in Hazelton," Volciak says of the Luzerne County neighboring town, eight miles away, that launched the career of Lou Barletta, the local congressman and an original ally of Donald Trump, who is now seeking to oust Democratic U.S. senator Bob Casey in 2018.

"We do have some manufacturing outside of the area, and distribution centers, but really the jobs are hard to come by and the ones that are here do not pay much. Makes for a real brain drain of young people," says Volciak as he heads into the Other Side.

Most visitors entering town for the first time will notice the cheery WELCOME TO FREELAND—PENNSYLVANIA'S HIGHEST BOROUGH sign, with its skyline silhouettes of steeples and towers as the backdrop. With

Freeland at just over 1,942 feet in elevation, the proclamation is likely untrue—the title could be more accurately claimed by many other locales far to the west—but it is legend for Freeland schoolkids as they grow up. Still, the views from the ridge are beautiful.

Most of the media and pundits were stunned when Donald Trump beat back Hillary Clinton in this county in 2016; but given the Democratic history here, "beat back" is too mild a term; he pummeled her.

For six presidential elections in a row, Luzerne County helped, or tried to help, place Democrats in the White House. In the two election cycles preceding the Trump-Clinton matchup, Luzerne gave Barack Obama its support.

In 2008, Obama beat Republican nominee John McCain by 9 percentage points here—and even John Kerry and Al Gore carried it before that. But things changed in 2016. Trump even dragged Republican senator Pat Toomey behind him for a local victory here—Toomey edged out his opponent Katie McGinty with just over 50 percent of the vote, 7 points behind Trump's number.

In 2016, the signs were visible everywhere in Luzerne that its support for Democrats was thinning—but few noticed. Pennsylvania has been the ultimate tease for Republicans since 1988, tempting nominee after nominee to dump money into the expensive state that would eventually prove wasted. Many experts thought Trump and his allies, such as the National Rifle Association, were falling victim to the Keystone State trap as they targeted it from the beginning of the general election campaign.

Pollster Wes Anderson, who worked for Trump's two largest allies among independent super PACs, spotted Pennsylvania's competitiveness earlier than most. In a poll completed just before Labor Day, Anderson found Trump losing the state by just one-tenth of 1 percentage point—and winning the northeast portion of the commonwealth that includes Luzerne County by 40 points. Media polls weren't as accurate. A CBS News poll in the field at the same time as Anderson's showed Clinton up by 8 points statewide—a margin that held until the end of October in that recurring media poll.[13]

"When we told people the margins we had found for Trump in

Northeast Pennsylvania at the end of the summer, no one believed us," Anderson says. "But they were right and they held."

If anyone had looked at the trends here before 2016 closely enough, they would have understood that Pennsylvania was ripe, finally, for change. Since the 2000 presidential contest between George W. Bush and Al Gore, the state had become 0.4 percent more Republican in every subsequent presidential election. But Trump's win here was overwhelming; he flipped Luzerne County—which gave Obama 52 percent of its vote four years earlier—to earn a whopping 58 percent of that same county in 2016.

He won in every single precinct except for a few in Pittston, Hazelton, and Wilkes-Barre.

"People were weary of the professional politician, but no one seemed to hear us say that," says Kochie. "We were here in plain sight if anyone cared to listen. We still are; that sentiment has not gone away. The professional reporters and professional Washington still does not get it. They drone on and on every day either on social media or on the networks, and report with just enough inference that you know they find his win not legitimate. It is as if our votes were not legitimate," he explains.

Kochie is a young man with a big heart and a passion for his community. He has also been president of the local chamber of commerce, and is just the kind of civic leader that you might have expected to opt for a more experienced and even-keeled presidential candidate than Donald Trump.

On this particular evening, he is also the chef at the restaurant that he has owned for eighteen years, since before he was old enough to legally drink a beer from the bar.

The place is lively. About twenty people sit enjoying their endless-spaghetti bowls in a restaurant that has paneling, a long bar filled with young people, an area for bands, and signs for upcoming events Kochie hosts at the tavern.

If Cheers were relocated to Freeland, this would be that place.

The Other Side has twelve beers on tap, carries forty-five different bottled beers, and really has that welcoming neighborhood bar feel that you often see portrayed on television, but rarely find in larger cities with wealthier populations. In those larger places, people are more transient, more likely to try the newest place or trend, rather than be loyal to one barstool and the bartender you've known since high school.

"We do lunch, dinner. We do bands, live entertainment. We do a lot of fund-raisers. Anything fun. A lot of different games. I can see the basketball hoop over there. That was from Final Four. It was a competition. Best out of twenty shots. We had a big basketball rim. We gave them away," he says.

He was born here, his parents were born here. He's not the guy who never leaves town, though; he travels extensively and makes visiting Europe a once-a-year adventure.

"I have a sense of responsibility to this town. And this place," he says of the tavern. "This is who I am married to. When she says 'jump,' I jump."

He lives upstairs, and his routine is that of a man who truly is married to his business. "Well, I wake up early, two flights up, have breakfast, come downstairs, check on things, place orders for fresh food for the day, clean up anything I may have missed from the night before, and then get ready for lunch and dinner."

He employs eighteen people, runs the business, is often the chef, and is heavily involved in bettering his community.

"It's fun," he says sincerely. "It has its challenges, but along with a lot of good rewards." The challenges, he says, are satisfying people: "keeping food fresh, homemade, not store-bought. Our meatballs are always fresh," he adds with pride. And they are, made in the southern Italian tradition, speckled with bread crumbs and spices, and kneaded continuously so that the meat is light and airy, despite its denseness.

"Spaghetti night is a seller for us, especially the meatballs. We have prime rib and lobster on the weekends. It's really good. Yep. Homemade soups. My mom loves making soups. She's a soup connoisseur. She likes all different kinds of stuff: chicken potpie soup, BLT soup, gnocchi soup, butternut squash."

Business, he says, is always a challenge. "You always got to keep up with the new things with the kids coming up, turning twenty-one, activities, something for them to do instead of just come out to a bar. We like to be more than just a bar, where you come out, shoot some pool. We can shoot pool here, darts, anything, we'll even do cornhole. We'll do beer pong. We'll have flip-cup. We'll have all kind of different games for them, and competitions. We have Beer Olympics coming at the end of this month. That's a lot of fun. We start on a Sunday morning and it goes until about four or five in the afternoon. It's a lot of fun."

After he joined the local chamber of commerce, he quickly rose to be its president. Why? He wants to move Freeland up. He has friends in this town who have made it, and friends who are struggling, and friends who have left.

"There's a limited scope to what people can do in this town based on their talents and their professions; that is why we have this brain drain. Those of us who have made it want to keep a good mix of people living in the community," he says.

Kochie is your standard businessman Republican: he's for lower taxes, fewer regulations, less government.

During the election he voted for Trump—though it took a while for him to get to him, because of his personality. The persistence of educated, civic-minded voters who had reservations about voting for Trump, but did it anyway, defied the largest exertions of the Hillary Clinton campaign, which spent millions targeting Romney voters in key states such as Pennsylvania who had hesitations about Trump. It ran an onslaught of testimonial TV ads and radio ads with self-professed lifelong Republicans promising to "put party aside" and vote for Clinton, even though they "may not agree with Hillary on everything."[14]

But in the end, Trump's business sense and bluntness appealed to Kochie, and the Clinton ads did not work.

"There was this sense of reality with him. It has gotten so in this country that you are not quite sure what you can say to people that might offend them. Things you would never think would make people offended. The politically correct stuff has gotten overboard. Certainly we needed corrections from crude or awful behavior, but we've gone overboard. You are afraid to talk to people. I didn't like the country's going that way," he says.

Kochie worries that the last few years under Obama made people more open to racism. "I don't like some of the things that were done. We're here in a small town where you could see lots of racism, but that's from people that don't get out and get on in the world. I don't care if you're pink, purple, black, blue, you're all the same, but I think there was a lot more stuff that would come up because Obama failed to use more common sense when talking about problems the country faces, like for instance when it comes to fighting terrorism. Just say what it is instead of trying to not offend people."

That reluctance, he says, was frustrating. He was also frustrated by how the unrest in Ferguson, Missouri, and Baltimore was handled by the White House. "I didn't like the way he handled the riots where all these small-business owners, especially in Baltimore, had their livelihoods destroyed for the riots, and he didn't do anything, just said, 'Just riot nicely.' No, that's somebody's livelihood you're ruining. Those people will never come back. Most of them African American small businessmen and -women who worked hard to start a business. They were just destroyed in an effort to not let the police do their job? If rioters came and did that here, I'd be done. I'd have to go find something else to do. That would just destroy me."

He also thinks that Trump might have the sense to understand how Obamacare has impacted businesspeople indirectly. "So my insurance went up almost a hundred dollars a month. Now think about that for a moment, that hundred dollars a month is twelve hundred dollars less I have a year to spend on things I like, like traveling or entertainment. Now, you multiply that by a couple of hundred people and that is a whole community that starts to have a loss in people using their services," he says.

"Obamacare impacted me, impacted everybody here. Everybody. It is making it hard for the average working person to get ahead. You can't. There's too many bills."

Kochie is very satisfied with Trump as president, saying he understands that disrupting a system that has been run by essentially the same class of people on both sides of the aisle, and news organizations that are used to being vaunted and not scrutinized, is going to make them attack him.

"He does not back down. I think he's still sticking to his guns. He shows every day that he is sticking up for the country. Honestly, I don't think four years is enough for any president to put something in effect to actually see how it's going to work. I was the president of the chamber for two years. It took two years to get the ball just started rolling again," he says of the local organization that lost its steam years ago.

"They needed somebody in there that I think was interested in the town and had a business and could see it from all around, not just in the center and look out for everybody. That's why I decided to do that," he says.

His first point of action: get others involved. "So we would ask people to join the chamber, and they would ask, 'What do we get with it? How does it benefit us?' And honestly, at the beginning I had no answer for that because we as an organization offered no tangible benefits. We wouldn't do anything except sending donation letters. I figured if we could get a little newspaper for the town where it could advertise all the business for a cheap price, maybe we could start there."

So he did.

Under his leadership, they started with reinvigorating the town's Memorial Day festivities. "We wanted to work on that. Build that up again," he says.

Then he started a local pub crawl to go along with that. "We have the pub run in Freeland, challenge for all the people to run around to different bars. I started working on that. I got a lady that had a printing company, not a printing company, an advertising company. And she came in and she started the *Freeland Progress*. The *Freeland Progress*, back in the day, was one of the newspapers that used to be in town. The first and last newspaper in town. I did a lot of research on that. So that is how we brought the newspaper back. Now all the businesspeople or anybody that's in the chamber are advertised in there, so that's a benefit. They can advertise cheap for a month. We started with a business-size ad at twenty-five dollars. The response was amazing."

He left the chamber presidency after two years, having doubled the membership, and is still heavily involved. His big goal now is to try to draw other businesses to the Main Street area.

"We always try, but it's hard to attract people here. We're having a hard time keeping people here. They're moving away, going to college, and the kids aren't coming back. My wing nights here on Thursdays used to be nothing but kids. Now it's not that way. I would see the kids and be able to say, 'Oh, okay, that's the future.' It's not like that anymore," he says.

"I used to see kids running around at seventeen or eighteen, get them when they turned twenty-one, and keep them when they turned twenty-five and got married," says Kochie. "That doesn't happen anymore. Now they're going to school before they're twenty-one and then they move. Bring people to Freeland? It's tough. There's nothing . . . What are you going to come for? To get a job here is tough, a good-paying job. There's nothing in the area. Freeland, nobody's coming to Freeland anytime soon. It's all, it's all really sad."

Kochie marvels at the fascination, in the East Coast's metropolitan areas, with how it might be possible that places like Freeland shocked the world by voting for Trump.

"People are still scratching their head about why people voted for Donald Trump. Well, here is the thing: we voted for ourselves, and that is the thing they missed. That is the thing they still miss. I turn on the television and they talk about how he brags, or this or that about him, and they still don't talk to us. They still don't hear us. They still don't get us. We are a part of America too, and we are a part of America that wants to be part of something that takes everyone forward. Takes us all together," he says.

The direction the country was taking—culturally, economically, spiritually—worried Kochie long before Trump came along. "We've always been able to be different, come from different places and still feel that pride that we were all in this together. That we are American and that means something special. It means hard work, it means diversity, it means embracing each other's traditions. Well, we got away from that and moved towards only some people's traditions and cultures matter, and the other people just need to go away.

"One of the reasons I think Trump did so well and attracted a lot of Democrats was because he's not very ideological. He's a get-in-there-and-do-things kind of guy. People in this town have told me that they are fed up with politics and politicians and just want someone to get in and do what needs to be done. And help everybody out. Some of the stuff is getting out of hand," he says.

Kochie admits he was surprised on election night. "Honestly, I didn't think he was going to win. I did not think so. When he did, I was like, 'Wow! A lot of people are feeling like we do.' That's what I really thought. People are getting fed up. Getting fed up with the news and what's going on and just all that nonsense.

"What I think people who aren't from mid-America do not still understand several months later is that this commitment to being part of this movement is just starting. We wanted to be part of something, part of a community that we feel as though we are giving back to, you know, a very American feeling, I think. And that is the core of this movement. And I think it's going to be a hell of a thing to break the bubble of Washington, but I think the only thing that has a chance of breaking it is this."

That's one of the things that people missed about this election, says Kochie. "We've talked about this. It was his message, 'Make America Great.'

"It was potent and powerful. It takes you to a better place. It's aspirational. And I think that Hillary's message strung together was flat. It didn't say, 'Come with me,'" he says.

"And aspirational is the heart of what makes America move forward all the time. Like you said," he says to Volciak.

Kochie leaves the interview to go organize the kitchen. The Other Side restaurant has cleared out—by now it's late in the evening—but the bar is still filled with regulars. Two couples are playing pool, and they order another round.

"I have to get the order ready for the food in the morning. It's lobster night tomorrow night. Have to go catch a few," he jokes, then disappears into the kitchen. But not before several locals pat him on the back and greet him.

"He's a good guy," says Volciak of Kochie as he finishes off his second bowl of spaghetti. "Really good guy. Really cares about the community, and honestly, I think that is why all of us voted for Trump. I think that is the part no one really got."

7
King Cyrus Christians

In his pre-political days, Donald Trump made regular appearances on the national radio show of shock jock Howard Stern, routinely going on air to talk about his sexual exploits or the anatomical features of starlets who struck Stern's fancy. His crassness continued onto the campaign trail, with his taunting of fellow Republican contender Carly Fiorina as ugly—telling a *Rolling Stone* writer, "Look at that face! Would anyone vote for that?"[1] Trump mocked a disabled reporter and fumbled through embarrassing explanations of his own thin religiosity.

Yet from the Iowa caucuses forward, Trump exceeded expectations with a strong performance among evangelical and fundamentalist Christians and conservative Catholic voters. In Iowa, where the respected Pew Research Center study on religious life in America found that 77 percent of adults call themselves Christians, and half of them are self-described conservative Christians, Trump won a respectable second in the nominating caucuses and a historic victory in the general election. In the Deep South's Bible Belt, Trump won every state except oil-patch Texas and Oklahoma—both of which stuck with Texas senator Ted Cruz. Trump's best early primary margins were in Alabama, Mississippi, and Louisiana, all heavily evangelical electorates where he topped 40 percent in multicandidate fields.[2]

In the general election, more revelations of Trump's lasciviousness emerged and still, conservative Christian voters stuck with the man who had not long ago been a pro-choice, pro–gay rights supporter of liberal Democrat Nancy Pelosi. Leaders of many evangelical Christian groups were quick to distance themselves during the campaign from Trump's personal values but reaffirmed their political bargain—they were willing to ride the Trump candidacy with all its bumps because he had explicitly promised to choose a Supreme Court nominee from a defined list of acceptable conservative possibilities. In the wake of the October release of the bawdy backstage tape with *Access Hollywood* host Billy Bush, Tony Perkins, head of the Family Research Council, said, "My personal support for Donald Trump has never been based upon shared values, it is based upon shared concerns."[3]

As the election progressed and Trump gathered more support from evangelicals than expected, some Christian observers likened his appeal to that of Cyrus the Great, a sixth-century BC pagan Persian king, who released enslaved Jews from generations of bondage in Babylon, enabling their return to Jerusalem where they would construct the temple that preceded the Herodian Temple Mount that still stands today.[4]

Christian motivational speaker Lance Wallnau, credited in some quarters with originating the King Cyrus analogy about Trump, wrote a book on it and said, "America has been unraveling for two decades and Christians are probably the people that are the most sensitive to it . . . the mercy of God intervened . . . and gave us an individual who has the willpower and the tenacity to be able to do a reset."[5]

Trump's appeal and ability to retain the support of so many seemingly incompatible conservative religious voters merit a deeper look at this archetype of Trump voters, the King Cyrus Christians. It is possible that Trump would have struggled to get these voters to trek to the polls had he not run against a villain to the cultural Right with the long pedigree of Hillary Clinton. It's also possible that four decades of culture war has just made these voters Republican, and active, under any circumstances. Trump, of all potential candidates, would seemingly have been the one to test that boundary.

The alliance between the billionaire and the believers, however transactional, has persisted well into Trump's presidency. The Great Revolt Survey indicates that 91 percent of the group approves of Trump's performance in office, and 65 percent trust him most to do what's right for the country, besting congressional Republicans, congressional Democrats, big business, and the news media on that question. Roughly two-thirds Protestant and one-third Catholic, and more conservative than the rest of Trump's coalition, this group of voters helped him roll up massive margins in rural counties across the Midwest, and held up his sagging numbers in the suburbs.

This group placed a high premium on Trump's promise to re-place Supreme Court justice Antonin Scalia with a conservative, and 72 percent of them believe "abortion should be made mostly illegal." Trump's first major accomplishment, the confirmation of conservative jurist Neil Gorsuch to the highest court in the land, ensured that the bargain Perkins and his fellow King Cyrus Christians made would at least be partly repaid.

Julie Bayles

Bristol, Kenosha County, Wisconsin

Julie Bayles did not decide she would vote for Donald Trump until the moment she walked into the voting booth on Election Day 2016.

"Even then I still had struggles with voting for him," she says.

The forty-four-year-old mother of seven took issue with Trump's coarse language and boorish behavior, and found them incompatible with the commands of her own Christian faith.

Ultimately, two things, she says, pushed her into his column once inside that voting booth: the belief that he was someone who would be a warrior for religious freedom, and that he would right the ship on national security and the economy.

"It was clear that despite his lack of virtues he was going to be a champion of religious liberties," she says.

"The attack on Christianity that has happened over the past few years in both the culture and with court decisions has been awful, and honestly, people of faith feel that personally," says Bayles, who ran a nonprofit ministry and thrift shop with her husband for seven years.

"I was looking for a warrior for our values, for righting the direction of the country. When he said he would appoint Supreme Court justices who would uphold the values of our country and our Constitution, I started to bend towards listening to what he stood for," she says.

Bayles is a dynamic force of nature, the mother of one daughter and six sons; she has been married to her husband, Donnie, since high school. Bayles is trim and fit, her raven hair is cut in a modern-day shag, and she is wearing dark blue jeans and a deep-purple collared blouse, the same one she wore in a family photo from earlier in the year displayed in her living room. She is beautiful inside and out.

One of her children, Seth, was diagnosed with a rare autoimmune disease when he was seven years old. "Seth's in the middle. He's got three above him and three below him. We have traveled to the Mayo Clinic constantly since 2009. The disease he has is very rare and he's been on the highest dose of low-dose chemotherapy for nine years; he swallows 196 pills a week, as well as patches, and injections, and all kinds of stuff, but he's thriving, he's surviving; from surviving to thriving, so we're just, we're grateful for every day," she says.

She holds her emotions in check, for now. She smiles. There is constant buoyancy in her cadence. This is a woman whose faith fills her spine with strength and optimism.

The Bayleses live in Bristol, in Wisconsin's Kenosha County, which straddles the exurbs of two major metropolitan centers, Milwaukee and Chicago. Their farm sits on 150 acres along U.S. Highway 45, a mostly rural road that takes you to Chicago's O'Hare International Airport forty-six miles to the south.

In 2016, this county—the onetime home of major auto plants owned by AMC and then Chrysler—broke a forty-four-year Democratic voting streak when it picked Donald Trump over Hillary Clinton by fewer than 300 votes. Not even Ronald Reagan, in his forty-nine-state reelection landslide, could carry Kenosha County for the GOP.

Bordered by Lake Michigan on the east, Kenosha County today has 168,183 people, and unlike a lot of counties that flipped its support from Barack Obama in 2012 to Donald Trump in 2016, it is growing, albeit more slowly than the national average.

Kenosha still feels Rust Belt industrial in its eastern portion, a result of the lakefront harbor and railroad lines that encouraged the development of factories in the last century.

The western portion of the county remains rural, and the growing central section, bisected by Interstate 94, which links it to Minneapolis, Madison, Milwaukee, and Chicago, is driving the county's growth. Within yards of the interstate is a bustling Amazon distribution center employing 2,000 people, and the corporate headquarters of packaging giant Uline, relocated from high-tax Illinois a few years ago and now employing 2,600 Kenosha Countians.[6] Smaller plants, such as Kenall Lighting, have joined the exodus from Illinois to Kenosha and post NOW HIRING signs brandishing opportunities not normally associated with Trump Country.

That growth fills up subdivisions and thriving nondenominational churches with big video screens and mood lighting in their auditoriums. Trump performed well in these growing precincts, outpacing Romney's 2012 surplus by 11 points in the fast-growing center of the county and by 15 points in the rural west, in addition to narrowing the margin of defeat for Republicans in the graying blue-collar city to the east.

Much has been made of the resonance of Trump's message among people who have seen their local economies crater. But for a key slice of his coalition, it was attacks on their values on the national stage by a culture careening leftward that drew voters to his bombast.

Perhaps no state in the Blue Wall that Trump turned Republican red better exemplifies the dual pull of cultural and economic concerns than Wisconsin.

Julie and Donnie Bayles, along with two of her adult voting children, could easily have been expected to stay home on Election Day when faced with the choice between the liberal Clinton and the secular Trump. Instead, they were part of a political tipping point in Wisconsin, a state in which 22 percent of the adult population is affiliated with an evangelical Protestant church and 71 percent overall identify as Christian.[7]

Wisconsin is not a transient state; it ranks fifth in the nation in its share of those born there who stay there—trailing only Sunbelt boom states Florida, Georgia, North Carolina, and California— owing in part to deep family connections and a traditional lifestyle.[8] Most of its people are the sons and daughters of the sons and daughters who settled here a hundred years ago, and most of them have lived here all of their lives, or left and returned to raise their families. Many can trace their family tree back generations on the same plot of land that they, or some member of their family, still inhabit.

Once a bastion of American socialism, and today home to the progressive idyll of Madison, Wisconsin had been stubbornly

Democratic for the better part of two generations. With a proud labor history, many of the Badger State's cultural conservatives could not get comfortable with Republican coziness with big business in elections prior.

It was one of only ten states won by Democrat Michael Dukakis in the 1988 presidential election and hadn't been won by any Republican since 1984. Trump's economic message rallied voters with manufacturing in their blood, but he also scored big among traditional-values voters seeking a restoration of cultural respect.

It is a state filled with national pride and nostalgia. Voters were looking for someone who spoke to their traditional cultures, someone who would protect those cultures.

Sill, evangelical voters, and traditional and observant Catholics, were perhaps some of the least likely to stay with Trump as his unconventionally harsh rhetoric and allegations of a sordid personal life poured out during the campaign. They didn't have to vote for Clinton; they could've just stayed home.

But some, like Bayles, ultimately stuck with the thrice-married Trump, albeit reluctantly, because "he was going to be a warrior for people of faith. He wasn't going to let us down, and that would begin with his Supreme Court choices," says Bayles, who attends CrossWay Community Church, a modern nondenominational mega-church with acoustic guitar and trap-set drum music and an evangelical approach to the Gospel.

Trump's lack of familiarity with even the basic tenets of Christian observance were on display during the primary campaign, even as he attempted to appeal to religious conservatives. In a forum sponsored by the Family Research Council, a socially conservative lobbying organization, in his second month as a candidate, Trump said he had never asked God for forgiveness—an assessment he re-upped six months later, putting him completely at odds with the central dicta of evangelical theology.[9]

In speaking to evangelical Liberty University in January 2016, Trump cited a verse from "Two Corinthians," earning mockery from those who know the book is Second Corinthians, and explained his communion practices in terms that some found flippant and theologically incorrect.

"When we go in church and when I drink my little wine, which is about the only wine I drink, and have my little cracker, I guess that's a form of asking for forgiveness," Trump said.[10]

Trump also had a checkered history on policy issues usually important to evangelicals and conservative Catholics: he had long taken the liberal positions on gay marriage and abortion, saying in 1999 that he was "very pro-choice" and that he "cringed" when hearing people even debate abortion.[11]

Yet exit polls showed that 81 percent of evangelical Christians supported Trump on Election Day, and a plurality of those Christians consistently supported him during the primary season, even over more proven socially conservative candidates.

"In the end that election came at a very consequential moment in the country; we have been heading in the wrong direction for years and a lot of us felt as though we had to do something to stop it," Bayles says, belying a sense of urgency that ultimately got her past her hang-ups about Trump's character.

The "consequential moment" Bayles mentioned is made manifest by an increasing tension between a society bent on secular tolerance and restrictions on the exercise of religion. Two of the lasting outcroppings of upheaval during the Obama era were the fallouts from the Supreme Court decision decreeing gay marriage the law of the land, and the insistence—imposed by the party-line passage of the Affordable Care Act—that contraception and abortion services be not only available, but required as coverage in employee or government-provided insurance programs.

The raft of similar litigation that later culminated in the Supreme Court's decision in *Obergefell v. Hodges*—overturning state bans on gay marriage in 2015—spawned a movement at the state level to protect the rights of wedding contractors such as bakers and florists who oppose gay marriage to refuse to participate in those ceremonies. The resulting Religious Freedom Restoration Acts—or RFRAs—were met with fierce resistance by liberal activists, who squeezed corporations to pressure the governors who had signed them in Indiana and Arkansas to back down. One of those governors, social conservative champion Mike Pence, would later become Trump's running mate.

The litigation spawned by the Affordable Care Act's reproductive procedure mandates sparked a similar legal war that culminated in *Burwell v. Hobby Lobby Stores,* in which a slim Supreme Court majority carved out a narrow religious liberty protection for closely held private companies, allowing the owners of those businesses to opt out of contraception and abortion mandates in Obamacare that violate deeply held religious convictions.

Those two cases, one in favor of religious liberty and one spawning a ferocious corporate and media campaign against it, brought the threat to the First Amendment's free exercise of religion clause into full focus for many evangelicals, just in time for the run-up to the 2016 election.

Then, on a mid-February Saturday in 2016, the composition of the Supreme Court moved to the top of the voting agenda for evangelicals and other conservatives. On that morning, just four days after New Hampshire's first-in-the-nation presidential primary, Supreme Court justice Antonin Scalia was found dead on a hunting trip in Texas—removing from the court its most ardent and articulate defender of religious liberty.

Though Trump had just decisively won a crowded contest in New Hampshire, the timing theoretically should have helped his main rival for the nomination; Texas senator Ted Cruz had cultivated a huge following among evangelicals, and made a big bet to focus on the rash of Southern state primaries in early March where religiously devout voters dominate.

Even Bayles was in Cruz's camp at that time.

"I was a big Ted Cruz fan," she says of the Texas senator who often talks about his faith when discussing any policy, social or not.

Bayles and other conservatives helped Cruz win the Badger State's primary decisively on April 15—Trump's most significant loss in the nomination calendar—but the front-runner consolidated his support in Indiana three weeks later to put Cruz away, leaving evangelicals to choose between only Trump, Clinton, and staying home. "And when it dwindled down to 'Wow, these are the two choices,' I was just kind of at a loss," Bayles says.

Even as Trump had surprised observers with his evangelical support in the populist South, the smart money still wagered he could not bring more reluctant evangelicals like Bayles a[...] obstacle for any Republican, since the GOP has hi[...] on nearly unanimous support among that group in [...] November.

Bayles, not shy about her hesitation regarding Tru[...], [...] a very long time. "I don't want to come across as disingenuous, as this person who was all-in from the very beginning; I wasn't. It was really hard," she says. "Just knowing about what was coming out about him being a womanizer and just his mouth and his whole demeanor just like didn't go with my belief system.

"That's not the way I talk. That's not the way we act. And I felt like I needed to be accountable to my children for his moral character."

Years ago, Bayles left rural Wisconsin as a young bride with her husband for Florida, and the change jolted her. "It was scary and I don't know how I retained the Midwest values down there. It's a whole different fast-paced culture of 'me, me, me' world. The West Palm Beach area, in our opinion, was not a place to raise children, so we homeschooled down there, and once we came back to Wisconsin it was like, yeah, this is where we're meant to be," she says. (Her husband, Donnie, is from the tiny town of Cameron, West Virginia, just outside of Wheeling, and had a similar worldview.)

"I wasn't raised knowing about politics whatsoever. I was never taught to vote, that it was an honor or responsibility, none of that. And like I said, getting married at seventeen, I was really figuring out adulthood by myself anyway," Bayles recalls.

"I got a job for a big telecommunications company, and I immediately, at eighteen, kind of broke into I would say, into their union."

Bayles admits she really didn't know what a union was or why she had to join it. "And [the union steward] said, 'Oh, you need to be in it, we have your back' and I just kind of signed on the dotted line and then they trained me to also become a union steward," she says.

It is easy to understand why she was recruited. Bayles has a contagious personality; you immediately want to be part of whatever she is doing. Right now that is volunteering in the community and doing whatever she can to make Seth's life better, but back then it was getting other people on board with the union.

"So I was pretty big into the union and I thought it was a great thing, but what I realized was they were telling me what to do, how to vote, and in fact, they actually drove me down and registered me to vote," she says. "I honestly remember the day. I was so naive and I kind of chuckle about it now. I said to the other union members, 'What's the difference between a Republican and a Democrat? I have to check one. What does that mean?' And they told me, 'Oh, you're a Democrat because you're working-class. Republicans are rich.' So I checked Democrat and that's really all the information I got; I just knew that I wasn't rich so I was a Democrat."

She admits that she was a dispassionate voter at that time in her life.

"Then I started going to church as a married adult. They talked about the importance of voting your values and that was the first time I ever heard that. They had a Christian voter guide and they never told me who to vote for, which I liked, because I was always told who to vote for with the union.

"But the church didn't tell me who to vote for, but they said, 'Look at these morals and values and if you agree with, you know, being pro-life, if you agree, you know, that the sanctity of human life is important, that the sanctity of marriage is important, these are the questions that were asked to each of the candidates.'

"And that was the first time I thought wow, I'm really empowered because I know what I stand for and now I can see what the person that's running for president is standing for and I get to make that decision. As I looked at what the candidates answered, I thought, 'Wait a second, that's closer to Republican, that's closer to Republican, actually I don't identify as a Democrat on any of these issues.' "

She briefly registered as an independent and then started to really be impressed with her local Republican representatives. "Paul Ryan is just my absolute favorite. He has taken the time to talk with me and I can't believe he's third in command for the president," she says of the Speaker of the House from nearby Janesville, who represents Kenosha County in Congress.

For seven years she and her husband ran a ministry and the Christian Mission Thrift Store, which was dedicated, Bayles says, to "spreading the love and message of Jesus Christ through the supporting of Gospel-centered church plants, mission trips, missionaries, and supplying resources for those called into full-time ministry."

All seven of her children were hands-on involved. "I can't remember anyone complaining about their portion of the work. Along with their devotion to their faith, as parents they impressed on their children the obligation to exercise their right to vote—conversations that came back to haunt Bayles as she pondered two nominees for president she both found lacking.

"Which is why it was so hard for me to tell them I didn't want to vote in the 2016 election," she says. "So I did have a lot of conversations with my children and I even went through the 'I'm just not gonna vote, because I just—I don't want to even, you know . . . I—I just can't,' and they were shocked because they were, like, 'Mom! You can't not vote! You know, that's horrible!'"

Her husband had a solution for reconciling her qualms, however, rooted in Trump's political strength. "He saw him as this protector," she says.

"So I did a lot of research on Christian . . . different pastors and whatnot, and just came to the realization that we're in a broken world. There's gonna be moral conflicts. There's no perfect candidate. And I kept hearing the term 'the lesser of two evils' and I hated that. I didn't want to just take the remnants of the lesser of two evils. I really wanted to base my vote on a conviction.

"So my conviction kind of came down to pro-life, which candidate is pro-life, and obviously . . . Planned Parenthood supported [Clinton] and we knew although people had said [Trump] wasn't pro-life from the beginning, but his vice president pick had a great history of protecting the unborn and marriage.

"And that's another thing," she says, interrupting her own train of thought. "I love Mike Pence. If it was Mike Pence for president, oh my word! I would be shouting from the rooftops. He's the most pro-life vice president I think in our country's history since *Roe v. Wade*. I mean, he is just an incredible guy."

Bayles had a history on Facebook in previous elections of vocally reminding her friends of the importance of voting. "I was huge on the Mitt Romney–Paul Ryan ticket on Facebook and just telling my kids as soon as they're able to vote, 'You've gotta exercise that God-given right.' "

And then in 2016 she went radio-silent. "People started wondering what was wrong. They wanted to know who I was voting for. 'What's going on? How come we haven't heard anything from you? You're not posting anything. Are you with anybody or not? Why are you not even stating your point? What's going on?' " she says of the barrage of questions her friends and family asked her.

"I'm not gonna be a hypocrite because I was the first one to, again, say, 'I would not vote for this man, this man doesn't represent me.' But even though I changed my mind . . . I just felt like I needed to keep that to myself, so to speak, if that makes sense.

"It was the hardest decision I think I've had to make as an adult in any voting process. It was so difficult. And I think that the reason why it was so difficult is because I don't take it lightly. This is important, this is our country. This is my children's, my seven children's, future. I don't take that lightly. And I'm accountable to God, to my children, to the unborn."

Bayles has to leave the interview; she has a daughter to pick up from cheerleading practice and a community outreach program she has to chair. As for Trump, she's still warming to him. "Funny, all of that anxiety, all of that praying, and it turns out I like him now much more than I did when I voted for him."

Why? He is making the right enemies.

"Of course, the Supreme Court pick [of Justice Neil Gorsuch], but also his sheer willpower in standing up to the traditional powers, it's refreshing. The tweets? Well, not so much, but everything else, pretty good."

Paul and Emily Cherry

Canton, Stark County, Ohio

Pastor Paul Cherry and his wife, Emily, only have one political disagreement: Paul thought Barack Obama was a talented orator, but Emily had to leave the room anytime the former president was on the television.

"He talked out of both sides of his mouth. It was just so phony and disingenuous to me that I'd just have to leave the room," she says.

"I know that's not very Christian of me . . . but he was dishonest. He just used pretty words so it fooled so many people, and every time he opened his mouth, he drove me nuts . . ." Her voice trails off.

Paul places his arm around her and smiles. "There is nothing wrong with what you said.

"I didn't like him," he continues, "but I also didn't hate him or something like that. But as a speaker, and with his personality, he seemed like somebody I could sit down and have a beer with, talk and be all right with." Paul's smile lingers, sparking her to smile back.

Both are still in that full bloom of being newlyweds one year after saying "I do." It is the second marriage for both.

"You know, as a minister, I read off transcripts and stuff; for me it was just like, this guy knows how to really speak to the people, like speak to the crowd, and get into it, so I respected that talent," he explains. "But as far as the foundation that Obama stood on, well, I disagreed with a lot that he stood for. He was not pro-life, he was not a champion of national security, he missed a lot on the economy, a lot of Americans fell behind on his watch."

Paul is the pastor of Friendship Community Church in Canton, a Southern Baptist ministry that holds its services at Cedar Elementary School on Ninth Street in downtown Canton, a city of 71,323, in the throes of the opioid epidemic that is ravaging Ohio. Two censuses ago, in 2000, Canton had 81,931 people.[12]

Emily's voice is deep, but measured; his is subtly charismatic. His sandy blond hair and neatly trimmed beard create a striking resemblance to the mature Leonardo DiCaprio. He is dedicated to the life he has chosen—to serving God and the community he lives in.

He has his work cut out for him.

Canton is a city that has not yet coped with its remake from a heavy industrial blue-collar town to a service-industry economy. The unemployment isn't astronomically high, but the new jobs created after the bulk of the heavy industry left the city, beginning in the 1980s, are well below what they used to be back when people made things here in Stark County. Like its largest city, Stark is losing population.

Economic deficiencies are obvious at every turn here; the poverty rate is over 31 percent, double the national average. All of the children in the city school system are eligible to receive free breakfast and lunch through the federal Community Eligibility Provision.[13] The district qualified because 40 percent of its student population are homeless, in foster care, or from a household on welfare or receiving food stamps.

A drive along Tuscarawas Street, downtown's main artery, toward a McDonald's can bring a visitor face-to-face with an open drug market outside the fast-food franchise.

"Crime follows poverty; so do drugs; people need help," Paul says.

Canton's violent crime rate is about three times worse than the national average.[14] And opioids? Between 2004 and 2016 there was a 603 percent increase in adults with opiate-use disorder in treatment in Stark County.[15]

"They used to do a lot of things here; this is a story of 'used-to-be's,' " Paul says.

The bright spot is just off the interstate cutting straight through the heart of the city, where the NFL is expanding the Hall of Fame's footprint. In 2016, the league brought on a sponsor, Johnson

Controls, a diversified technology company, for naming rights for a $500 million city-within-a-city project that creates a state-of-the-art "smart village," an entertainment extension of the Hall of Fame experience.

Outside the grid of Canton, Stark County's rolling hills and farmland are a sharp contrast to the decay inside the city. There is even a little unincorporated town called Trump along the old Lincoln Highway.

Trump won big here—the evidence that this upset was coming was visible if one was looking closely. Ohioans do not choose a political party when they register to vote, only when they participate in primaries. In 2016, 64 percent of Stark Countians who chose to participate in a presidential primary chose a Republican ballot, up from just 42 percent of county voters who had picked the GOP primary in the 2014 gubernatorial year primary. Ohio Secretary of State Jon Husted's office told the Canton newspaper that records indicated 5,572 Democrats from past elections switched to the GOP primary in 2016, compared to only 824 Republicans who switched to the Clinton-Sanders primary. Three-fifths of the new primary voters with no previous partisan history also chose the Republican primary.[16]

Trump ultimately clobbered Clinton 56 percent to 39 percent in this county, the same place that Barack Obama won twice and even John Kerry won in 2004 while losing Ohio and the nation. That kind of political upheaval does not happen because things are going well, and every stat in Stark County bears that out.

Paul was born in Norwalk, in North Central Ohio. His parents divorced when he was an infant. "My mom remarried, so I never had any recollection of that town," he says. The new family moved to Mansfield; his stepfather worked as a computer programmer and his mother went back to school to be a nurse. For a long period of his childhood—because of allegations against his dad that Paul does not get into—Paul never saw his father.

"Eventually those allegations were proven false and I moved in with him at the age of sixteen. I immediately went from a white-collar, middle-class family to a working-class situation. My father was blue collar, worked in the factories in maintenance and as an industrial electrician," he says.

Paul explains that his mother's home was much more financially stable. "Whereas my dad's was, I never wanted for anything, but I didn't have the same things I did at Mom's. But I learned something incredibly valuable that shaped who I am today, and that is you worked hard for what you had and you appreciate what you had."

He did not immediately attend college after high school. "I worked for a while and I started out slow, taking night classes at the Ohio State branch in Mansfield." He eventually saved enough to attend Ohio Christian University, south of Columbus, where he got two degrees, "one in world religions and a bachelor's degree in leadership," he says.

"I had a calling to ministry, and that school fit my lifestyle. I still worked full-time, went to school full-time, and flipped houses on the side to pay for school."

Paul snags a French fry off Emily's plate; they are having dinner at John's Bar & Grille, a Canton staple for seventy years. It's owned by the Varavvas family; three generations work there. Two of those generations are working this evening, and the wood-paneled tavern is packed. Many of the staff have been here for thirty-plus years. It is the kind of place where everybody knows your name and your business, whether you like that or not.

Paul has been working since he moved in with his dad at sixteen. "We had a local Best Western hotel; I rode my bike down with my best friend and we used to clean rooms, housekeeping, and work in the Laundromat and sweep the parking lot. I mean, I did whatever they asked us to do, for whatever—it was at the time five bucks an hour, I think.

"I've always had a job. Like through high school, I paid for my car insurance, I paid for my fuel, I paid for my car. I was taught to be responsible and nothing was free, you know. You work hard and I've just done that my whole life," he says.

He played football and soccer in high school; the discipline also helped shape him. "I think it teaches you to put the effort in. If you want to accomplish a task, it's not going to be given, and, I mean, not only do you have to train yourself psychologically, mentally, I guess you could say, but you had to do it physically and you had to do it with others, so you know, team effort. So, I guess that works out in the real world, when you're working in a company together with people."

Both Emily and Paul were intuitively drawn to the Republican Party. "I've always been a Republican. I have voted for Democrats, locally," he says.

"Same here," says Emily. The attractive brunette with shoulder-length, softly wavy hair takes a call from the babysitter; she has to leave soon to care for their blended family.

Paul works two full-time jobs right now. "I am a minister full-time and I also work full-time as a maintenance manager within a nursing home." He says he met Emily at Alcoholics Anonymous.

"Paul!" she says, seemingly aghast. "Geez, he tells everyone that. Would you mind telling the real story?" They both fall into deep laughter at his ribbing.

"We met online actually," he says. "I had two friends that had successful relationships on Christian Mingle, so they had a free sign-up on Christian Mingle. So they threw me on the Internet and I met her when I was trying to shut off the membership because it was blowing my phone up."

"I was so nervous," Emily says, as her bright green eyes well with tears at the memory.

Emily was born in Cleveland, and her parents moved to Canton when she was an infant. Her father was a metallurgist and engineer; her mother was a stay-at-home mom for years before she went back to nursing school at the University of Akron. "My mom always tells people that if you always want to have a job, go into health care, become a nurse or do something in health care," she says.

Emily's family is very tight-knit. "Big family dinners on weekends and holidays; we always joked that anything could become an event and it was just an excuse to get the entire family together, and, you know, we still do that. We still get together on the holidays, and it's a huge meal, huge production, the spread is always good, if you leave hungry it's your own fault."

Emily attended all twelve years of her schooling at a private school in Canton called Heritage Christian. She then went off to the

University of Mount Union for business administration. Both her and her husband's lives have been intertwined with their deep faith.

When it came time to vote in 2016, neither went for Donald Trump as their first pick. Paul liked Senator Marco Rubio, Emily liked everyone; both say they were looking for strength.

"I didn't think it was going to be Trump, I'll be honest. I just thought that was just a no-show," the pastor says, even though he voted for him in the Ohio primary that wound up being seriously contested only by Trump and Ohio governor John Kasich.

"I didn't really have a front-runner. I didn't think Trump was gonna be it. At first I didn't think he was gonna be the one. It just got down to the point where I looked at him and started listening to what he had to say, and like Emily always says, I liked what he said about America and what we need in this country," says Paul.

The fact that Trump was able to easily convert two people like the Cherrys, for whom faith is so central to their voting patterns, is testament to the desperation many conservatives felt after eight years of Obama and a Republican Congress they believed had not been able to successfully thwart him. The potential for Trump to be a disruptor, a force from outside politics who might be stronger than those in politics, offered the prospect of a successful pushback to many who craved it.

"I have been deeply rattled about the direction our country has taken, and I was really looking for a defender, a protector of our liberties if you will, someone who spoke to the issues that have been put on the back burner for years. The Iran deal, calling Fort Hood a workplace violence, how we treated Israel, Syria, religious liberties always seemed to be under attack . . . ," Emily says, peeling off the list of issues that had resonated with her.

Trump came more easily to Emily than to Paul. "I liked him," she says. "He's got that business mind, where he doesn't take crap from anybody, and heck, all we have been taking is crap. There was nobody for me that came out strong except him, and I said, 'That's my candidate.'"

In Paul's church he sees the toll that drugs, crime, and hopelessness have taken on "otherwise good people," he says.

"We as a country cannot just let our fellow Americans be left behind, dismissed because someone in Washington or Silicon Valley has decided their time has come and gone."

The pastor was also shaken by the country's lack of fortitude in protecting "our greatest treasure," he says. "That, of course, is our people; it is like we have been disposable to the Democrats. We need leaders who don't consider us a political calculation."

Faith and God are central to the Cherrys' lives. As their first-year anniversary as a married couple approached, Emily wrote a Facebook post that held nothing back in recounting their early dating years:

God centered, God blessed, and totally God orchestrated!! Three years ago today, I was sitting at work on a Tuesday happy, excited, and completely trying to figure out in what ways Paul was screwed up and not perfect for me. Over the next couple weeks, after continuing to try to find reasons to not be with this amazing man, God continued to push us together and show that He has a plan for our lives together, forever. It's not always been easy these past three years, but I would not trade one single day or go back and do anything different. My best friend, confidant, support system, lover, and husband, among so much more.

While Paul's support of Trump came later than Emily's, it has been hardened by what he perceives to be unfair treatment from the media.

"You know, I don't listen to the media anymore. I don't trust it [at] all, and it's not because I'm told not to trust it, it's just, it's so blatant and obvious now. It's just trash news, you know?

"You can tell by the first paragraph, you know, whether or not it's worth even reading, because it starts out, you know, how Trump has screwed up in the first six months or first year or whatever. I'm not reading that, you know? Like, I don't expect my president to be perfect. I know he's like gonna make mistakes. Nobody's perfect."

As both a parent and a pastor, Paul says he deeply worries about what he sees in society and culture when it comes to the demand for free stuff. "It seems like what I see from the Democratic Party is, let's play to that group. 'We'll get you free college.' I worked my butt off to pay for college. And they get a free vote. That is not creating a strong country, that is not creating good people—where is that rugged individualism streak? We need lessons of strength, not promises of what you can get for doing nothing," he says.

"That is my biggest worry going forward, that lack of strength, of virtue, of standing up for a belief system and values and religious liberties. I worry about young people not having that drive to better themselves. The entitlement thing is so very much there, I see it in my own kids. I find myself, as a parent, fighting it, even though I'm not teaching it.

"I am hoping that fighting spirit becomes part of our culture and some of that entitlement culture starts to lose face; that is what I want going forward, what I wanted to start with Trump."

Neil Shaffer

Rural Howard County, Iowa

One hundred and fifty years ago, ten Norwegian families descended on this open land to build their lives and expand their families. They were young, courageous, devout, and determined to carve out a decent life filled with family, community, and worship of God. They came by foot, covered wagon, and on horseback.

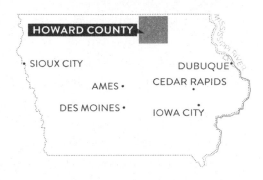

They brought with them oxen, tools, supplies, and all of their meager belongings from the West, a unique directional distinction from the rest of the early settlers. Originally from Wisconsin, this group had initially settled in South Dakota, but found the region unsafe. They went eastward across the new state of Iowa and settled along Crane Creek, where a large tract of land sat as-yet unused because of the weak density of the soil.

They were soon joined by more immigrants from Norway; most came here without much more than a trunk or two from home, but they all made sure they brought a series of important books with them: a Bible, a hymnbook, and, for the children, catechism lessons.

"God's Word and his presence was everything to those early settlers," says Neil Shaffer, a trustee of the Jerico Evangelical Lutheran Church and direct descendant of those early Norwegian settlers who were part of the same congregation that still thrives today.

Shaffer's great-grandfather, Ole J. Anderson, helped build the sturdy white clapboard house of worship in 1913. It is the fourth structure this devout group of farmers and settlers have used, and has been central to their lives for 150 years. His mother, Mavis O. Shaffer, at ninety years of age, is the longest continuous member of the church.

On the anniversary marking the congregation's sesquicentennial, the Reverend Craig A. Ferkenstad said as part of his sermon, "We gather here today, not to laud the founders of this congregation— but to give thanks for those who passed on the faith to us, and to remember the leaders who spoke the Word of God to you. It is by God's grace that we teach and preach the same Word of the Bible and the same Gospel as was preached 150 years ago, because without God's grace, we would have ruined everything long ago.

"God's Word is everything. It is why this congregation was formed. It is why we continue today. And now, as for you, continue in what you have learned and have become convinced of, because you know those from whom you learned it, and how from infancy you have known the Holy Scriptures, which are able to make you wise for salvation through faith in Christ Jesus."

For six generations the Shaffer family has worshipped at this same Evangelical Lutheran Church in Lawler, Iowa; for six generations they have farmed the land in the area; and for six generations they have helped the immaculate structure retain its austere beauty.

"We did $55,000 in restoration work to the steeple and bell tower, plus a new handicapped entrance to the basement—all paid by donations by the time the projects were completed," says Shaffer. "Since I am a trustee of the church, I headed up the projects. In my spare time," he deadpans. Shaffer is not a man who has much downtime, let alone spare time.

"My father's family grew up in central Iowa, so he moved up here with his parents and then my parents met. My mom still lives on the farm yet. I was dairy farming up until last year and sold our dairy cows. But the last sixteen years, I've worked for the Soil and Water Conservation District as an environmental specialist in watershed projects."

Shaffer has lived in Howard County all of his life, halfway between the small towns of Lawler and Cresco. The only time he came close to leaving was right after high school. "My plan was to go to the military. Growing up, I had several uncles who fought in World War II and grew up listening to war stories in the South Pacific, and had one uncle that landed at Normandy. My idea was I was going to the military, and then to college for four years, but it was right in the midst of the farm crisis, mid-eighties; the only thing that made us money was the dairy. My dad was sixty-two at the time." His voice trails off as he explains his father's age factoring into his decision to stay and help.

The 1980s brought the American farmer to his knees; the crisis was a convergence of events—two major droughts, years of monstrous accumulated debt, and the roller-coaster uncertainty of commodity prices—that resulted in hundreds of family farms collapsing almost daily.

By the end of the decade, nearly 300,000 farmers defaulted on their loans, and more banks failed in 1985 than in all the years since the Great Depression.[17] The impact was devastating. It was the beginning of the end of many rural Main Streets across America, especially in Iowa; farmers and their families no longer had incomes to spend on local goods, either because their money was scarce or they had literally lost the farm.

White crosses dotted abandoned farmsteads—emotional and stark reminders left by the owners that they had fallen victim to the financial circumstances of the decade. It was a time of great instability in the heartland, and many of those scars still have not begun to heal. Even today, a generation later, Iowa has sixty-five counties with fewer than 20,000 people, and only six with more than 100,000—small-town Iowa is Iowa.[18]

Shaffer watched everything sink around him and understood he was needed on the farm. "If they would have sold that, we had huge debt, and I don't think we could have made it without the dairy cows. I thought, 'Well, I'll milk cows for a few years.' Then we got the bank paid off and it was kind of nice you got to keep the whole milk check. Then my folks got older, and then, well, I just love what I do now. I work with farmers every day, and I'm working to improve the environment."

Shaffer works for the Howard County Soil and Water Conservation District. "I am a watershed project coordinator. I work to improve water quality on a tributary of the Upper Iowa River called Silver Creek," he explains.

As a solid, rock-ribbed conservative, he chuckles at the notion that conservatives do not want to protect the environment. "I mean, we are called 'conservatives,' we want to conserve the environment, and as someone whose faith is very important to their lives I am tasked to be a good steward of the earth," he says of his evangelical beliefs.

The funding for his job comes from the EPA, the money funneled to Iowa's Department of Natural Resources, then on to his local Soil and Water Conservation District. "In essence, I use EPA funds to cost-share projects for local farmers like manure puts, grasses, waterway and wetland restoration."

Shaffer is one of six children, and family and faith have always been the driving force in his life. "We are a very close-knit family. You talk about family dinners; every Sunday we went to either an aunt's house or uncle's, or they were at our house. I think there was more sense of community when families got together a lot more. It's kind of a distant thing now. The next generation's very busy. You don't see that connection," he says, sighing.

"Growing up, I mean, we went to church every Sunday together too. Faith is still a very important part of my life."

In 2008, Barack Obama won 62 percent of the vote over John McCain here in tiny Howard County—one of Iowa's smallest. Obama's support didn't budge much in 2012, when the president won 59 percent of the county's vote, defeating Mitt Romney. Four years later, Trump won 58 percent of the traditionally Democratic county's vote—a feat that would not have been possible without rock-solid support among evangelicals for the thrice-married philanderer and regular guest on the racy Howard Stern radio show.

Exit polls conducted for national news networks showed that Trump beat Clinton 80 percent to 16 percent among self-identifying evangelical or born-again white voters, including a 70 percent to 25 percent margin in Iowa. That national margin was better than the 78-21 advantage Mitt Romney mustered among white evangel-icals in 2012. (Romney's Mormon faith was theologically alien to many evangelicals, but his devoutness and personal comportment should have made him a better match than Trump.)[19]

Howard County's 42-point swing in margin from 2012 to 2016 made it the third-most-volatile county in the entire country, trailing only Clark County, Missouri, and Elliott County, Kentucky. Overall, thirty-two Iowa counties switched party allegiances from 2012 to 2016, more than in any other state in the country.

The swing in votes in Howard is notable because it's a county that doesn't really have an active, official Republican Party "apparatus," as that term is traditionally understood—the one it does have is run by Shaffer, who says they are often left to their own devices by the state party.

"We've been kind of an independent organization for twenty years; we can't rely on our state, national, or our state party. I couldn't even get a Romney sign. I had to go down to the sign shop and have them make us one so we had one for our fair booth. That's how disorganized they were," he says.

Sitting in the meeting room of the Howard County Farm Bureau on First Avenue, Shaffer, at fifty, has sandy brown hair, glasses, an infectious smile, and the calm, deliberate voice of someone who spends his time educating people. This room is typically reserved for meetings about conservation issues important to this farming community, from how to best protect water quality, to field practices such as restoring wetlands and using the bioreactors that play a crucial role in Iowa farming.

Conservation talks, events, webinars, lectures, and hands-on advice from ag experts fill up a big part of the yearly calendar on the wall; there are also reminders for the Farm Service Agency crop certification deadline and the Mighty Howard County Fair in June—and when the baby pigs and cows will be at the fair.

Shaffer says that politics was always part of his family's discussion. "Always has been, always has been. My parents were staunch Republicans. My dad passed away about thirteen years ago from cancer. They both grew up in, well, actually, Dad's family were FDR Democrats, but my mother's family were out there for Alf Landon and that," he says of the obscure Republican Kansas governor who ran against FDR in 1936 and went down in the greatest electoral landslide since the beginning of the current two-party system in the 1850s. Roosevelt beat Landon in every state except Maine and Vermont, and won 523 electoral votes.

"Yeah, they were pretty die-hard Republican. My folks always voted. I remember we had a little one-room schoolhouse down the road and they'd go vote, come back, and we'd always watch the election returns. The first election I remember is the Republican Convention, and I was watching Ford and Reagan. My folks were actually Reagan fans back in 1976. The first election I voted in—I just missed getting to vote for Reagan that year. We had a picture of Reagan hanging on our wall. Catholic families had JFK on the wall, we had Reagan," he says.

"Most of my friends are Catholic. This community is probably sixty percent Roman Catholic, and probably thirty percent Lutheran, then ten percent Methodist, others. But faith has always been something. Even my friends now, most of them are pretty good churchgoers," he says. The political alliance between socially conservative Catholics and socially conservative Protestant evangelicals has always been intermittent, with many Catholics voting their blue-collar economic outlook as often as their views on abortion—but the convergence of those two factors in the Trump coalition has big ramifications in Iowa.

The congressman representing Howard County is second-termer Rod Blum, a Dubuque software entrepreneur who first won election in 2014, breaking an eight-year Democratic grip on the northeast Iowa district, and was then easily reelected by 8 points in 2016, in spite of heavy targeting by national Democrats.

The community in Howard County and all of northern and eastern Iowa has changed; and agriculture has changed since the late 1970s, becoming more consolidated. "When I was a kid, there was a farm every 160 acres. They were diversified, they had pigs, cattle, milk cows, chickens. One of my things was to collect eggs. We sold eggs. The egg truck came around and picked up eggs at farms. There was probably three or four hundred dairies even up until the seventies. Now agriculture's gotten much bigger. The sense of community out in the rural areas is fading."

Why? There are so few family farms left. "There are mostly corporate. I would say half of the farmsteads have been leveled in just the last twenty years. Farms just got bigger. Commodity prices kind of drove a lot of that. And, for me, 160 acres, milking forty cows, you couldn't make a living at that. That's why I went into town and started working with the conservation groups." So the family sold off all of their dairy cows.

"My mother still owns all of the land. It's the family farm. She's the matriarch of the farming establishment. So now we just raise corn and soybeans. We just have a custom hire done. It's too expensive to try and do it on your own. The investment of what it costs to put in a crop is just unbelievable. I paid fifteen thousand dollars for corn and soybean seed and some years if we got eight or nine thousand for our soybean crop we were lucky. It's big stakes now. You're investing four to five hundred dollars an acre into your crops. And tight margins. Last year farmers, if they made fifty dollars an acre on their crop they were looking good. Things are getting very tight. The last two years, most of the ag in our area survived because we had outstanding yields, because our prices have dropped so much. This year, we're starting to wonder. We haven't had the best ideal planting season. There's a lot of nervous people out there. There's nervous people in the banking industry," he says.

For Shaffer, eight years under Barack Obama's policies felt like prison. "I've worked within government. I could see how things were changing and how the environmental extremists' view was coming into our daily actions, and process, making things much more difficult to get something done.

"I also felt from the first get-go of Obama was that the country's sliding backwards. Government interference. Just, I almost want to say, a moral decay. This attitude of entitlement for people seemed to be getting worse and worse every year. The direction of the country really has me concerned. It was one of the driving forces for me in this election.

"Liberty, especially religious liberty, was always under attack. I felt like there was no one to protect people who held traditional values. It was really all very backwards. You cannot force people to do things that go against the fundamentals of their religion as long as it is not illegal. That is just not what we are in this country, and yet that is exactly what we started to become.

"I also think there is such an elitist attitude and a smugness. Well, that's not how we are here. Whether you're a Democrat or Republican, or Catholic or Lutheran, we're an extended family and we wouldn't treat people like that. It just had that attitude, especially toward the Midwest."

Shaffer's first choice was not Donald Trump. "Oh no, it was Ben Carson," he says. "I have been tired for years of the party bosses telling us we have to give the next person in line the nomination. They did that to us with John McCain and Mitt Romney, and this time I had had enough. I wanted someone who would actually stand up for us, protect our liberties."

Like many Iowans, showered with attention from presidential wannabes eager to impress in the state whose caucuses kick off the nominating process every four years, Shaffer can rattle off minute details about his feelings toward almost everyone who ran in 2016.

When Trump entered, he was uneasy. "I was a very big skeptic. I was just not into him. I tried to somewhat be a bit neutral, because I'm the chair of the county party, but, I started out, I was a big Ben Carson fan. I was for Carson, but I was like, he just doesn't have the drive. He's a nice guy, I love what he says, but he just don't have the fire. Then I jumped to Rand Paul; I like his dad. We've had these straw poll votes in Iowa and I would always end up voting for his dad, because I just loved the enthusiasm. I have a bit of a libertarian streak to me," he says.

"Well, after I went to Rand Paul, then I thought, 'Eh, he's not doing anything. He's not even a person.' Then I really got onto Marco Rubio. A good friend of mine, young guy, was so enthusiastic. I thought, 'Man, I'm going to get involved there.' That's who I actually caucused for, was Marco Rubio. Then the wheels pretty much fell off his bus too. I didn't like how he, he seemed petty, just unpolished. I thought, 'Well, I'll have to give him a few more years.' Then I was really kind of in limbo. They're all dropping out and I am left with Trump."

He pauses, rolls his eyes, and then breaks out into a wide grin.

"Then you hear, 'Oh, we can't be for him, the way he talks and everything.' Then, what really changed it for me was when he came out with that list of Supreme Court nominees. Then it was over, all over—I was in," Shaffer says of Trump's gambit to consolidate conservative votes as the GOP nomination process wound down in May

2016: he released a list of judges he'd use, if elected, to pick the replacement for Justice Antonin Scalia.

"Right then I said, 'I don't care what you think of the man, I don't care what he said, if all he does is put one, then I'll be for it.' From that point, that's what I always told people."

Trump's gambit worked, and not just to get Shaffer. By the end of May, Trump had secured the endorsement of the Supreme Court–minded National Rifle Association, which would go on to spend tens of millions on his behalf in the election and become his biggest ally. Separate from any formal group, Trump had also created a rallying cry for evangelical voters across the country who had been put off by his bawdy language and rough Manhattan ways.

It was an awakening for Shaffer. "All of a sudden I started seeing people who were lifelong Democrats talking about how they were not going to vote for Hillary."

For these voters, spooked by a decade of court cases such as the Ninth Circuit Court of Appeals ruling that a high-school football coach, Joseph Kennedy, had no First Amendment right to kneel and briefly pray at the 50-yard line after a football game—one of many rulings that drew ever-thicker lines around the extent to which religious beliefs may be used as a Constitutional defense against the majority's secular priorities. There suddenly was a tangible, and seemingly achievable, transaction justifying a vote for Trump.

Five months later, when a tape was made public of Trump on a hot mic backstage, speaking in the most vulgar terms about his attempts at adultery, plenty of evangelicals stuck with him.

Republican pollster Wes Anderson of OnMessage Inc., in his post-election survey of eight presidential target states, found that 52 percent of Trump's voters cited the Supreme Court vacancy as an "extremely important" factor in deciding their vote, compared to 43 percent of Clinton voters who assigned it such importance—both are large numbers for a single issue, but the intensity clearly favored Trump.[20]

Trump, for his part, held up his end of the bargain by nominating appellate court judge Neil Gorsuch to fill the Supreme Court seat left vacant by Scalia. Gorsuch was not only a judge who'd been on the initial list that won Shaffer over to Trump; he was also a judge who had ruled in favor of the evangelical-owned Hobby Lobby chain of retail stores in its bid to seek a religious liberty exemption from the contraception coverage mandates in Obama's health care law. The precision of the political payback was not lost on evangelicals.

Shaffer says that as long as Trump continues to have a positive impact on the courts, his support is not going anywhere. "And I am pretty sure I am not alone. I don't think that institutional America understands how much we have split from them, and the courts and the protection of religious liberty is a big part of that. The amount of people I saw and talked to who never voted before and who are thrilled with him is a nuance they did not get.

"I'm an election precinct official, so I work election days. That Election Day in 2016 we probably had 127 people [who] came in to register to vote; we have same-day voting in Iowa. These people were from eighteen years old to, I think the oldest one was eighty years old. There were people who hadn't voted for thirty, forty years. They show up in our book as inactive. It was those people. You could just tell, they were there because they wanted to vote for someone. And they have not changed that sentiment. This is a very traditional community; we were looking for a warrior for us.

"I was so excited to vote for Trump by the time we got into October that, we have early voting here, my mom and I, we voted, I'm sure I voted as soon as you could request a ballot. We voted. I never do that. I'm kind of traditional and I work elections. I was going to work that day. I wanted to vote so badly for him," he says.

"I cannot emphasize this enough because I really, really did not want to vote for him. This was a big turnaround. I came a huge long way because, even up until I saw that list of the Supreme Court judges I was dreading what the summer was going to bring. Then I was, wait a minute, this is going to fire up people. We also have a community of people that are, I would say I'm a moderate libertarian streak to me, but we do have some pretty conservative Republicans. Bless their hearts, but they always seem to pick the losing candidate, then they have sour grapes. At the end of the season, they just don't vote because they are so fed up and feel disenchanted. I ran into a couple of them and they were getting Trump signs; it's like, what happened?

You would think that Trump would be about the most opposite of them, but they saw that Supreme Court and knew what that was."

Shaffer has always been a big fan of watching the Supreme Court. "I felt like Obama put a bunch of mediocre people in, and Clinton too, he put mediocre people in there. I'd much rather have Thurgood Marshall and Brennan on there than Sotomayor or Kagan. They're no large figures. I'd rather have a super-liberal thundering person, but I also want a thundering Republican conservative. And Bush let us down. Souter, oh, my god, Souter, even to an extent Kennedy. And Roberts, that was probably one of the biggest letdowns. That's when I saw the list and who was on that list. You didn't see any John Robertses or Anthony Kennedys or Souters."

With two more justices in their eighties, Gorsuch may not be the last of Trump's appointees, a prospect that excites Shaffer. "Support for Trump is only getting stronger. The way you see Trump treated now, I'm more on his side. I wasn't, I was pretty lukewarm even going into the fall until that. The political class on both sides of the aisle and the media have shown their true colors," he says. "It just makes me like him more. It is as simple as that."

"When Obama came along and he started this culture change. 'This is how you have to act. This is how you have to think.' Everyone has to think his way or it is unacceptable. My whole idea growing up was, free speech, freedom of expression was you just can't scream fire in a crowded theater. When they start saying from the pulpit, your pastors or your priest can't say certain things, that's not America. That's something they've created out of this culture of acceptance and you're a bigot if you don't accept everything the way I am. There's moral standards and there's a line that you can walk, but also it is that you can't force it down people's throats. We just felt for the last eight years we were spoon-fed this liberal cultural crap."

It's nice, Shaffer says, to have a president that has the country's back. "And not apologizing for every imagined slight."

8
Silent Suburban Moms

If any group in the ultimate Donald Trump coalition was unexpected, it was the group of suburban women who stuck with him after a year's worth of campaigning designed to cleave them away from the Republican column.

With Hillary Clinton seeking to break the glass ceiling and become the first female president, and a boorish septuagenarian billionaire on the other ticket, it would have seemed only natural that the 2016 election would see a gender gap far larger than normal, with women siding with the Democratic Party in even greater numbers. Except that's not what happened.

From Clinton's first day on the national stage as a fresh college graduate who gave a widely noted commencement address at Wellesley College, to her tenure as a globally respected secretary of state, she was seen as the poster image of the women's movement—the paragon of the barrier-breaking generation. Her second campaign for president ran on that premise exactly, targeting women in both parties with explicitly gender-based appeals. On the attack, her campaign's targets were educated Republicans and independents in the suburbs whose sensibilities were offended by Trump's coarse manner and impulsive, often inappropriate, rhetoric.

Clinton's strategy worked to a point, but not nearly well enough to secure her the presidency. While Trump's margin among college-educated white women was below the Republican norm, those defections were not enough to deny him the electoral votes of every swing state in the Great Lakes region, plus Florida and North Carolina. Because she and her campaign team bet their entire strategy on this group and failed to get the margin they needed, the Silent Suburban Mom is an important archetype in the Trump coalition.

Younger than most of the coalition, less religiously conservative, one out of four in this group reported they had voted for Obama in either 2008 or 2012, according to the Great Revolt Survey of Trump voters in the Great Lakes swing states. Almost half of them were uncomfortable telling friends they were voting for Trump during the campaign, because they feared disapproval. They're less pro-life than the rest of the Trump coalition, but only slightly so. They are also less likely to cite the Supreme Court as a critical factor in their vote for Trump.

As long as Trump is the face of the emerging populist-conservative coalition, this group will remain on its margins—and at the center of the electoral combat between the two parties.

Cindy Sacco

Washington Township, Macomb County, Michigan

Twenty-eight miles separates the life Cindy Sacco and her husband once had in the city of Detroit proper and the one she has now in Washington Township, Michigan, located on the northwest tip of Macomb County.

Years after growing up along the famed Seven Mile Road as the daughter of a Detroit city police officer, working at her grandmother's lunch counter—and ultimately owning the lunch counter with her husband, Bob—she still considers herself a Detroiter. For her, it's an identity that transcends an address. You sometimes hear that identity in the music of the famous artists born in the county, from Kid Rock to Eminem to Uncle Kracker.

Halfway between home and the diner is Eight Mile Road—the not-invisible dividing line celebrated and lamented in popular music that has long served as a psychological, cultural, economic, and racial border between the urban core of the predominantly black city and the whiter, middle-to-upper-class suburbanites who escaped the city's decay.

The farther north you travel in Macomb County, away from Eight Mile Road, the post–World War II blue-collar suburbs slowly give way to more affluent suburbs and newer, trendier housing stock. With a population of 867,730, Macomb is no longer one homogenous place, but the bonds between the county's north and south, both culturally and politically, remain strong.

Unlike in suburban enclaves in other parts of the country, people in Washington Township rarely identify themselves as anything other than someone from Detroit. Perhaps one of the most uniquely misunderstood aspects of this region's racial tension is the nostalgia that both blacks and whites have for Old Detroit.

"I will always be that girl from East Detroit," says Sacco of the Macomb suburb closest to the city.

Her current home farther north is lovely, the third one she and her husband have bought since migrating here in the 1970s. Located in the pristine suburbs of northwest Macomb, they are a stone's throw from their working-class roots but on the cusp of the exurbs.

This is prime real estate—once the home of orchards filled with apples, cornfields, and berry farms, it is now home to successful suburbanites, nearly all with blue-collar roots, who made it out of the city in the 1970s on more than just sheer willpower; they worked two jobs, they worked overtime, they took out loans; in short, they did everything they legally could to move out and up.

Macomb sits perpendicularly across two trends that run concurrently in most other American suburbs. It is much more affluent than the national average, but also less educated. Mid-decade census estimates show that only 23 percent of the county has a college degree—the national average is nearly 30 percent—but the annual median household income is $55,931, 10 percent above the statewide median in Michigan.[1]

For decades, both those figures were driven by good union jobs in the auto industry. The ideal of physical labor producing a solid and reliable middle-class lifestyle is part of the place's identity, and Sacco's.

"We busted our behinds," she says. "Everything you see here we worked very hard for," Sacco says of her immaculate Macomb home filled with original artwork, custom window treatments, and an elegant mix of traditional and antique furnishings.

The community where her home is located is also exceptional. Stony Creek Metropark surrounds it; so do two golf courses. A pristine white, octagonal cupola sits on the top of this house, designed in the mid-2000s in the Early American Federalist tradition.

Time has treated Sacco well; at sixty-six, her deep chestnut hair is thick and frames her broad, warm face attractively. She is gracious, pragmatic, and directly to-the-point, like many Midwesterners of her generation. She is the exact voter nearly every pollster in America misunderstood in the 2016 presidential election—a suburban woman of Hillary Clinton's generation. Pollsters assumed Trump's crass conduct with women would hurt him with these female voters. It did—but not enough to give the slim margin of victory to Clinton.

Exit polls show that 53 percent of white women voted for Trump, including more independent-minded suburban voters like Sacco than almost any pre-election survey projected.

She was one of those voters hiding in plain sight—unwilling, as she says, to be "unheard in the voting booth." Until her recent retirement she was a card-carrying member of the American Federation of State County and Municipal Employees union (AFSCME), and drove a school bus.

Her dream as a young woman was to finish college and become an art teacher, but before she could finish, she and her husband got the opportunity to purchase the B&M—the family lunch counter named after her grandparents Bob and Mary, who owned it in Detroit's heyday.

"When we were first married we took over my grandmother's lunch counter along East Seven Mile in Detroit. We ran it together for five years until I found out I was pregnant with twins, then we sold it," Sacco says.

Three years and three kids later, they got a call from the city of Detroit; the new owner had failed to pay the taxes, the water bill, and the electricity. Because the sale had been a land contract sale—a quirky arrangement that allowed homeowners and businesses to "sell" homes and businesses no one wanted to buy when the neighborhoods started collapsing—the business came back to Cindy and Bob.

It was a pattern that repeated for the Saccos three times—in the longest stretch during which the business was theirs, from 1980 to 1985, Cindy ran the restaurant, commuting every day back and forth between the suburbs and East Seven Mile while Bob got the children off to school.

"He was in law school then, so he would get the kids ready and drive the nearly one hundred miles to [law school in] Lansing, and I would be home right after they got home from school," she says. The diner was only open until 4:00 p.m.

Every time they got the business back, it was in worse condition, surrounded by a neighborhood that had deteriorated a little more.

After a series of robberies on their last tenure of ownership, Cindy had had enough; so had Bob. "I was worried about her constantly," he says, sitting across from her in their sunroom.

They boarded the diner up and eventually sold it in 1985 to a man named Alvin Taylor, who still operates it today as Taylor Made Burgers. Cindy explains that she took the job as the school bus driver when her husband first started out as an attorney, because he had no benefits. She kept that job, even after Bob began to achieve personal success, because she loved it.

"And I was able to be home with the kids when they were home. I had the same days off they did, it was the perfect balance. And I enjoyed it, which is why I never quit. I loved driving the kids, I loved getting them safely to and from school. I enjoyed talking to the parents," she says.

Sacco grew up in a Democratic family in a Democratic city, worked for a union that lived and breathed Democratic politics. She spent most of her adult life voting mostly Democrat, but that started to change as she got older. "Then I just flipped back and forth. Safety and security were big issues for me, so I would vote the person, especially locally."

Safety and security are still at the top of her list when it comes time to vote. "I do not think that people understood there are many suburban women who vote based on who makes them believe they will keep them, their children, their grandchildren, and their communities safe," she says.

"People laugh if you say you worry about a terror attack happening again, like September 11—their argument is, that level of attack would never happen in Michigan. And I wonder why they don't understand that September 11 had a very emotional impact for people living hundreds of miles away from Ground Zero," Sacco says. "Our countrymen and -women . . . perished there doing nothing more than going to their jobs on a Tuesday morning. They are part of the fabric of the entire country. That is real pain, to see that happen to people in our country.

"I am concerned for all of us, and I think that we had been

weak and too politically correct during the Obama administration," she says.

"The same goes for self-defense; I want someone in office that will protect my right to bear arms and protect the fundamentals of the Second Amendment."

Longtime Macomb County Republican campaign operative Jamie Roe says that cultural connection on gut-level issues is what put Trump in position to snap the GOP's drought in Michigan. "They thought this guy had their back," he said in a telephone interview. "Those people who were tired of having the liberal establishment look down their noses at them, when they saw the establishment and the media attack Trump, it made him stronger."

But perhaps showing that even Macomb is subject to some of the same social pressures that other suburbs its size experience, Sacco says she rarely told anyone that she was voting for Trump in the fall of 2016. "The general understanding among people who either did not like him, or do not know anyone who has lived in a place like Macomb County, was his conduct and comments would eliminate him from consideration by women," she says. "That is fine, I suppose; what they do not understand is that women are more worried about the economy than they are about his crass delivery of words. Even if your life is going well, you worry about it for your children. You worry that you could be one deep recession or economic downturn from losing what you worked so hard for."

Among men, Roe thinks, Trump's unorthodox and edgy, even offensive, communication style was a big part of his appeal to the group of voters that can swing to either party in Macomb County. "The guy has been around construction sites his entire life, and he has respected the work those guys did," Roe says. "The blunt way he talks connected with them."

Trump made three campaign stops in Macomb County in the run-up to the 2016 election, and carried most of its communities on Election Day. In Washington Township, where Sacco lives, Trump won in a landslide in all ten precincts—defeating Clinton 67.1 percent to 27.4 percent.

Trump won the county overall by 12 points, after Barack Obama had beaten John McCain by 16 points here and Mitt Romney by 4.

Trump's 54 percent was the best presidential showing by a Republican in Macomb in twenty-eight years.

More stinging for Democrats, Trump's winning margin in Macomb of 48,348 votes was good enough to swing the entire state, with its sixteen electoral votes, by a margin of 10,704. Clinton didn't even need anything like Obama's 2012 Macomb County margin of 16,103 to win the state—she just needed to not lose it big.[2]

Trump's three visits to Macomb County were not unique—Bill Clinton came three times in 1992, and his opponent, incumbent president George H. W. Bush, came twice.[3]

Hillary Clinton came to Macomb County too, to give a jobs speech at a community college, but not until after a *Detroit News* statewide poll had found her trailing in the county in early August.[4] She made another last-ditch trip to Detroit proper in the campaign's closing days.

"Macomb County . . . is full of ticket splitters. They will vote for the people who split the ticket, the person they think will do the best job. Whether it's local, whether it's state legislator, whether it's federal," explains Sacco.

Democratic pollster Stan Greenberg, who served as one of Bill Clinton's top advisers, has been a longtime student and chronicler of Macomb County's evolving politics. In his book *Middle Class Dreams,* Greenberg recalls being hired by local Democratic leaders in 1985 to study the group of people now made famous as "Reagan Democrats"—longtime blue-collar party loyalists who had twice broken ranks to support a Republican for president, with Macomb County considered the epicenter of a broader national movement.

Greenberg's book was written in 1995, a decade after his initial research, but it could have just as easily been written about the Trump voter. Recalling his earliest Macomb focus groups of Reagan voters, Greenberg described their animus to both parties: "The Republicans thought mainly about 'big business,' and the Democrats concentrated mainly on the minority groups. . . . These workers saw themselves as members of a new minority class that was ignored by the government but forced to support social programs that did not benefit them."[5]

Greenberg now believes Trump has made a major mistake by

allying with Paul Ryan's attempts to roll back the Affordable Care Act—and that attacks on Republicans for trying to cut Medicaid will be potent in the midterms.

A thread through all of Greenberg's Macomb research, including a post-election study he did for Democracy Corps in 2017, is that the swing voter in this part of the Rust Belt is not averse to government on philosophical grounds, and is keenly sensitive to appeals to both patriotism and strength.[6]

In 1995, Greenberg wrote, "Ronald Reagan sided with the small against the big. He was seen to be waging a sincere and determined struggle against big and inexorable forces."

Sacco saw the same in Trump, as early as the first Republican primary debate in 2015.

"I loved the slogan, 'Make America Great Again,' and second, he was not going to bend and bow to political correctness. Those were probably the first two things," Sacco says. "Third thing, he was a very successful independent-minded person, who did not need to run for president, but did, out of his, I feel, dedication and debt to the greatness of the nation. He saw it. He stood out. He wasn't afraid to say what everybody was thinking . . . Truth is very appealing."

Greenberg noted that the populist resentment in Macomb extended beyond big government. "They identified with things small, and suspected 'big' and 'powerful' institutions of any kind—labor and business, government and both political parties."[7]

Today, sitting in her suburban Macomb home, Sacco says detachment extends now to big media outlets, whose personalities she perceives to be culturally disconnected from her worldview.

"Here is what I do not understand: Why do they shun people who have faith, who believe in God? And I don't think that's fair, that's not right. I don't go around picking on people who don't have faith and try to degrade them, so I wish they wouldn't do that," she says.

As attested by Greenberg's borderline-obsessive writings about Macomb—President Clinton reportedly would teasingly ask his pollster if the county had more electoral votes than Florida—the populism that Macomb has embodied in the American political lexicon is not a new phenomenon, but a lasting one. Sacco, for one, sees herself as part of something that will outlast the election that put the place back in the spotlight.

"What I feel isn't an anomaly; this movement unequivocally goes on long past Trump, and this is going to be a continuing battle. This fascinating group of people who placed him in the White House is because a variety of different people wanted to be part of something bigger than themselves," she says.

"It means it makes me more important. It makes the individual more important, believing that they are contributing directly or indirectly in whatever they're doing."

Sacco is not someone to sit still; she now volunteers three days a week at a senior center. "I just love working with the seniors. I lost my mom, five years ago, and I was still driving the bus at the time and I started to think it's probably time to do something else."

And so she did. "There are 250 residents and I know everybody's name," she says, becoming animated. She clearly loves what she does; it connects her to the mother she lost and the grandmother whose lunch counter she and her husband bought. "They do Zumba, and chair Zumba, chair dancing, because some of them can't stand up. Line dancing, they do it in the chair. I run bingo three times a week. We serve a lot of liquor. Cocktail party, wine and cheese," she says, laughing.

The voters of Macomb County have been volatile over the last three decades, switching from lifetimes of Democratic allegiance to Reagan to Bill Clinton and Obama and then back to Trump; but if Sacco is representative, Republicans now may have a chance to solidify the county in this new conservative-populist fusion in the wake of a decades-long leftward Democratic drift. "You know, I personally will never turn back. I don't agree with what every conservative or Republican or independent thinks, and I haven't always liked the way that Trump has talked, but I think the importance of his list of Supreme Court nominees was and is so huge going forward, that I cannot imagine that not being the driving force on my support going forward," she says.

Sacco has been a firsthand witness to the essential core of the U.S. economy changing. No place in America has been as rocked by the twin forces of automation and importation as has Detroit, leaving corroding factories, demolished homes, and human displacement.

For people like Sacco who have made their lives in Macomb County, the personal cost was always right in front of them.

"The sorrow of those changes are everywhere," she says.

"We are tired of these disturbances marginalizing American workers that have scraped out of their hometowns and either scattered away from families or left trying to re-create something that is gone. No one has guided us through this ruthless transition. Trump identified what we already knew."

This time, though, something different happened. "We banded together. It's going to take a lot to extricate that."

Patty Bloomstine

Frontier, Erie County, Pennsylvania
Due west from the clutter of fast-food restaurants, cottages, and budget motels concentrated around the entrance to Presque Isle State Park, a picturesque neighborhood named Frontier emerges along Eighth Avenue toward South Shoreline Drive.

Pretty boulevards with majestic oaks lining the streets are punctuated with grassy islands separating the traffic to give the place a park-like feel. Streets with the names Monaca, Shawnee, and Mohawk are filled with brick homes built from the late 1920s to the mid-twentieth century.

The Frontier neighborhood is a suburban haven annexed by the city of Erie in strict accordance to the deed of the original property owner, William Scott, a wealthy Gilded Age robber baron who wanted his rural farmland to eventually be laid out as a subdivision to make Erie "more beautiful."

Patty Bloomstine's home on Columbia Circle hugs a ridge that has a breathtaking view of Lake Erie's Presque Isle Bay. Three classic red, wooden Adirondack chairs sit at the property line; directly below them, the steep drop to the shoreline gives way to Ferncliff Beach and the Erie Yacht Club.

On this balmy spring afternoon, sailboats glide in and out of their slips; the breeze is pitch-perfect for a cruise on this sheltered part of the shallowest of the Great Lakes.

The home Patty shares with her husband, Chris, and son, Max, is airy, full of light; the decor is moderate but elegant, family photos are abundant, and in the living room her dog naps silently in front of the fireplace.

Bloomstine grew up not far from this, Erie's premier neighborhood, and so did her husband. Both their families live within a stone's throw of their house. "Except my sister, who lives in Belgium. She is a teacher on the NATO base," Patty explains.

Bloomstine is engaging, animated, very funny, and fast. One almost needs to take notes on an index card to keep up with her conversation as she bounces from one observation to another. From the outside she looks like the picture of health. Her thick mid-length chestnut hair curves smoothly around her neck and her skin is luminous, with only a faint hint of makeup—and scant is evidence that she tires easily.

The Bloomstine family is comfortable, educated, professional, well-mannered, and suburban through and through. At fifty-five, Patty is a respected civic volunteer, a social worker who put off her career to be a stay-at-home parent, and more recently, a breast cancer survivor. She's active and optimistic, so the casual observer might never suspect it.

Bloomstine is exactly the kind of voter who was at the top of Hillary Clinton's persuasion-target list during the 2016 campaign. In swing states such as Pennsylvania, televisions were jammed full of ads aimed squarely at one slice of the electorate: white women with college degrees. The Clinton campaign calculated that this group, which typically tilts Republican but is less conservative than the rest of the GOP's base, would be especially put off by Trump's string of insensitive and crude verbal explosions.

Clinton ran an ad, called "Role Models," that seemed to show the perspective of kids watching Trump curse and use inappropriate language from the podium, designed to make their mothers think twice about voting for him. It ran another ad, "Mirrors," with teenage girls looking into mirrors as Trump's abusive comments about women's figures play in the audio—including "a person who's flat-chested is very hard to be a 10."[8] Clinton used one of the three presidential debates to pick a fight over Trump's negative comments shaming a former Miss Universe winner for her weight gain.

After that debate, a senior Clinton campaign official told *The Washington Post,* "We know that white suburban women are critical for both parties . . . and the lowest hanging fruit for expansion among that group is more likely to be college-educated white women."[9]

A poll taken in late September by *The Washington Post* and ABC

News found that Trump trailed among white women overall by 2 points—and that survey was taken two weeks before the release of the *Access Hollywood* backstage tape, in which Trump spoke vulgarly and abusively about his attempts at sexual exploits with a woman who was not his wife. In the wake of that incident, many Republican elected officials, including prominent women such as Senator Kelly Ayotte, renounced Trump in the strongest of terms. Even Senate Majority Leader Mitch McConnell, never one prone to strong language, called it "repugnant."[10]

Clinton used that audio in a brutal online ad in the campaign's final week, pairing it with old footage of the much younger Trump saying, "Putting a wife to work is a very dangerous thing," and "When I come home and dinner's not ready, I go through the roof."[11]

Clinton's all-out push to aim her campaign's closing argument at suburban women fell short, if exit polling was accurate. The polls taken by a national news media consortium as voters were leaving their precincts on Election Day found that Trump won white women by 9 points—7 points better than where he stood in the *Washington Post*/ABC News poll in late September.

The exit surveys, which are conducted by interviewing randomly selected voters as they leave polling places, found Clinton winning with white college-degreed women by 7 points, 51-44, a margin not nearly large enough to offset her 61-34 loss among non-college-educated white women.[12] Clinton's overall showing of 43 percent with white women was scant improvement over Barack Obama's 2012 performance of 42 percent of the white female vote, in spite of the fact that she aimed a major share of her campaign's resources at that group.[13]

Even if Clinton's campaign did not work, all evidence points to the fact that it almost did. In the crucial presidential swing states, nearly one in five Trump voters say that at some point during the campaign they were embarrassed to tell their friends or relatives they were voting for him, for fear of disapproval. Sixty-one percent of these "shy Trump voters"—so named for the long-observed trend in the United Kingdom of a hidden vote for the stodgy and uncool Conservative Party—were college-educated, and they were disproportionately female. Among all college-educated white women who voted for Trump, according to Wes Anderson's post-election survey in swing states, 29 percent reported reluctance to share their support even with family.

In the weeks leading up to Election Day, Bloomstine found herself going from watching the news every day to not watching at all. "I just found myself becoming negatively affected by the constant predictions that [Trump] was going to lose, and by the inferences made by reporters every time they reported on him. The smallest thing became a big negative," she says.

Then the biggest negative of all landed on Friday night, October 7—the *Access Hollywood* backstage tape was released. By this point, Bloomstine had gone from being a supporter of Trump to a campaign volunteer.

"It was on a weekend. I went down to the campaign office to make calls and find out if there was anything I could do, when the look on everyone's face told me something was terribly wrong," she says.

The other volunteers at the campaign office told her news had been unraveling that a tape existed of Trump bragging in explicit and vulgar terms about groping and kissing women during a 2005 conversation with then–*Access Hollywood* host Billy Bush.

"It was captured on a hot mic so there was no denying it happened," says Bloomstine. "This wasn't the media being the media. This was real and the pit of my gut just hurt."

She assessed the situation and found she personally could come to terms with it because of the length of time that had passed since the incident, and his apology. "But there were other people who were slipping away from him because of the vulgarity of what he said. There were many of my friends, people I socialize with, who were turned off enough about it that it could have impacted how they were going to vote that November.

"There were plenty of people I know who stalled, who really gave it a second and third look. The people and friends that I spoke with about it, ultimately they came back and voted for him."

Accordingly, the greatest amount of social peer pressure for women to oppose Trump came in well-off, well-educated neighborhoods— places where Trump underperformed the Republican average and any prospective Trump voter would have intrinsically known before the election from her own social interactions that she was hopelessly outnumbered. So why did just enough suburban women stick with him, in spite of the social consequences and Clinton's best efforts to persuade them?

Pollster Wes Anderson, who took that post-election survey that found the "shy Trump voters," attributes some of the resilience of Trump's vote among suburban women to the potent pull of what he calls the "echo of labor"—the strict code of patriotism and manufacturing work and skepticism of welfare that was imbued in the children of the industrial age now past.

That might explain how Patty Bloomstine got to Trump.

"We bought the house less than ten years ago. Over a hundred years ago it was where the Kahkwa Club was located," she says, referring to the now prestigious private golf club that began on this site in the 1880s as a social club centered on aquatic sports.

Bloomstine lives now on what used to be a playground for Erie's industrial rich, but she grew up in a working-class-Democrat household: "Totally blue-collar, Dad was a machinist, had one job his whole life from school to retirement. Mom stayed home with the six of us. We all went to Our Lady of Peace Catholic School."

Her father and mother are still Democrats. "I knew Dad was going to vote for Clinton. I brought the absentee ballots to them, knowing very well at least he would be voting for her. So I said, 'Dad, no matter who I support, you have to vote whatever way you want to vote,'" she explains.

And so he did, but "the funny thing is now my father has changed his mind; he is happy with Trump. Can you believe that? He likes him now; a big part of that switch for my father is the way the press and establishment politicians dislike him—that and his take-charge attitude."

Her father also really doesn't like the way the local paper, the *Erie Times-News,* treats Trump. "He just canceled his subscription, which he has had for over fifty years, all over the way they have reported on him. It takes a lot to crater that kind of loyalty from a paper, but they did."

Both Bloomstine and her mother voted for Trump—though she had to persuade her mother. So did her husband, Chris, who owns an insurance company in town with his family.

"Chris always said it's going to be Trump. And I looked at him like he had ten heads. I thought it would be Ted Cruz or Carly Fiorina," she says. "I liked her because I thought she'd be a good fit against Clinton, at first, and because she's a businesswoman. Smart. Not completely over-the-top. I thought she'd be able to appeal to a lot more people. And then when things started happening, there was a shift and I said, 'You know what,' I was immediately on board. 'He's going to win. Mark my words, I'm telling you. He's going to be one of the best presidents we've ever had.' "

Her seventeen-year-old son, Max, enters the living room—he is attentive to his mom, brings her a shawl and a bottle of water. Outside, a storm is forming in the distance and the breeze has kicked up. A flurry of sailboats make their way back to their slips as the sky, cloudless just moments before, turns an inky indigo in the west.

Erie is the fourth largest of the five Great Lakes, but its shallow depth and the prominent wind along its longitude make the western part of the lake experience significant storm surges year-round.

Max is part of Generation Z, the newest cohort after the much-hyped millennials. "I loved following this election because, based on the history I have studied, it is unlike anything that has happened before. I honestly wished I could have participated," says Max, who is deciding between whether he should attend a university in Pittsburgh or in Rochester, New York, for engineering.

Max likes Trump, but not for the same reasons his mother does. "I like his independence from political parties"—an anti-organizational hallmark of this new generation.

To say his mother operates on a whole different level of optimism and sheer willpower is an understatement. "I never have bad days," she says. "Even with cancer. It is not a big deal. It's all good. Never thought, never, never once, it wasn't a death sentence. There was actually good things with chemo. We never had a bad day driving to Cleveland. My husband, I had great support. Huge amount of friends. I had food brought to my house every day for my family. The outpouring from people I barely knew. Unbelievable."

The diagnosis brought everyone together, Max says, quietly.

Bloomstine was diagnosed in July 2015. "I had this lump, and I'm like, 'It hurts.' It's weird, in March. Didn't do anything about it."

In July, she went for a checkup and the doctor immediately ordered a sonogram. "The doctor tells me I have breast cancer. And I'm like, 'Okay.' And he goes, 'Huh?' I'm like, 'That's okay, give me my records. I'll go to Cleveland, not a big deal.' "

Two weeks later she has a double mastectomy. "And then I started chemo that September. Every two weeks I had to go back to Cleveland. And then, to be honest, the worst part was my hair."

"Yeah, that was bad," Max says.

Bloomstine switches subjects with ease. "This neighborhood is not Frontier proper," she says of the prestigious area, perhaps a hint of her blue-collar self-identity showing through, "or maybe it is."

"There's a lot of Democrats even here. Our neighborhood used to be more Republican, our area. As a matter of fact, Kathy Dahlkemper, who's our county executive, is from this area," she says of the onetime moderate Democrat who was swept into Congress and the House majority during the 2006 midterm wave election, and swept out during the Republican House midterm wave of 2010.

"To say I have disdain for her, that doesn't sound Christian, right? But I'm just telling you, she just drives me crazy because we were all on board—gave her money for her first campaign when she was in Congress, and then she goes to Washington just to become a Nancy Pelosi wannabe. I am telling you . . . ," she says, biting her tongue.

Lightning streaks across the sky in the distance; though the storm stays due west, the rumble of thunder seems to shake the house.

"That is the reason she lost. She is the reason I changed political parties. She didn't get it. I believed she was going to be exactly what the country needs, what the community needs; she understands how we think, and then she supports Obamacare.

"I went from a passive political observer, to a warrior. I got full-throttle involved," she says of her support for Mike Kelly, a businessman from Butler, Pennsylvania, when he ran against the Erie Democrat in 2010.

Bloomstine is animated; it is clear this was personal for her. "I needed to make a difference. I put my money where my mouth is.

I guess my biggest impetus is what am I leaving my son?" She alludes to policy changes the Democratic majority in 2009 and 2010 made with Obamacare, and the massive surge in federal spending in the wake of the 2008 recession.

"That was the beginning of putting the country on the wrong track; it placed the economy on the wrong track. You can see the evidence of that everywhere around here. How could I just sit back and not get involved? I have an obligation to my son, to my community," she says. "My husband is a small-business owner that caters to this community. If this community is not doing well, the ripple effect hurts everyone; we have to right the ship."

That drive for change from the economic stagnation of the Obama era in communities like Erie may have doomed Clinton from the start.

Bloomstine says she wants for her son what her parents wanted for her and her five siblings. "To be able to do better than we did, to achieve more, and to be able to move back home after college and be surrounded by family if he wants that."

"I definitely want that," the teenager interjects. "I love Erie. I want to be part of not bringing it back, but reinventing it. I don't know what its potential is; I do know I want to be part of it. I didn't know the Erie my parents knew; I know the Erie in decline. But I do know I love the ability to make a difference, remake it, be part of it."

Bloomstine smiles, then tears well in her eyes; it is clear he has never articulated that to her before. "I had no idea," she says, and then the woman who hardly stops talking pauses, and for a long time.

"I want you to be and go wherever the world and your talents take you," she tells him. "I am honored that you think that might be right here at home."

"We need a new mindset in Washington," Bloomstine says. "This is my thing when I say that I truly could be an independent. I lean Republican, for sure . . . but I think the one thing that Trump will always get credit for is that he proved that our votes matter. No matter what party we were from, our votes matter. And I haven't felt that way in a very long time."

Sally Tedrow

Keokuk, Lee County, Iowa

Nestled in her home in the only residential enclave of this struggling Mississippi River town, Sally Tedrow admits she struggled with her vote for Donald Trump.

"I really did. It wasn't easy. All of my friends from church were really upset about it," she says.

Tedrow, who is very involved in her United Methodist Church, felt the heat from some of her peers in the pew. "When the *Access Hollywood* tape came out, it was really hard to tell some people that I had not lost my marbles," she says; but she eventually held steady for the very unorthodox Republican nominee.

"My friend at church thinks there's something wrong with me because I don't love Hillary Clinton. Because I not only voted for Trump but have started to really like him."

She pauses, then suddenly her poodle, who has been sitting on her lap, makes a beeline for the screen door as a neighbor passes by.

"Dora!" Tedrow says quietly but sternly. Tail between her legs, Dora returns immediately to her lap.

"And I'll tell you honestly. I didn't vote *for* Donald Trump. I voted *against* Hillary Clinton. I thought if I didn't vote for Donald Trump, I would make it possible for Hillary to win. In other words, if I didn't vote at all. I thought, I did not want to do that."

Pollster Wes Anderson, who did opinion research in 2016 for Trump's two largest independent supporters, the National Rifle Association and Rebuilding America Now, a Trump-dedicated super PAC, says that vehement opposition to Clinton was the glue that kept what he calls the "shy Trump voter" in place.

"These women may not have decided to vote for Trump until late in the race, but most had decided much earlier that they were definitely not voting for Clinton," says Anderson, whose eight-state post-election survey indicates that nearly one-fifth of Trump's voters, and more than a quarter of the women who voted for him, report having been reluctant to tell friends or family they were voting for Trump, for fear of social reprisal.

Tedrow hardened into a Clinton opponent, but it was a migration. "I had every intention to vote for Hillary Clinton in 2016 in the beginning," she admits. "I think the thing I liked about her most of all was that she was a very intelligent woman. You could see that in how she formed some of her ideas on foreign affairs and some domestic issues. And I liked the fact that she's a very strong woman.

"So I thought I would vote for Hillary, but by midsummer that year it became clear that voting for her was not going to work for me," she says.

What changed her mind?

"I felt like she was not honest. I felt like she didn't have a very strong message to me as to exactly what she was going to do. I studied, I watched all of her speeches, I went to see her when she was here [in Keokuk, January 2016], and her response to most people's questions was 'Yes, we'll check on that.' Or 'We will definitely check on that.' And maybe she did check on it, but I doubt it."

With terrorists ratcheting up attacks on civilians in Europe and the economy lagging in this, Iowa's second-highest county for unemployment, Tedrow decided Hillary was stuck.

"I didn't feel that anything would change at all in terms of our economy improving or our security," she says. "I just thought we were going on a downhill slide, and I thought that would just continue if Hillary got in. I didn't think she was going to change a thing."

And seeing Hillary in action did nothing to allay that sense of inertia. "She was just going through the motions. She was incredibly dishonest right to people's face, about issues they deeply cared about.

"When people point to her e-mails and Comey as the reason she lost votes, I don't think they were paying attention to what people were thinking; the direction of the country was awful, just awful."

By spring, Tedrow had taken interest in a new candidate—the

one who was taking the Republican nomination by storm. "When Donald Trump came out with his list of Supreme Court justices—for me that was a game changer," Tedrow says, finding something concrete to go with a more general sense.

"But I do like Donald Trump's ideas." She smiles for the first time, before giving her hedge.

"I just wish he had a softer manner about him sometimes," Tedrow says gingerly. "He embarrasses me. That's not exactly the word to say, but, oh gosh, I think you could've said the same thing much kinder and much gentler."

The city limits of Keokuk in Lee County, Iowa, are the southeasternmost tip of the state, next to Missouri and Illinois, hugged by the nostalgic embrace of the curving Mississippi River that shaped its past, and shadowed by the distance from metropolitan America that clouds its future.

Tedrow lives in a lovely little bedroom community of sleepy Keokuk, where the homes are neatly cared for in a town that is waiting to understand its identity going forward. Tedrow's home is modest, but skillfully decorated; as she sits in her modern taupe easy chair, she is surrounded by tasteful antiques, candles, and photographs. Her red maple hardwood floors gleam in the late-spring sun shining through her French doors. She is dressed in a lovely buttercup-yellow sweater with floral embroidered piping. Her sandy blond hair is cut stylishly short, and at seventy-three, she looks to be a woman fifteen years younger.

"I grew up on a farm. We struggled financially all of the time. I guess we were lower-middle-class. I married a farmer; I lost him in a motorcycle accident ten years ago. It's, it's still painful," she says.

Tedrow explains that she had often gravitated to Democrats in the voting booth, before souring.

"I voted for Bill Clinton twice and I voted for Obama twice. I really liked Obama. I thought he was new and refreshing and I liked him personally. I wanted him to be successful," she says.

His policies, though, she struggled with. "I did not like his foreign policy. I did not like the way that he handled his foreign policy. That was my main concern. And the direction of the country, he did not seem to have a handle on that, or if he did, well, then his idea of what the direction of the county should go wasn't very well thought out.

"The economic problems of this country were not Obama's creation, but he did nothing to apply the brakes. In fact, if anything he put the gas pedal on them. The regulations that hurt farming and . . . energy impacted the small towns . . . more so than they were already hurting; it was like shoveling salt on big wounds," she says.

All over this faded river town, smaller now in population than it was a century and a half ago, economic concerns drive conversations about politics. Obama won the place handily, thanks to voters like Tedrow, racking up a 16-point margin each time he was on the ballot. In fact, Democratic nominees carried the county by 15 percent or more in every election dating back to 1988—before Trump flipped that math upside-down and won 55 percent to Clinton's 39 percent.[14]

Despite her reluctance to vote for Trump, Tedrow says she oddly finds herself warming to him as a president.

"You know, I have to admit I like him more now than I did as a candidate. On the issues I care about he is strong. He comes from a place of strength when he talks about our economy becoming dominant again. And on security issues he has proven to be steady," she says, her statement underscoring the irony of the moment: the same unease about America's place in the world that ushered Obama into office persisted after his election, eventually preventing his secretary of state from succeeding him.

"America's prestige in the world and even here at home has dwindled, in my estimation. I think there's some of us grassroot people, obviously, that are proud of America. And I don't think that that was the message that America was sending," Tedrow says.

"And I think 'Make America Great Again' was a wonderful slogan. You know, we used to be all about God and country and we've kind of got away from that, a lot of people have. I think this Donald Trump made it possible to go back to feeling like that."

Part of what has made Trump more appealing, in Tedrow's estimation, is how the media and the party establishments on both sides treat him. She sympathized with Trump with every shot they took.

"They show him shaking hands with the President Macron of France, and they were criticizing him because his handshake was too long. It was a white-knuckle handshake before he let go. Really? Really? That's all you've got to talk about? He's in a very important meeting about NATO and everything, and all they could talk about is that he held the president of France's hand too long and made his knuckles turn white. Isn't that ridiculous?" Tedrow asks.

Since Trump's election on the strength of his vote in Midwestern locales such as Lee County, Trump voters like Tedrow have watched as news reporters attribute fictional motives to them that they don't recognize—forgetting that many of these exact people delivered the votes that put Obama into office.

"I find myself very frustrated with the television. I just turn it off. During the campaign, I watched a lot of news, a lot of news. I watched a lot of the political stuff, and I did that up until the election and now it's got so ridiculous, so, so ridiculous. So slanted. But I get very frustrated with it, so I just turn it off. I think, I don't need those things going around in my head, you know?"

As coverage of Trump has become more hyperbolic and more antagonistic, it only stands to reason that voters—even mild-mannered Methodist matrons like Tedrow—could pass lasting judgment on the news networks, just as they checked out on the Republican Party establishment and then Hillary Clinton. If the Trump coalition broke two large institutions in American life, it's not a stretch to imagine it breaking another.

9

A Culture Craving Respect

In the short span of a generation, the face and focus of the Democratic Party nationally has shifted from a glorification of the working-class ethos to multiculturalist militancy pushed by the Far Left of the party.

That stark change in the priorities of the American political Left has at a minimum powered the shotgun marriage of populism to conservatism, a connection unthinkable even twenty years ago.

It was just five elections ago that none other than today's elitist Al Gore tried to defeat the scion of the Bush Dynasty in 2000 with what NBC News called "a populist call to arms." In accepting the Democratic nomination that year, Gore thundered from the convention podium, "They're for the powerful and we're for the people."[1] Gore's gambit didn't quite work, but none other than the house organ of the elite, *The New York Times*, spotted it for what it was—a play for the same votes that Trump would later steal from the Democrats, the "swing voters in battleground states in the Midwest."[2]

Gore was clumsily trying to do what his predecessor had done reflexively—attend to the economic ambitions and anxieties of the working class and on cultural grounds. Bill Clinton's standard stump speech during the primary season of his first race for president in 1992 bore as much resemblance to Donald Trump's announcement as it did to his wife's standard speech of 2016.

The former president's speech was pillared on nationalism and a critique of the economic and political elites who had taken actions contrary to the best interests of middle-class America:

> The ideal that if you work hard and play by the rules you'll be rewarded, you'll do a little better next year than you did last year, your kids will do better than you. But that idea has been devastated for millions of Americans. How did this happen? I would argue it happened for two reasons. No. 1: We lost our economic leadership. Other nations began to do some things better than we do, and their economies started growing faster and faster as ours slowed down. Big, Simple Ideas. No. 2, and this is why I'm running for President: We elected people to high office who had the wrong response to the problem.[3]
>
> —Bill Clinton, April 22, 1992, Johnstown, PA

By the time the next Clinton launched her second presidential campaign in 2016, her speech was not a paean to the middle-class work ethic as much as a pandering checklist to clusters of the self-styled oppressed. She attacked Republicans who "shame and blame women," put immigrants "at risk of deportation," "turn their backs on gay people who love each other," and "reject what it takes to build an inclusive economy . . . an inclusive society."[4]

Hillary Clinton ended her kickoff speech with an extended riff about gender politics and her own potential to break the glass ceiling, a more self-centered than audience-centered thesis:

> I wish my mother could have been with us longer. I wish she could have seen Chelsea become a mother herself. I wish she could have met Charlotte. I wish she could have seen the America we're going to build together. . . . An America where a father can tell his daughter: yes, you can be anything you want to be. Even President of the United States.[5]

Bill Clinton closed his 1992 stump speech in the opposite manner, with a clarion to a cause instead of a call to a candidacy: ". . . this election is about you. It isn't about me. It's about you and your problems and your promise and your future, and all these little kids who are here tonight."[6]

Hillary Clinton's campaign message was fueled by social wedges and cultural grievance; Bill's stump speech didn't mention any hot-button cultural issues at all—just kitchen-table economics and the middle-class ethos. The closest he got to Hillary's approach was pledging to provide "a basic health-care package to all." That jarring juxtaposition, by a married couple no less, is a fitting measurement for the distance traversed by the national political and cultural dialogue of the American Left over the twenty-four-year span.

Within a generation, the religiosity that was once honored by both parties became mocked by one as merely a basis of bigotry. Angst about financial insecurity was derided by coastal elites in both parties as the last wheezing of an outmoded appendage on the global economic animal. Even in the wake of their decisive role in the elections, Rust Belt voters watched on cable television as the Left and journalists pigeonholed their rebellion as an ugly bout of white nationalism, doubling down on all the elitist snobbery those voters sought to rebuke.

As relevant as the comparison between the two Clintons' speeches is, politicians, even the famous ones, don't create national cultural movements; they follow them. Hillary Clinton's migration from chief adviser for her husband's homage to work and responsibility, to her own campaign of campus-style thought policing, demographic score-settling, and forced redistribution reflected not just changes in her approach but changes in the society at large.

Political scientist Charles Murray, in his landmark 2012 book *Coming Apart,* attributed this growing disconnect to a widening gulf between the setters of cultural norms and the scattered millions of workaday Americans. Murray's book began with an explanation of "The Formation of a New Upper Class" that "increasingly consists of people who were born into upper-middle-class families and have never lived outside the upper-middle-class bubble." Murray's premise that this bubbling effect foretold ongoing cultural schism due to the prominence of the new upper class in culture, commerce, and government: "the danger increases that people who have so much influence on the course of the nation have little direct experience with the lives of ordinary Americans, and make their judgments about what's good for other people based on their own highly atypical lives."

Murray noted that the epicenters of this new upper class, what he calls the "narrow elite—people with national influence," coincided with what he called the "Big Four" centers of cultural impact: New York, Los Angeles, San Francisco, and Washington, DC—the places that drive entertainment, technological innovation, government, global finance, and the mass media.[7]

The emerging populist-conservative coalition is in no small measure a resistance to the mores and power of those Big Four clusters—and the Democratic message of the Obama era has proven to be a purely distilled insistence on conformity to the values, societal norms, and priorities of that hyper-educated, metropolitan class.

A liberalism that seeks to spread cosmopolitan relativism to the masses, by force if necessary, instead of spreading economic equality, was destined to leave a decisive slice of the American electorate in search of a new home. It took an outsider to the conservative tent like Trump to throw out the welcome mat for them.

It is not incidental that naked nationalism was an admitted feature of Trump's campaign message and was, at the same time, a pejorative used by his opponents in describing it. Many of the influencers in the new upper class that Murray describes consider themselves citizens of the world first, and denizens of a single nation second—a self-description made possible by the rise of technology, and the mobility and liberal arts education that only affluence can provide. Murray, blaming this gap partly on cognitive abilities separation, said: "Many in the intellectual wing of the new upper class feel more comfortable around their intellectual colleagues from other countries than they do with Americans who aren't intellectuals."[8]

This sentiment of schism is not one the new upper class, as the primary purveyors of content delivered via news and entertainment, feels obligated to hide—which inevitably is pushing the nation toward equal, and opposite, reactions.

Murray's thesis from 2012, that the American economy and education system has become a great sorting engine that drives the cultural divide, virtually anticipated the 2016 election returns four years later.

Mid-decade census data projects that eleven of the eighteen American jurisdictions with the highest concentrations of bachelor's degrees are in Manhattan, the San Francisco suburbs, and Washington, DC, and its immediate environs. Trump's net election margin was worse than Romney's margin in all eleven of those counties—and it was double-digits worse in nine of them.[9]

In fact, Trump's margin was weaker than Romney's in 86 of the 100 most educated counties in the country—a fact that held true regardless of the jurisdiction's normal partisan leanings.

This juxtaposition between the 2016 elections and all its recent predecessors is evident in virtually every state in the country. Counties with rates of educational-attainment density higher than the national average performed better for Hillary in defeat than they had for Obama in victory, and counties with rates of bachelor's degrees below the national average of 29.8 percent moved toward the Republicans.

The driver of this split is not the college education itself, but the social pressure that comes with living exclusively among other college graduates—and the political liberation that comes for college graduates who have a more educationally diverse orbit.

As the Rotary Reliables group of Trump voters demonstrate, the herding effect trumps education levels. Educated voters who socialize, work, or serve among those with only a high school degree are more likely to reflect the political views of that peer group. Meanwhile, college-educated voters in places with a preponderance of double-degree households are likely to conform to their neighborhood dinner party consensus and eschew Trumpism, even if they otherwise lean Republican.

Among the voters surrounded by other degree holders, 2016 saw migration even among what had been the most Republican of suburbs. Booming Williamson County, Tennessee, the wealthiest county in that state and the purest suburban bedroom of Nashville, was 11 points weaker for Trump than for Romney, even as the Volunteer State as a whole gave Trump a much better margin than Romney. Similarly, Johnson County, Kansas, the most gilded suburb of Kansas City, gave Trump a bare plurality, 47 percent to 44 percent, after having given Romney an 18-point margin in 2012. Collin County, Texas, the ruby-red corporate headquarters of Frito-Lay, J. C. Penney, and Dr Pepper, gave Hillary Clinton the largest share it had given any Democratic candidate for president since 1976.

The reverse was true on the opposite end of the spectrum as well—in the 1,500 American counties with the sparsest concentrations of bachelor's degrees, Trump's net margin bettered Romney's in all but 51.[10]

This shift was most noticeable in rural counties with small populations. Two-thirds of the nation's 3,100-plus counties have fewer than 50,000 people; Trump lost only 197 of them while Romney and Bush had both lost more than 300. But it held true even in suburbs with lower-than-average concentrations of bachelor's degrees.

In suburban Denver, Trump's margin was 8 points stronger than Romney's in blue-collar, traditionally Democratic Adams County, while he ran 4 points worse than Romney in swingy Arapahoe County next door, and 8 points worse in neighboring Douglas County. All three jurisdictions are bedroom communities of the same city. The difference? College education levels. The population of Douglas, ruby-red Republican in most elections, has a bachelor's degree incidence of 56.6 percent, while Arapahoe's is 40 percent and Adams's is 22.2 percent—well below the national average of 29.8 percent. This schism is evident not only at the macro level of counting votes and sheepskins, but at the professional level as well.

The high-tech sector gravitated to Hillary Clinton with financial support by nearly a 19:1 ratio, according to data cited by the ESPN-owned number-crunching blog FiveThirtyEight.com.[11]

The entertainment sector, already heavily Democratic in its political leanings, moved even further left in going against Trump. Industry magazine *Variety* cited data showing entertainment figures gave $22 million to Clinton and her super PACs, and less than $290,000 to Trump. "Showbiz is heavily in favor of Hillary Clinton. That is not surprising," wrote *Variety* editor Ted Johnson on Election Day. "But what is different from previous years is just how lopsided the level of support is."[12]

Technology companies and Hollywood infect the political discourse through a slow drip, but journalism drives it on a daily basis; and while Republicans have long argued there is a media bias against them, the evidence points even more strongly toward it in the Trump-Clinton race.

In trying to put his finger on a definition of media myopia in 2016's election, political data journalist Nate Silver cited research by academicians John Woolley and Gerhard Peters showing that of the major newspapers to endorse either Romney or Obama in 2012, nearly half of them, 46 percent, went with the Republican. Meanwhile, only 3 percent of major endorsing newspapers in 2016 went with Trump.[13]

While it is not completely fair to presume editorial biases always bleed into the newsroom itself, Silver argues that the most elite beat reporters were at a minimum guilty of not noticing what was happening in swing states. "National reporters often flew into these states with pre-baked narratives," Silver wrote. And "the top news sources (such as the *Times, The Washington Post* and *Politico*) have earned progressively more influence over the last decade," as local newspaper staffs and circulations have shrunk, giving those elite misses more weight.[14] Silver's observations of the consequences of the ongoing funnel of media influence just as easily could have been made by Murray, years in advance.

Leading national journalists missed the potential efficacy of Trump's grievance appeal because they exemplified, professionally and personally, the other end of the complaint. Trump's campaign went straight at the idea that cultural power was stacked against voters who live outside the elite zip codes. In his victory speech after a key early primary in Nevada, Trump said famously, "I love the poorly educated," a remark that drew swift rebuke from mainstream media outlets but never hurt Trump electorally with his new coalition. Trump, an Ivy Leaguer himself, understood his audience even at that early stage of the nomination process.[15]

Trump's weakest jurisdictions in the Republican primaries mirrored the kinds of places where he would underperform Romney in November: the most credentialed of suburbs, which are home to the bulk of the Republican leadership and donor base. In Georgia, Trump lost only 5 of the state's 159 counties, and they were all in suburban Atlanta or the college town of Athens. In perhaps his most consequential primary victory, in South Carolina, Trump lost only the state capital of Columbia and the most cosmopolitan city, Charleston. Trump lost Wisconsin's primary, his most notable stumble, because he couldn't crack a 25 percent ceiling in the suburbs of Milwaukee.

Despite Trump's rarely broken string of state primary and caucus victories, he was unable to attract the bandwagon support of Republican elected officials—scoring just eleven congressmen, only one of the GOP's fifty-four then-senators, and just three sitting governors.[16] One reason Trump failed to get support from Republican elected officials was his mold-breaking nonideological approach, but another is the fact that it was simply not socially acceptable to support him among the country's thought leaders—a group that included donors and strategists in both parties. Even in the pitchfork-era GOP, the professional strategists and fund-raisers who color the opinions of elected leaders live in the kind of higher-income, college-educated suburbs that proved to be Trump's worst ground.

That split result between the densely populated locales and the sparsely populated locales in the Republican nomination contest demonstrated that the GOP itself is not immune to the tug of the larger cultural forces powering its new governing coalition.

The emerging schism between the intensity of support for Republican candidates who represent this populist-conservative fusion in rural and industrial areas, and the newly competitive nature of educated suburbs that previously tilted Republican, is the core axis of our new politics.

Democrats used this schism to score a big victory in the first statewide test of post-Trump politics, the Virginia governor's election of 2017. Buoyed by a 24 percent increase in turnout over the previous election four years ago in the suburbs outside Washington, DC, among the most educated places in the nation, Democrats were able to win the Old Dominion's governorship in a rout. The Republican nominee for governor ran up Trump-like margins in the state's rural counties and small towns, but even a 13 percent increase in turnout there was insufficient to overcome the anti-Trump consolidation of the state's most educated suburbs.

Democrats are betting that the realignment the Trump coalition presents will have added benefits for them in dense jurisdictions everywhere, even the most exurban reaches of the country's metropolises—the "outer ring" places where people have traditionally moved to find lower property taxes, safer streets, and cheaper houses, bringing with them the historically Republican outlook that drives those impulses.

The challenge for Republicans is to keep the Trump coalition intact in rural and small-town geography, while preserving the pre-Trump partisan breakdown of suburbia—a feat that will require keeping longtime Republicans voting their party and newer Trump voters voting their cause. The tax cut passed by Trump and congressional Republicans in late 2017 will be the policy hook on which the GOP seeks to hang this effort. These competing objectives will color the strategies of both parties for the next two to three national election cycles. But it's not just political operatives who must make strategies that factor in the competing social pressures in a fast-sorting nation.

The consequences of the divide flow down a one-way street, according to Murray: "It is not a problem if truck drivers cannot empathize with the priorities of Yale professors. It is a problem if Yale professors, or producers of network news programs, or CEOs of great corporations, or presidential advisers cannot empathize with the priorities of truck drivers."[17]

The decision makers of cultural institutions and corporate brands tend to reside not just in more educated places, but in the *most* educated places—the handful of places Murray tagged as the most important "Super Zips," in the toniest neighborhoods of New York, Washington, San Francisco, and Los Angeles. If the people who make branding, news, and political decisions are immersed in environments hostile to a coalition that represents a governing majority of the nation, cultural schism is the most likely outcome.

As those with access to the megaphones of culture become more hegemonic, and less sympathetic or even less cognizant of the opposite half of America that lives outside its enclaves, it becomes inevitable that a siege mentality will set in among the consumers who see less of their values and priorities in the dominant culture. Otherness becomes manifest in collective action, particularly in electoral politics, and in 2016 that action found its vehicle in Donald Trump.

The driving construct of otherness, manifest by Trump voters in both the Republican primaries and the general election, is at its core driven by perceptions of respect.

"We spent all of our lives doing the right things; we pay our taxes, we give back to our communities, we volunteer at our churches, coached or served on the PTA at our kids' schools. And we voted for President Obama and still we are ridiculed. Still we are considered racists. There is no respect for anyone who is just average and trying to do the right things," says Cindy Hutchins, the store owner and nurse in Baldwin, Michigan.

"Our culture in Hollywood or in the media gives off the distinct air of disregard to people who live in the middle of the country. As if we have no value or do not contribute to the betterment of society. It's frustrating. It really wants to make you stand up and yell 'We count,' except of course we don't. At least not in their eyes," explains Amy Giles-Maurer in Kenosha, Wisconsin.

"All hard work has value. All people eventually contribute to the fabric of the country. But live in a small or medium-size town and you would think we were dragging the country down. What we do here matters. We aren't a country just made up of large metropolitan areas—our politics and our culture up until now has dictated that we are less than in the scale of importance and value," says Michael Martin, a Rotary Reliable, in Erie, Pennsylvania.

"Even nearly a year after Trump won, the political class is fighting to respect the voters who put them in office; we are either part of a cult, or dumb, or whatever the insult du jour is, and that becomes part of the culture," explains Trump voter Rick Novotny, in Erie.

Data indicates the Trump voters who perceived a lack of respect were right. The Pew Research Center's poll one week out from Election Day found that "Clinton backers—particularly highly educated ones—have more difficulty respecting Trump supporters than the other way around," wrote Pew's John Gramlich. Fifty-eight percent of Clinton's backers agreed with the statement "I have a hard time respecting someone who supports Donald Trump for president," while only 40 percent of Trump voters said the same of her supporters.[18]

This mentality of a cultural siege was made manifest in the campaign. Unlike in campaigns during the three decades prior, traditional culture battle lines such as abortion, gay marriage, criminal justice, and welfare policy took less spotlight in 2016 than a security issue that overlaps with culture: immigration, both from nations to our south and from the Muslim Middle East.

Trump's nonpolitical, often coarse language on this issue served as an attractant for the kinds of marginal voters who were previously unmotivated by more conventional Republican candidates such as Mitt Romney, who awkwardly talked of "self-deportation" as an immigration policy, and John McCain, who had at times been the Senate's leading GOP advocate of a pathway to citizenship for undocumented immigrants. And contrary to pundits' expectations, this harder-edged approach may not have cost Trump votes he otherwise would have received among Latinos—exit poll data showed a comparable Democratic margin among that group in both 2012 and 2016, though Hillary Clinton's Latino pollsters disagreed with that number.[19]

But Trump's approach to border issues did change the way Democrats and media figures, and in some cases prominent Republicans, reacted to him. When Trump first called for temporary curbs on Muslim immigration in late 2015, he used blanket terms based on religion alone and the reaction to him was as coarse as his own approach. Former governor Jeb Bush called him "unhinged," Clinton called him "reprehensible, prejudiced," Senator Bernie Sanders called his speech "racism and xenophobia," and Democratic governor Martin O'Malley labeled it "fascist."[20]

Trump's actual plan evolved over time from a religious test to a short-term ban on immigrants of any religion from seven enemy or failed states—but its effect on the campaign itself was arguably driven not by his specific details but by the siege effect generated by the reaction to Trump. Trump's critics on border subjects galvanized many Trump voters. They saw one candidate, who shared their anxiety about immigration's potential connections to domestic terrorism, being attacked by an entire political and media establishment that blew off that concern as bigotry.

This pattern was repeated through many other campaign episodes triggered by Trump's imprudent, and inherently impolitic, tweets or remarks. He falsely said a judge sitting in a case against him had a conflict due to his "Mexican heritage"; he got into a days-long dispute with the family of a killed-in-action Muslim soldier after they spoke against him at the Democratic National Convention; and, mere weeks after he launched his campaign, he implied that illegal immigrants were disproportionately responsible for the nation's rapes.[21] Each time Trump rocked the crowded campaign media landscape with a bombastic, racially charged statement, he commandeered the attention of the political world for days afterward and drew counterfire that his most loyal supporters interpreted as overreaction.

Clinton's most extreme and costly overreaction came two months out from the election. She told a crowd of donors that "you could put half of Trump's supporters into what I call the 'basket of deplorables.' . . . The racist, sexist, homophobic, xenophobic, Islamophobic, you name it." A survey conducted by *The Washington Post* and ABC News soon thereafter found that nearly two-thirds of registered voters—including almost half of Democrats—found her labels to be unfair. And for a certain strain of Trump voter, this polarization, fueled by the left-wing reaction to the Trump action, became motivational.

"Nobody ever likes being called a racist. It is the worst possible thing you can call someone, especially someone like me who has raised several children of a variety of races. They just say that because they don't know how to understand someone doing something different than what they have done. It stops the conversation instantly. And it is just awful. Awful," says Renee Dibble in Ashtabula, Ohio.

The professional Left focuses heavily on race-related questions in analyzing the Trump vote, but race-tinged subjects were rarely cited by Trump voters interviewed for this book. The Great Revolt Survey asked 2,000 Trump voters in the five Midwestern swing states to rank four key Trump campaign promises in order of importance to their vote, and his pledge to build a wall on the Mexican border was ranked a distant fourth place.

	% SAYING MOST IMPORTANT	MEAN RANK
Bringing back manufacturing jobs to America	34%	1.98
Protecting Medicare and Social Security	30%	2.28
Putting conservative justices on the U.S. Supreme Court	28%	2.49
Building a wall on our border with Mexico	7%	3.25

Trump's comments about the southern border with Mexico no doubt also caused cross-pressure in his coalition, helping him with the populists but harming him with a bedrock group in any winning Republican coalition: the people the Democracy Fund's Emily Ekins calls "Free Marketeers." These voters support more legal immigration and made up 25 percent of Trump's vote in her study, which tellingly shows that these more traditional Republicans actually mirror Democratic attitudes toward African Americans, Latinos, immigrants, and on race in general. However, they did find common ground with Trump on the newer subject of the temporary ban on Muslim immigration.[22]

By broadening the immigration debate to include not just hopeful economic asylum seekers from Central and South America—to focus also on potential terrorists—Trump found a way to unite much of the Republican Party on an issue that had divided it recently. This accomplishment will likely get him no credit by his internal critics who blanch at his intentionally crude and divisive rhetoric on immigration topics.

Pre-election and post-election portraits of the Trump coalition too often shortchanged this complexity of its subgroups' motivations, and the cross-pressures between them. The political accomplishment of Trump's candidacy may be his ability to fuse together two or more wings of voters who came to him for often-conflicting reasons.

10
Pragmatism Before Ideology

Whether it was by design, by impulse, or by instinct, Trump's often ad hoc campaign had one disciplined aspect, a single tenet that made him unique among presidential candidates in 2016: he was an exciting pragmatist.

History is littered with losers from both parties who were unable to make a focus on competence interesting. The money line from Governor Michael Dukakis's acceptance speech at the 1988 Atlanta Democratic Convention was "This election is not about ideology, it is about competence."[1] Senator Bob Dole, a Washington pragmatist if there ever was one, posited his campaign against the myth-weaving romantic Bill Clinton—to use Dole's words almost exactly—as one embodying "a certain wisdom" wrought by "the gracious compensation of age."[2] Dole and Dukakis, like Walter Mondale before them and John McCain after them, found that the pastels of pragmatism are a sorry opponent for bold colors of an ideological cause. But Trump managed to not only eschew ideology and win; he mocked it, even in the philosophical hothouse of a Republican primary.

"I watch the speeches of these people, and they say the sun will rise, the moon will set, all sorts of wonderful things will happen. And people are saying, 'What's going on? I just want a job. Just get me a job. I don't need the rhetoric. I want a job,' " Trump said in his announcement speech, mocking his new colleagues in the political profession.

Trump's announcement speech included the word "deal" twelve times, and some form of the word "negotiate" ten times. Trump managed to make mere promises of management sexy because he used it as a common cudgel against disparate forces his voters resisted, from Barack Obama—and by proxy, Hillary Clinton—to China, to multinational corporations: "We have all the cards, but we don't know how to use them. We don't even know that we have the cards, because our leaders don't understand the game."[3]

The fact that Trump was obviously not motivated by ideology was the source of most Republican primary attacks against him—from magazines such as the *National Review,* to his opponents, to Freedom Caucus congressmen who camped out on MSNBC in front of willing cameras chronicling the Republican rift. Former Texas governor Rick Perry, who would later join Trump's cabinet, said in the summer of 2015 that "Donald Trump's candidacy is a cancer on conservatism, and it must be clearly diagnosed, excised, and discarded." For conservative thought leaders, the problem with Trump was not merely the boorishness that outraged the pundit class but his inability to articulate, and perhaps even comprehend, the theoretical construct behind the movement he was in the process of hijacking.

Conservatives had for decades taken it as a cause worth martyrdom to decry the rise of the welfare state—the House Republicans voted year after year on budget resolutions, which did not have the effect of law but instead stated the will of the majority to fundamentally alter Medicare. But Trump from his first day as a candidate promised, in the style of the best Democrats, to preserve Social Security and Medicare unaltered. Conservatives entered the 2016 race having spent the bulk of three campaigns building a congressional majority on the solitary idea of repealing Obamacare; Trump promised, "I am going to take care of everybody. . . . The government's gonna pay for it." Conservatives, save the darker libertarian corner of the movement, had spent decades defending a muscular approach to advancing democracy overseas; Trump spoke fondly of dictators and had spent the entire Bush era railing against the GOP's policies in Asia.

In the stretch run of his nomination process against right-wing stalwart Senator Ted Cruz, Trump took the subject head-on during an interview with ABC's George Stephanopoulos. "I'm a conservative. But don't forget this is called the Republican Party. It's not called the Conservative Party." Trump came to the contest from New York, where, notably, a separate and feisty Conservative Party does exist in state campaigns and has its own line on the ballot.

Trump's apostasy on so many conservative tenets, and his refusal to deconstruct the intellectual underpinnings of nanny-state liberalism, made him a ripe target in the primary that was overcome by his wholesale ownership of the antiestablishment zeitgeist that had come to rival ideology as a metric for Republican primaries in the post-Bush era. More even than Cruz and Senator Rand Paul, both of whom had built Senate careers on opposition to the body's Republican leadership, Trump understood that the bulk of Republican voters had become just as hostile to the GOP's own leadership as they historically had been to the Democrats. His conquest of the GOP hierarchy in the nomination process was the logical conclusion of the guerilla movement that began in April 2009 with the first Tea Party protests.

Not four months into Obama's presidency, those protests against his policies came not from the institutions of Republicanism but from a new, organic movement. The loose group of political guerillas deliberately did not affiliate with the GOP directly, because it took as much umbrage at the Wall Street bailout engineered by the Bush administration in its waning days, in addition to the domestic spending spree steered by a Congress led by Speaker Dennis Hastert. The subsequent 2010 primary upsets by Tea Party candidates in Senate and gubernatorial primaries coast-to-coast forged a new matrix of Republican primary campaigning—one in which "outside" became a proxy for "Right," and "inside" translated to "Left."

Most of those underdog outsiders who won Senate primaries by railing against the political establishment with Tea Party help— including Marco Rubio and Governor Rick Scott in Florida—did so as conservatives, but not only because they were conservatives. Trump went one short step further, enacting a primary strategy in which outsider credentials were not a veneer for ideological stripes but a replacement for them.

There is ample evidence to suggest that the nonideological nature of his campaign served as fuel to drive new, or at least infrequent, voters to the polls on his behalf.

The Great Revolt Survey found that the new voters and infrequent voters who flocked to Trump, the Perot-istas discussed in earlier chapters, were decidedly less conservative than the rest of the Trump coalition, and they ranked the ideological clarion of the 2016 election—the vacancy on the Supreme Court—lower than any other archetype did in vote-determining importance. This research is echoed in survey work done on an 8,000-person longitudinal panel by Emily Ekins for the Democracy Fund. Ekins found that Trump's most loyal voters "are more fiscally liberal" than the more traditional Republicans in his coalition, the kinds of voters who make up the Rotary Reliables and King Cyrus Christians. Trump's most loyal backers are more likely than traditional Republicans to favor raising taxes on households earning $200,000 or more, and to oppose cuts to Medicare; and even more likely to be alarmed about global warming. Ekins concluded that this type of voter was not only Trump's strongest tribe in the early Republican primaries, but also the group most likely to have defected from the Democrats since 2012.[4]

Trump benefited from this surge of new or infrequent GOP primary voters who participated in the 2016 nomination process. The first three contests, in Iowa, New Hampshire, and South Carolina, were 24 percent larger than in 2012.[5] The Pew Research Center's study of the primaries found a higher rate of participation than in any previous GOP contest since primaries became the norm in 1980—with a notable drop-off in participation after Trump had effectively sealed the nomination.[6] In forty-two of forty-seven state nominating contests (the other three states held conventions), the Republican primary was larger than it had been in either of the prior two cycles, and in most cases much larger. The first GOP contest, in Iowa, drew 180,000 caucus participants, shattering the 2012 record by nearly 50 percent.[7] The Republican contests outdrew the Democratic contests in Michigan, Wisconsin, and Ohio by 60 percent, presaging the states' November status as surprising battlegrounds.[8]

Mainstream media analysts watched state after state ring up record Republican primary turnout and wrote it off as inconsequential. Respected number cruncher Shane Goldmacher devoted a long

Politico piece in May 2016 to the title and thesis that "Donald Trump Is Not Expanding the GOP," based on his read that the people Trump was drawing to the primary process were reliable Republican voters, people who had just not bothered to participate in many primaries before. But the post-election evidence pointed to the contrary.[9]

In Pennsylvania, more than 61,500 Democrats switched their party registration ahead of that state's primary, a gain of more new Republicans than the previous four years combined, according to news reports.[10] Turnout in the Keystone State's GOP primary topped 1.5 million people—nearly double the participation in both 2008 and 2012. This kind of voter, crossing over from the traditionally Democratic camp, gave Trump another bump in the general election as well. In the five Great Lakes states overall, turnout was down in urban counties by 1.6 percent as a share of voting age population, but up 2 percent in the suburbs, up 4 percent in the exurbs, and up 1 percent in rural counties.[11]

Trump's red-hot pragmatism helped draw people to the polls who otherwise might not have voted. A small but important group of Trump's November voters are younger, nonideological, infrequent voters. They hold few opinions on political issues but were attracted to Trump's emphasis on deal-making.[12]

Even Obama conceded Trump's pragmatism in the wake of Trump's general election, albeit after a campaign in which Democrats had derided Trump as a right-winger to the point of fascism. "I also think that he is coming to this office with fewer set hard-and-fast policy prescriptions than a lot of other presidents might be arriving with," Obama said. "I don't think he is ideological. I think ultimately, he's pragmatic in that way. And that can serve him well."[13]

The question of whether Trump has remade, or can remake, the Republican Party on a less-ideological but more-strident forge is one that will persist past his presidency. After an era in which a sizable share of the Republican base, not to mention its often-checked-out margins and its most recent converts, had been disillusioned by the efficacy of more ideologically conservative politicians, from George Bush to Paul Ryan, Trump's new coalition may have been the only path back to presidential parity for the GOP.

11

Localism, Not Globalism

I f the 2016 elections demonstrated the potential of a new coalition of populists and conservatives, then the question for upcoming elections is: What will it take to keep that coalition together or break it apart?

Many of Donald Trump's supporters are willing to vote for Democrats: some did in 2008 or 2012 to elevate Barack Obama, and others did in 2016, down-ballot. In Pennsylvania, which was arguably Trump's most important and hard-fought state victory, Democrats narrowly missed capturing a U.S. Senate seat on which they had spent heavily. Their candidate, Katie McGinty, ran ahead of Hillary Clinton in what is known in the state as "the T" for its geographic shape, covering the bulk of the state's landmass outside the southeast and southwest corners. McGinty outpolled Clinton in forty-eight of the fifty counties that have fewer than 200,000 in population—earning 32,668 more votes than the former secretary of state there. That rural and small-town gap between Clinton and a losing candidate underneath her on the ballot accounted for over half of her statewide shortfall against Trump.

For the last three decades the Republican playbook for attracting voters has had only two approaches—robust gut-level conservatism or a vanilla chamber of commerce–style corporatism that politely rejected conservatism's sharper edges. Trump motivated the lost tribe of the GOP majority by using neither of those two approaches.

So what kind of coherent approach, separate from personal appeals from Trump himself, is likely to attract those voters in future elections?

The connective tissue of the Trump movement is nationalism, but a proper understanding of that tie necessarily encompasses more than the 1930s caricature the term conveys when expressed as a liberal sneer. The motivation for the nationalism of today's populists is a lot closer to the so-called locavore impulse of the shoppers at Whole Foods, the upscale chain of organic grocery stores, than to the dictators of the Second and Third Worlds.

When you walk the produce aisles or seafood counter of a Whole Foods, or of any other upscale grocer today, you are bombarded with information about the place of origin of each fresh item. The retailers realize that their affluent clientele will spend extra money to buy perishable items that have been "sustainably grown" in a nearby region. Presumably, some make this choice for taste reasons alone. But for other consumers this affinity is the expression of consciousness of the atmosphere-polluting petroleum their purchased goods consume in transit. For some, it's a mostly uninvestigated belief in the natural superiority—or at least in the boutique possibility—of American growing practices over those in Mexico or South America.

This last attraction is primarily philosophical, and driven by a value that places localism above globalism. Ironically, it's the same value that moves Trump voters who are demographically quite different from the suburban Whole Foods crowd.

The new populism is a movement against bigness. It distrusts big government, big corporations, big media conglomerates, and, perhaps more than anything else, big multinational agreements and organizations. Just as the Whole Foods shopper is leery of the pesticide practices of a Mexican agribusiness, the Trumpian populist has no confidence that the Brussels bureaucrat will make economic decisions that consider the well-being of the American blue-collar worker.

The mistrust of multinational bigness underpins the attraction for this populist voter to Trump's border security and Muslim travel ban policies—not to mention his wariness of Bushian coalition wars pursuing democracy for other nations. It is stoked when Trump promises, as he did in his announcement speech and routinely on the campaign trail, to bully corporate executives who seek to off-shore manufacturing:

> I would call up the head of Ford, who I know. If I was president, I'd say, "Congratulations. I understand that you're building a nice $2.5 billion car factory in Mexico and that you're going to take your cars and sell them to the United States zero tax, just flow them across the border." And you say to yourself, "How does that help us," right? "How does that help us? Where is that good?" It's not. So I would say, "Congratulations. That's the good news. Let me give you the bad news. Every car and every truck and every part manufactured in this plant that comes across the border, we're going to charge you a 35-percent tax, and that tax is going to be paid simultaneously with the transaction, and that's it. . . . So under President Trump, here's what would happen: The head of Ford will call me back, I would say within an hour after I told them the bad news. But it could be he'd want to be cool, and he'll wait until the next day. You know, they want to be a little cool. And he'll say, "Please, please, please." He'll beg for a little while, and I'll say, "No interest." Then he'll call all sorts of political people, and I'll say, "Sorry, fellas. No interest," because I don't need anybody's money. It's nice. I don't need anybody's money.[1]
>
> —Donald Trump, June 16, 2015

This evolution of the Republican coalition away from global-ism, or at a minimum multinationalism, was not instant, but it is no less than striking. From Richard Nixon to Ronald Reagan through both President Bushes, most national Republicans were committed globalists. The American commitment to the North Atlantic Treaty Organization was seen as the bulwark against communism, and the consensus in favor of multilateral free-trade agreements was questioned only by the party's fringe.

In 1999, when then-governor George W. Bush announced he was running for president with a brief 1,800-word speech, he used part of it to champion his international economic view, saying, "We'll be prosperous if we embrace free trade. . . . The fearful build walls. The confident demolish them."[2]

In 2016, not only did Donald Trump oppose the pending trade-deal-of-the-moment, the Trans-Pacific Partnership, but most GOP senators running for reelection did likewise, including Rob Portman of Ohio and Pat Toomey of Pennsylvania. Earlier in their careers, Portman had been the U.S. trade representative for President George W. Bush, and Toomey had presided over the Club for Growth at a time when that special-interest group policed Republican primaries with heavy expenditures against candidates who were soft on trade agreements. The notion a decade and a half ago that Portman and Toomey might campaign for fellow Republicans who opposed a deal like the TPP, much less oppose it themselves in their own races, would have been laughable. But that's how far and fast the Republican center of gravity has moved on this issue. Equally striking was the fact that TPP's lone enthusiastic defender on the political stage was the country's leading Democrat, Barack Obama, and that the 2016 Democratic nominee's opposition to the deal was more muted than her opponent's.

Obama's tenure—from his campaign rally in front of hundreds of thousands of Berliners even before he was elected in 2008, through the controversial deal he brokered with other world powers to lift economic sanctions on Iran in his last two years—was laced with a philosophy that all American government actions abroad should be undertaken with multinational blessing, a position that would have given an older generation of Democratic politicians great pause.

The onset of the Obama presidency heralded the arrival at the top echelons of Democratic Party leadership of a generation whose identity was forged in the period after the anti–Vietnam War protests of the late 1960s and early 1970s. That protest movement was joined at the hip with a domestic civil rights movement and a bureaucratic experiment that was originally known as the War on Poverty, a moniker chosen by President Lyndon Johnson's administration. Though Johnson served less than two full terms, he successfully inaugurated a vast expansion of the welfare state, creating Medicare, Medicaid, and the programs that led to the construction of government-owned public housing projects in every city in the nation—a cradle-to-grave government social safety net based on a faith in technocratic social engineering as a means to lift people out of poverty.

The young Americans whose political sensibilities were imprinted during the Johnson presidency, and in opposition to the Richard Nixon administration that followed it, adopted a post-Vietnam worldview that said America could ill afford the expense of multinational commitments abroad, and that the nation would be better off spending those resources elevating the fortunes of the underclass domestically.

Obama was too young to be a part of the protest generation himself, but he was the political heir to the philosophy it engendered, and his administration's priorities were their logical postmodern expression. Born to parents of different nationalities and formed professionally as a community organizer, he found the roots of poverty, abroad and at home, in the exploitative colonial policies of the previous century. His cohort's antidote to what it sees as imperialism is a renewed commitment to global governmental egalitarianism, in which the United States is but one chair around the table of the family of nations. Through this lens, there are no superpowers and therefore no tolerance for unilateralism, even by nations with relatively more at stake or more resources to affect a problem. This schism was expressed in the 2012 campaign in a disagreement between Obama and Romney over the notion of "American exceptionalism"—the doctrine that the United States holds an objective, morally superior place among nations for its commitment to opportunity, equality, and individual liberty. Obama refused to endorse the doctrine, except in wordplay that affirmed its opposite, insisting that America's exceptionalism is nothing more than a viewpoint shared by other nations about themselves. Romney, a cheerleader by nature, reveled in goading Obama for this deviation from a notion at the heart of the national mythology to which most prior presidents had paid homage.

Understanding this shift is simple if one reads the political scientist Charles Murray's conclusions about the new upper class who live in the "Super Zips"—those neighborhoods that are home to the people who drive decisions at most commercial and media institutions, and now the Democratic Party. Murray's contention is that these people are more likely than others in the United States to identify as global citizens first and Americans second, which colors an understanding of the new Democratic consensus for multilateral governance.

The Pew Research Center's semiannual foreign policy survey showed that by the spring of 2016, views on U.S. engagement in the global economy had bifurcated sharply along educational-attainment lines. Sixty percent of Americans with postgraduate degrees surveyed were more likely to think the U.S. role in the global economy is a good thing, creating new markets and growth, while only 36 percent of those with a high school degree or less said the same, with 36 percent of postgrads and 56 percent of the less-educated saying global economic engagement lowers wages and costs jobs.[3]

The Republican coalition has begun to take a dim view of multilateralism in international affairs. Four out of five Trump voters in the Midwestern swing states reported in the Great Revolt Survey that the United States should make its own decisions in international affairs and challenge other nations to follow, rather than following the example of European nations and fully participating in international organizations such as the United Nations.

The transformation of the American political divide along the lines of relative cosmopolitanism is evident in the diminution of blue-collar influence on internal Democratic priorities as well.

When Walter Mondale was the Democratic candidate for president, he proudly took the endorsement in 1983 of a 13.7-million member AFL-CIO, for an election that would have 92 million votes cast. When Hillary Clinton got the union umbrella's baton in 2016, it had just 12.5 million members in an electorate 48 percent larger, involving 136 million votes.[4] Of the AFL-CIO's overall number, more than a quarter are now in the government wing, either through the American Federation of Teachers or the American Federation of State County and Municipal Employees Union.[5] The leaders of the traditional, physical, blue-collar unions simply do not have the numbers to wield the structural clout within the Democratic Party that they did even in the recent past.

The realignment has run along the management side of the labor divide as well, with titans of America's largest industries moving toward the Democrats and driving more of their decision making. That shift occurred in congruence with the economy's slide away from companies that make products in the United States for export, to companies that make products overseas and import them back here, or companies that don't make tangible physical products at all.

When Bill Clinton first ran for president in 1992, the top ten names in the Fortune 500 list of America's largest corporations were little altered from the previous postwar decades: General Motors, ExxonMobil, Ford Motor, IBM, General Electric, Mobil, Altria Group, DuPont, Texaco, and Chevron. Seven of those same companies had been in the top ten since 1972, and six had stayed in the top ten from as far back as 1962. By the time Clinton's wife became the Democratic nominee in 2016, the list had dramatically changed, with only ExxonMobil, General Motors, and Ford as carryovers from 1992. The others were replaced by the likes of importers Walmart and Apple along with health care giants McKesson, United-Health Group, and CVS Health, and multi-sector investor Berkshire Hathaway.[6]

Instead of a group of hard-hatted domestic manufacturers, today the American corporate pantheon relies on Asian labor coupled with domestic knowledge in the finance, marketing, logistics, and engineering spheres.

1962 FORTUNE 25	1992 FORTUNE 25	2016 FORTUNE TOP 25
1. General Motors	1. General Motors	1. Walmart
2. Exxon	2. Exxon	2. ExxonMobil
3. Ford Motor	3. Ford Motor	3. Apple
4. General Electric	4. IBM	4. Berkshire Hathaway
5. Mobil	5. General Electric	5. McKesson
6. U.S. Steel	6. Mobil	6. UnitedHealth Group
7. Texaco	7. Altria Group (Kraft)	7. CVS Health
8. Gulf Oil	8. DuPont	8. General Motors
9. AT&T	9. Texaco	9. Ford Motor
10. Esmark	10. Chevron	10. AT&T
11. DuPont	11. Chrysler	11. General Electric
12. Chrysler	12. Boeing	12. AmerisourceBergen
13. Gen. Dynamics	13. Procter & Gamble	13. Verizon
14. Chevron	14. Amoco	14. Chevron
15. Bethlehem Steel	15. Shell Oil	15. Costco

16. Amoco	16. United Technologies	16. Fannie Mae
17. CBS	17. PepsiCo	17. Kroger
18. Shell Oil	18. Eastman Kodak	18. Amazon.com
19. Boeing	19. ConAgra Foods	19. Walgreens Boots
20. Kraft	20. Dow Chemical	20. HP
21. Armour	21. McDonnell Douglas	21. Cardinal Health
22. IBM	22. Xerox	22. Express Scripts
23. Navistar	23. Atlantic Richfield	23. JPMorgan Chase
24. Union Carbide	24. Marathon Oil	24. Boeing
25. Procter & Gamble	25. Nabisco Group	25. Microsoft

The companies at the top of the American economic heap today are run by people far left of their predecessors, most notably Warren Buffett of Berkshire Hathaway, who is trotted out as a reliable Democratic shill in policy debates every year.

Even before Trump and his politically incorrect crassness arrived on the scene, the kinetic energy in America's emerging corporate C-suites was moving leftward. A *New York Times* analysis found that in presidential donations in the 2012 election, Obama got 91 percent of the checks from Apple employees, 89 percent of those written by eBay employees, and 81 percent of those from Microsoft donors.[7] The tech sector, captive to West Coast sensibilities and angled toward the Pacific Rim in its outlook, is inherently more international than the smokestack manufacturers it replaced. And the rise of health care behemoths, highly regulated and dependent on government-negotiated payers such as Medicare and Medicaid, inherently must view government as a collaborative rather than purely combative business agent. Not surprisingly, before Trump had even accepted his nomination in Cleveland, Clinton rolled out a list of fifty CEO-types who were endorsing her, including some nominal or former Republicans such as ex–General Motors CEO Dan Akerson.[8]

A key to projecting the potential staying power of the Trump-made alliance between populists and conservatives is understanding not just the changing influences within that coalition, but the forces pushing Democrats further toward the multinational worldview that enabled the coalition to form.

The seeds of the Republican divorce from corporatism were sown even before the rise of Big Tech and Big Health.

Presaging 2016's wholesale realignment of GOP candidates toward skepticism of trade deals were other skirmishes in the same vein. In 1998, business groups became agitated at House Republicans, led by then-Speaker Newt Gingrich, for holding up funding of the International Monetary Fund over religious persecution practices in China. Gingrich's office shot back that "the Republican Party is the party of small business, mom-and-pop storefronts and mainstream entrepreneurs."[9]

But the divorce was not immediate. In 2000, in what history might record as the last major trade fight on the battle lines of prior decades, a Democratic president (Clinton) and a Republican Congress allied with most corporate interests, and against the AFL-CIO and many Christian conservative groups, to pass what were known as Permanent Normal Trade Relations with China. In the wake of that law—which cleared the way for long-term relationships between Chinese exporters and U.S. customers—a flood of outsourcing decisions increased U.S. imports from China from $8 billion to $40 billion over fifteen years, dwarfing the domestic manufacturing job losses attributed to NAFTA in the 1990s.[10] Decades later, Trump-loving voters in Middle America still routinely cite these deals, and the local job losses they engendered, as drivers of their disenchantment with prototypical politicians in both parties.

The elected leaders of small-government conservatism grew more estranged from their natural corporate allies when they discovered the titans of commerce were summer soldiers in the war on the welfare and regulatory state, often content to cut side deals with the masters of government that protected their narrow lanes of the market—like when drug companies and hospital chains helped "underwrite a multi-million dollar television campaign" pushing Obama's comprehensive health care takeover into law.[11]

With populism ascending and globalism descending on the Republican horizon, Democrats are going to get the better of these deals from big business more often, even as they argue for a larger state and rail against corporate profit-taking.

Democrats for eleven elections in a row have nominated

establishment statists for president who have been content to work within the concrete walls of the economic temple. As liberal as Barack Obama was at the personal level, he filled his administration with ruthless pragmatists, such as former White House chief of staff Rahm Emanuel, who were more than willing to cut deals with corporations and their lobbyists. Under Obama, as long as corporate America allied with liberals on cultural matters domestically and on multilateralism abroad, their anti-consumer mergers and their influence on regulatory policy could be tolerated by a Democratic administration.

The next generation of Democrats may not be as amenable.

Democratic senators Bernie Sanders, Elizabeth Warren, and Kamala Harris all espouse a more confiscatory and less collaborative liberalism than Obama or the Clintons did, and they now command a larger share of voices in the Democratic chorus than their self-styled progressive predecessors did.

Trump-era Democrats, embittered by the defeat of an establishment candidate like Clinton, are already moving so far left on tax rates and regulations that they could reset the compass of business political calculus leftward. And President Trump's actual policies, such as his regulatory relief push and the massive corporate and personal tax cut he negotiated with the Republican Congress at the end of 2017, should in theory make business leaders warmer to a government with Trump's coalition in charge. But the more likely scenario is that the CEOs follow the social pressure in Murray's Super Zips to keep drifting leftward themselves, following the Democratic politicians—and that the populist-conservative alliance is strengthened in reaction.

Republican elected officials are now accustomed to a world in which their most reliable business allies are not large publicly traded corporations, but smaller entrepreneurs and large family-owned, privately held companies in the retail and energy sectors. These newer companies, still entrepreneurial in nature, are still controlled by their founders, or their founders' progeny—people in Murray's new upper class to be sure, but headquartered in the country's interior, far from the cocktail parties and lacrosse tournaments frequented by people in the coastal-state Super Zips.

Their company names are still blue-chip, but their outlook is different from the older brands on the global stock exchanges—names like Koch Industries, Amway, Continental Resources, Pilot Flying J, Love's Travel Stops, Menards, Sheetz, and Kohler.

These companies are run by executives who are less buffeted by social pressure, and are not subject to stockholder or investor rebellions led by activist liberals.

As the Trump administration progressed through its first year, executives who had first agreed to serve on the president's economic councils resigned in protest as liberal backlash to him has mounted. In just one week in August 2017, Trump lost the CEOs of Merck, Intel, and Under Armour, and promptly abolished the advisory groups they had left—a move that left the house organ of corporate America, *The Wall Street Journal*'s editorial page, aghast. "The disdain for the President in the media and Hollywood isn't surprising, and Mr. Trump wears it like a badge of honor. But the business community is, or ought to be, a natural part of a Republican President's governing coalition," the editors wrote—sparing the executives themselves from criticism for cowering to pressure from liberal activists.[12]

The larger question for executives on both sides of the new political divide is not about politics but about customers. It only stands to reason that the kinds of voters who seek to alter corporate political behavior will not forever be coming just from the Left.

It seems only logical that voters who brought havoc into the political system in rebellion against political correctness and central decision-making by stale institutions could eventually see the same faults in their consumer brands. The first nonpolitical shock wave of this rebellion was engineered by Trump himself in the fall of 2017 in the one cultural arena that had previously been most impervious to political partisanship—the National Football League.

A year after former San Francisco quarterback Colin Kaepernick launched a sparsely adopted protest movement against police brutality, Trump polarized the entire nation around the fault line. In a September 2017 speech in Huntsville, Alabama, Trump railed against the NFL players who were following Kaepernick's lead by kneeling during the playing of the national anthem before games. Trump's riff, unconnected to the main purpose of his speech, set off simultaneous firestorms on both sides, shifting the debate away from the protesters' stated purpose to a debate on patriotism itself. "Wouldn't you love to see one of these NFL owners when somebody disrespects our flag to say get that son of a bitch off the field right now, he's fired," Trump proclaimed, to roars of approval from his red-state crowd.[13]

The NFL, headquartered on Park Avenue in New York and influenced corporately by brand and media leaders in the Super Zips detached from Trump's coalition, fought back furiously at first, with the league and its allies in the sports media defending the anthem protesters against the president's scorn. But a significant number of NFL fans took Trump's side, and after a swift plummet in television ratings for league broadcasts, the league relented. Just nineteen days after Trump's speech in Alabama, NFL commissioner Roger Goodell sent a letter to the league's owners stating, "Like many of our fans, we believe that everyone should stand for the national anthem."[14] The television ratings damage may not be easily fixed. By January 2018, the showcase second weekend of the league's postseason attracted 94 million viewers, down from 144 million a year before.[15] The online public polling firm Morning Consult asked 300,000 respondents to rank the top thirty brands in the fourth quarter of 2017, and among Republicans, the NFL was viewed as the least favorable, ranking below even the liberal TV network MSNBC.[16]

Al Michaels, the veteran broadcaster who anchors the NFL's showcase prime-time telecast each week, gave Trump much of the credit for the shift: "Once the president made those remarks in Alabama, at that particular point it was like throwing a match into a gas tank."[17]

Chances are, the NFL won't be the last gas tank to combust under the friction of the colliding mores of coastal brands and heartland populists.

12
What Comes Next

Since he descended the escalator in the lobby of Trump Tower in the summer of 2015, Donald Trump's political trajectory has been impossible to project for even the most seasoned prognosticators. After he defied predictions from left, right, and center, it is perhaps hubris for anyone to attempt to project the direction his coalition might take. But the short-term future of the Republican Party and the conservative movement depends on it—and it is fair and important to ask if the societal fallout from the 2016 election has already fundamentally altered other institutions as well.

Regardless of what happens in the coming 2018 elections, the GOP's success in fusing populism and conservatism is not debatable. Republicans now control more state capitols than at any time in history, with 34 of the 50 governorships and more than 4,000 of the nation's 7,300 state legislative seats. The GOP Senate majority could plausibly threaten its historic high point of 55 after the 2018 midterms, and the GOP House majority margin of 24 seats is already the third largest in history. This combination of two of the great modern American political strains of thought—populism and conservatism—was in process long before Trump, and will likely long outlast him.

Democrats, having walked through the purifying fire of defeat in the South and Rust Belt, have few voices left that can check the virulently liberal impulses of the party's elite leadership. The electoral track record of the Obama era indicates that the faster Democrats march leftward on cultural issues, the better they do in liberal coastal bastions, even as more votes in the country's interior states become available to Republicans. Unchecked by the need to accommodate centrists in their own party, the Democrats continually redefine the litmus tests for acceptable liberalism, ranging from sensitivity over the stigmatism of Islam, to the migration of the historic fight for gay rights to a newer quest for transgender rights and an ever-lengthening acronym to describe them, to race-baiting political action that seeks to paint the motives of large swaths of Americans who consider themselves amply tolerant with the broad brush of bigotry.

This obsession with the redefinition of cultural norms has come at a price for Democrats. Beyond the people it offends, it denies Democratic candidates time to discuss the pocketbook issues that swing voters are more likely to use in guiding their votes. According to the post-2008 Democratic dogma, this setback will be more than made up for by demographic math. The theory advanced by those who endorse what journalist Ron Brownstein dubbed, in the wake of Obama's second victory, "the coalition of the ascendant" believe that America's coming nonwhite majority, the emerging numerical clout of the millennial generation, and the increasing prevalence of college education make it unnecessary for Democrats to dilute their secular, pluralistic, cultural liberalism—enforced by the courts and the executive branch. This argument holds that Democrats will soon no longer need swing voters, and the aging cohorts that make up blue-collar, religiously devout, and uneducated sub-cells of the American electorate are fading so fast in their electoral share that they need not be attended.

Brownstein, who originally described this coalition of the ascendant as also having "just enough blue-collar whites in the Midwest," says Democrats' shortfall in this category cost them the 2016 election. "Before Election Day I wrote that the risk for Hillary Clinton is that she'd fall in the gap between the party's past and its future," Brownstein says.

Brownstein, who recites census data and exit polls the way some rattle off sports scores of their favorite teams, believes that Democrats will attempt to patch this gap in the short term by adding economic issues back into the party's playbook. That's exactly what Democratic pollster Stan Greenberg—the original chronicler of the Macomb County, Michigan, transformation from the domain of Teamsters bosses to the hotbed of Reagan Democrats—is betting on.

Greenberg has hopes for the economic manifesto rolled out in the summer of 2017 by Democratic congressional leaders Senator Chuck Schumer and Representative Nancy Pelosi—dubbed "A Better Deal" to evoke comparisons to the similarly named "New Deal" and "Fair Deal" economic programs of Presidents Franklin Roosevelt and Harry Truman. Long an advocate of a message of economic populism within the Democratic consultant class, Greenberg believes that Trump's coalition can be broken by attacking congressional Republican plans to rein in entitlement spending, coupled with corporate accountability and job training promises on the positive side.

In touting the Schumer-Pelosi program, Greenberg asserts that the plan "is only on economics"—with none of the identity politics that dominated Hillary Clinton's campaign. *Newsweek*'s Matt Cooper gave voice to skepticism within Democratic ranks that the poll-tested plan will take hold. "The Better Deal, even if it's composed of respectable Democratic ideas, may seem too bloodless for the Bernie Sanders left and might be too easily lampooned by the Republican right."[1]

This kind of bifurcation of the Democratic campaign message has been overcome before, by none other than Barack Obama in his contentious reelection campaign.

"While I basically believe in the idea of the coalition of the ascendant, the Democratic political coalition required an act of political levitation," Brownstein concludes, noting that Obama did just that, and he did it by running two parallel campaigns. "They had run better among blue-collar whites in the Midwest than they had run among blue-collar whites nationally," Brownstein says. "In the Sunbelt [Obama] was running a cultural liberal campaign and in the Rust Belt he was running an economic populist campaign [against Mitt Romney]. In the Midwest there was a resonance to a guy getting out of the limo and all the jobs going away."

Clinton's campaign gave up on the bifurcation—much to the

consternation of Greenberg, who says he urged them as late as early October to close the campaign on middle-class economics.

Brownstein says that the fault line inside the Democratic Party in the short term is over this same question of strategy. "The core debate is how much of non-urban and blue-collar and white America can Democrats expect to win back on economic grounds once they've become a homogenous liberal party on cultural issues," he says. "I believe there is a fundamental limit to how much ground you can regain . . . on economic issues."

The homogenization of the Democratic Party on cultural issues, now reinforced by the coastal urban monopoly on the levers of power inside the party—and the stridency of the activists who have driven it—is but one factor in the polarization of the two parties and the fusion of conservatism and populism on the Right. Global economic forces and changes in communications patterns pushed and cemented the divide, and in short order.

Richard Edelman, CEO of the global public relations and corporate branding company that bears his last name, dates the beginning of polarization and populism's rise to 2006 as the communications world in the United States was being upended. "You saw populism start in 2006," Edelman says. "It coincides exactly with the idea of peer-to-peer horizontal communication being more credible than vertical." That timeline also coincides with the proliferation of the smartphone, the device that puts the entire search capacity of the Internet in the palms of most Americans at all hours of the day and night. The first BlackBerry with a color screen and track ball for easy Internet navigation debuted in 2006, and Apple's iPhone was introduced in early 2007.

Now, news consumers of all political persuasions have no need for the filter of brand-name news organizations. "Four out of five people only read or see that which they agree with," Edelman says. "Sixty percent of people say they prefer search [engines] to human editors. They are living in a world of self-reference, and their number-one credible source is a person like yourself."

Edelman, who annually conducts a study of trust in brands and institutions, says the consequence of this empowerment of the individual led to populism because it shattered the premise of expertise.

"What's happened in the world is we've moved from a pyramid of influence," Edelman says. "There were three presumptions in that: the elites had better information, the elites acted in the interest of the mass, and I could be one of the elites someday. All of those are out the window."

With more Americans consuming news only from sources with which they agree, it's only natural that Democratic opinion leaders would be pushed left and Republican leaders pushed right—and that cultural issues, with brighter lines, would come to dominate over economic issues, with grayer divisions between the ideologies.

Edelman says the resulting loss of trust in institutions is not confined to the populists and the Right, either. "It's become transversal. Fifty percent of those who have high-income, college-plus-educated, and five-plus media a day, they don't trust institutions either. It's not a mass-class divide. It's not a left-right thing."

An undeniable consequence of this silo-ing of information is the decline in the economic viability and the public reach of traditional media sources. The past decade has seen a domino effect of newspaper closures and cutbacks. Proud historic mastheads like the *Times-Picayune* of New Orleans are no longer even put into print every day. Newsroom employment that had peaked at 56,900 in 1990 was down to 32,900 by the end of 2014 in the long-running annual survey by the American Society of News Editors. By 2016, the society was no longer even counting.[2]

In the Obama era, the conservative-oriented Fox News Channel became the nation's number-one-rated cable news source and the forum for opposition to the president; in the Trump era, the left-wing fervor of prime time and morning hosts on MSNBC has led that channel's ratings to surpass Fox's. *The New York Times* and CNN, meanwhile, have turned their fiercely confrontational coverage of the Trump administration into marketing campaigns for the outlets themselves—with the *Times* even paying to run ads during Hollywood's Academy Awards ceremony telecast in February 2017, the paper's first television ad in seven years.[3]

Technology entrepreneur Mark Cuban, who stars on the reality TV show *Shark Tank* and owns the NBA's Dallas Mavericks basketball team, says we should not worry about this polarization of news sources and the decline in their credibility. "What we are seeing in politics is very analogous to how sports media has been for decades, very contentious, very partisan, very angry," Cuban wrote in response to questions over e-mail. "We are a nation that likes to take sides and get very vocal when we agree or disagree when our team wins or loses."

This reinforcing echo chamber has come at a cost to Democrats in the present. Some countries, such as France and Israel, conduct national presidential elections without regard to geographic divisions. But the American federal compromise dating back to the Constitution's ratification in the eighteenth century made our presidential elections state-based, requiring a political party to have its strength spread out among a diverse group of geographic locales.

In 2016, Clinton shrunk the footprint of the Democratic Party dramatically, winning only 489 of the nation's more than 3,000 counties; her husband had won nearly half the United States' counties or county equivalents, 1,526, in 1996. Clinton exceeded Obama's 2012 vote total in 364 counties, but she only picked off 22 counties that had been carried by Mitt Romney, while Trump won 220 counties that had been won by Obama.[4] Those counties where Trump outperformed his Republican predecessor were concentrated in the industrial heartland of the country, along the northern border in what had previously been called the Democrats' Blue Wall, as shown on the map on page 286.

In 2016, the Democratic coalition that claimed a plurality of the national vote was concentrated in two narrow strips of coastal real estate, bounded by I-95 and I-5, and the urban centers scattered in between. Clinton, in defeat, claimed larger local wins than Obama had in Los Angeles, New York, Chicago, Washington, San Francisco, and San Diego, but got no additional electoral votes for the bonus. Clinton's national popular vote margin was produced in the country's three largest cities alone—in states she could have won without even winning those cities at all.

"In the long run, Republicans have a demographic problem and Democrats have a geographic problem," says Brownstein, who believes that while Trump's bombastic style may yield near-term victories for Republicans, it will leave the party permanently behind among the millennial generation. "I think Trump represents this enormous gamble because he comes at this moment of transition. A majority of public school students are nonwhite. Shortly after 2020 a majority of the population will be nonwhite. There's no doubt his vision has this potential to increase margins among whites, but I just don't see how that's sustainable."

The theory of the coming dominance of the coalition of the ascendant—specifically racial minorities, millennials, immigrants, and the highly educated whites who take a multiculturalist, globalist view—is one that has been adopted not just by the Democratic Party but also by major national brands. After decades of avoiding political controversy, it is now normal to see national consumer brand companies such as Delta, Starbucks, Target, or Dick's Sporting Goods weigh in on hot-button social and political issues, and almost always on the liberal side.

When challenged at a shareholder meeting about Starbucks' decision to corporately back a state gay marriage referendum—and the boycott by conservatives that decision sparked—the company's CEO, Howard Schultz, challenged any shareholder who disagreed to divest his stock. "It is not an economic decision to me," Schultz reportedly said. "We want to embrace diversity. Of all kinds."[5]

Press reports show that Target, the national discount chain, saw sales decline in the three quarters after a boycott petition was signed by 1.4 million people following the company's announcement in April 2016 that transgender customers would be allowed to use the bathroom of their choice while at Target outlets.[6]

Public pollster Morning Consult found fast backlash against companies that cut business ties with the National Rifle Association in the wake of the Parkland, Florida, school shooting. One such company, Enterprise Rent-A-Car, saw its net favorability rating cut in half overall, driven by Republicans' rating of the firm crashing from a net positive rating of 52 percent before the action, to a net negative rating of 9 percent after.[7]

Greenberg, Cuban, and Brownstein agree that protests like these, and the potential for more backlash from Trump voters, will not deter brand leaders from siding with the cultural Left.

"I believe corporate America is betting that Trump isn't long for the road, that Trump is largely driven by anxiety about changing demography, and that ultimately demography wins," says Brownstein, citing the coming clout of millennials, who have yet to hit their peak consumer-spending years. "That's their future consumer and they think it is more important, indispensable even, to be seen as welcoming that and in no way seen as holding it back. I think they are making a clear generational bet."

Cuban says that Trump is not a unifying enough force to build a coalition that can change economics enough to make brand leaders reverse course. "With Trump, it's him. There is no team. There is no one else with him. That puts a time limit on his stay in office. That makes it a countdown rather than a systemic change."

That presents a central question about Trump's effect: Was his coalition the product of a candidacy or did he, as a candidate, benefit from a cause that succeeded in spite of him?

The Trump voters interviewed for this book clearly believe that they are part of a cause that is larger than a president, and one that began before the last election. The sense of mission to right the wrongs put upon middle-class Americans by the indifference of big business, big media, and big government is expressed independently of their trust in a man most admit is flawed. But the fact that their private, anonymous survey responses indicate a far greater level of trust in Trump than in congressional Republicans—and the intensity of the galvanization his presidency has engendered among Democrats—has to make Republican leaders in Congress and the party structure more than a little nervous about their chances of keeping populists and conservatives pulling in the same direction, and with the same shared effort, for long.

Well into the first year of the Trump presidency, the tension between him and Republican congressional leaders was higher than one would expect from a president still in what should have been the honeymoon phase. Having shown no hesitance to deride wayward incumbent Republican lawmakers by name, with the same or greater heat as he does Democrats, Trump may be adding more anchors to his marketplace positioning as a pragmatic outsider.

Democratic strategists are making a big bet on their ability to lash Trump's personal negatives to every congressional Republican on the midterm ballot in 2018, but if Trump succeeds in continuing to define himself separately from, and as a check on, both parties, that strategy may be perilous for Democrats. Conversely, if Trump's bluster and nonstop controversy demoralizes the normal-order conservatives while his occasional railing against congressional Republicans demotivates his most ardent, but irregularly voting, devotees, the GOP could find itself squeezed between the catalyzing heat of the party's new energy source and the mathematical reality of difficult coalition politics.

The same group of voters in the swing states of the Great Lakes region swept both the Democrats in 2008 and the Republicans in 2016 to complete control of both branches of the federal government. The migration of these voters—first in the congressional elections of 2010 and 2014, and then ultimately to Trump's side in 2016—has fundamentally altered the American political landscape for the foreseeable future. Democratic political experts have decided to try to outrun this revolt and form a new coalition of the self-styled enlightened that looks far different from the New Deal framework on which the party functioned for nearly a century.

The demand of these newly mobile populist voters for cultural respect, their resistance to multilateralism abroad and multiculturalism at home, their siege-like defiance of the loudest voices in American corporate and societal life, and the intensity of the Left's reaction to them, will now animate not just our politics but our nation's debates about commercial and societal norms.

"What happened in 2016 is only the beginning; in fact, the truth is it is not even that, because there is no turning back," says Ed Harry, the former union boss from northeast Pennsylvania, punching his hands into the pockets of his Penn State sweatshirt as if to drive home an important point.

"And honestly, it is bigger than Trump. I'll be watching him to make sure he does not screw this up . . . but whatever he does, as far as this goes"—he motions all around him, to no one in particular—"well, I don't think there is any way to put what happened in 2016 back into some neat place. This is the new normal, people just don't know that yet. Or maybe they just don't want to know."

Acknowledgments

As first-time authors, we had the good fortune of not knowing what we did not know when we began this process. That gave us the courage to stick with our expertise. We did what we know how to do, and then, by trial and error, we squeezed that into the book in its final form. Now that we know the magnitude of this task, we are even more grateful to Tina Constable of Crown Forum for taking a chance on us and for believing in the concept of this storytelling. In our very first meeting, we knew Tina was the right leader for the project and understood that the new populist-conservative coalition was being under-explained by prevailing media narratives.

Mary Reynics was a supportive and savvy editor who melded with us from the start and innately knew the sensibilities of the real people brought forward in this book even though she had not personally met them.

Our agents, Keith Urbahn and Matt Latimer, have our thanks for sensing the potential of this story and for being brave enough to take an unusual dual-author concept to market. Rookie authors could not have been in better hands. They and their firm, Javelin, continue to do more than anyone to advance the smart translation of politics to the reading public.

Blaise Hazelwood and Tim Saler of Grassroots Targeting LLC deserve a major public thank-you for their tireless diligence in helping us determine—and then crunch—the numbers that mattered to this story. Their firm is simply the best in the political data business. Once crunched, the data in the book was carefully handled, sorted, re-sorted, and double-checked throughout the writing process by Sarah Binion, with the able assistance of Allison Masters—a juggling act made more difficult by constantly changing instructions from us.

The endnotes of this book are chock full of citations for the online treasure trove uselectionatlas.org, curated for decades as a hobby by Dave Leip. His labor of love has become the gold standard for historical county-level election data and, like all authors in this genre, we are grateful to him for his service.

The Great Revolt Survey of Trump voters in the Great Lakes undertaken for this book would not have been possible without the patience and expertise of Wes Anderson, Rick Heyn, Kyle McGherin, Kayla Dunlap, and Joel Ransbottom. Their willingness to think outside the pack of political pollsters kept them dialed in to the 2016 election as it happened, and their experience in asking the right questions gave our Great Revolt Survey unmatched precision.

On the ground, we got incredible help opening doors in the ten counties we feature by a list of people too long to delineate, but a handful that just have to be mentioned: Scott Bolstad, Jamie Roe, Rudy Guy, Tim Albrecht, Kathryn Whittington, Jill Gilmore, Terry Schrepfer, and Matt Augustine. We tapped every relationship either one of us had in these five states to make sure we got wide exposure to the people who best translated the story of this changing coalition.

Our coworkers and employers, the *Washington Examiner,* CNN, *New York Post,* and OnMessage, Inc., deserve ample thanks for giving us the time and flexibility to work on this project even while the grinding of the gears of the next election already could be heard.

Thanks also must go out to friends outside the political realm who, in casual conversations even before the 2016 election, set off mental switches in both our minds that started this project in motion—among them Chip Hudnall, Frankie Davis, Paul Sracic—and every single person interviewed along the way. Early draft critique by Alex Castellanos made our thinking sharper. Michael Nelson, Marc Pohlman, and especially Daniel Cullen offered important encouragement, feedback, and book-writing tips to their old student Todd, whom they've never stopped teaching.

And a special acknowledgment to Frank Craig, a longtime newsman who took a risk hiring an unpolished Zito years ago and taught her to trust her instincts. Craig then gave her the room she needed to cover national politics on the ground and along the backroads of America when everyone else was begging to join the pack on the bus.

Last, and most important, no project as time-consuming as this one is completed without someone paying the cost of lost time. Both our families gave up some of our time, attention, and focus that rightly belonged to them, and we're grateful for their unconditional support of the project.

Appendix

Data and a Note on Methodology

This book makes multiple references to two important data sources: a geographical analysis of Trump's vote by county and the national electorate by population tiers, and the Great Revolt Survey of Rust Belt Trump voters.

A broader exposition of these two data sets follows.

The analysis of Trump's vote by population tiers is one of the best ways of understanding the trends in American politics as it realigns along not just regional lines, but educational and density faults as well. More than any recent election, the 2016 contest showed a polarization between those who live in dense cosmopolitan communities with higher-than-average education levels, and those who live in rural, exurban, and industrial locales that as a rule have less density, lower-than-average education levels, and less transience. Interestingly, the data suggests strongly that the emerging schism is not related merely to the income and education levels of an individual voter, but to the income and education levels of those who live around them. Voting is an inherently communal and social process, and social pressures are driving American politics as much as, or more than, demography— and that fundamental difference is a major part of the story of the miscalculations made by Clinton's campaign, Republican political experts, and media analysts in the run-up to the 2016 balloting.

The divisions of counties by population used in this book's analysis are as follows, utilizing the Census Bureau's 2016 population estimates for categorization—treating independent cities as county units for this purpose and excluding Alaskan jurisdictions, where census data and electoral jurisdictions are not aligned:

Mega Counties of more than 1,000,000
Extra Large Counties of 400,000–1,000,000
Large Counties of 200,000–400,000
Medium Counties of 100,000–200,000
Small Counties of 50,000–100,000
Rural Counties of fewer than 50,000

COUNTY SIZE	AVERAGE TRUMP MARGIN MINUS AVERAGE ROMNEY MARGIN IN COUNTIES WITH ABOVE-AVERAGE BACHELOR'S DEGREE HOLDERS	AVERAGE TRUMP MARGIN MINUS AVERAGE ROMNEY MARGIN IN COUNTIES WITH BELOW-AVERAGE BACHELOR'S DEGREE HOLDERS	NET GAP	TOTAL POPULATION	SHARE OF US POPULATION	# OF COUNTIES
Mega	-6.1%	-1.5%	4.6%	91,675,113	28%	44
Extra Large	-3.5%	4.4%	7.9%	83,172,109	26%	129
Large	-3.7%	5.0%	8.6%	43,663,268	29%	157
Medium	0.4%	9.9%	9.5%	37,409,571	16%	265
Small	1.6%	10.4%	8.8%	27,304,177	12%	388
Rural	0.0%	14.0%	14.0%	39,893,920	12%	2157

The individual voters featured in this book come from ten counties that switched allegiances from Barack Obama in 2012 to Donald Trump in 2016, in the five pivotal Great Lakes or Rust Belt states of Michigan, Ohio, Pennsylvania, Wisconsin, and Iowa. Those counties were chosen to ensure as much variety among the population tiers listed above as is possible.

There were no Mega Counties in these five states that switched allegiances. In fact, of the forty-four Mega Counties nationwide, only Suffolk County on middle-class Long Island, New York, switched from Obama to Trump. Macomb County, Michigan, in metro Detroit is an Extra Large County and typical of the cast of that entire tier, which tends to consist of midsize cities or suburbs of large cities.

Stark County, Ohio, which includes the city of Canton, and Luzerne County, Pennsylvania, which includes the city of Wilkes-Barre,
are both Large Counties in our classification and typical of the
smaller, not-quite-urban population centers that pervade that group
nationwide.

Kenosha County, Wisconsin, is a prototypical Medium County—a
growing place that sends commuters to two distant metropolitan
centers, Chicago and Milwaukee. Erie County, Pennsylvania, represents another common Medium County type—an urban area that is
losing population and no longer carries the political weight it once
did in its state.

Ashtabula County, Ohio, population 98,231, is a representative
Small County—a place with an industrial past and an agricultural
component as well.

The book includes interviews from four Rural Counties—all with
unique attributes—which is fitting, considering that Trump's coalition is more rural than any other winning effort in the current era.
Lee County, Iowa, is an industrial county along the Mississippi River
that has two old small towns; Howard County, Iowa, is one of that
state's smallest jurisdictions and sits squarely in the northern agricultural belt of the state; Vernon County, Wisconsin, is a Mississippi
River county that is rapidly changing, and even growing in spite of
its distance from any metropolitan area, thanks to its toehold in the
organic agriculture of the future; tiny Lake County, Michigan, is
featured because it spent decades as a lone Democratic holdout in
that state's very Republican north woods region.

COUNTY	POPULATION	BACHELOR'S DEGREE	TRUMP %	CLINTON %	ROMNEY %	OBAMA %	GOP NET MARGIN GAIN '12-'16	TRUMP MARGIN	ROMNEY MARGIN	'16 PRIMARY WINNER	'16 PRIMARY 2ND
Lee, IA	34,615	15.5%	55%	38%	41%	57%	32%	16%	-15%	Trump, 31%	Cruz, 25%
Howard, IA	9,332	12.8%	57%	37%	39%	60%	41%	20%	-21%	Trump, 31%	Cruz, 29%
Macomb, MI	867,730	23.3%	54%	42%	47%	51%	16%	12%	-4%	Trump, 48%	Kasich, 22%
Lake, MI	11,496	9.4%	59%	36%	47%	52%	28%	23%	-5%	Trump, 51%	Cruz, 24%
Ashtabula, OH	98,231	13.3%	57%	38%	42%	55%	32%	19%	-13%	Trump, 44%	Kasich, 38%
Stark, OH	373,612	21.9%	56%	39%	49%	49%	18%	17%	0%	Kasich, 48%	Trump, 38%
Erie, PA	276,207	26.1%	48%	46%	41%	57%	18%	2%	-16%	Trump, 52%	Cruz, 25%
Luzerne, PA	316,383	21.4%	58%	39%	47%	52%	24%	19%	-5%	Trump, 77%	Cruz, 13%
Kenosha, WI	168,183	24.5%	47%	47%	43%	55%	13%	0%	-12%	Trump, 42%	Cruz, 41%
Vernon, WI	30,814	20.5%	49%	45%	42%	56%	19%	4%	-15%	Trump, 47%	Cruz, 37%

COUNTY	MCCAIN '08	OBAMA	G.W. BUSH '04	KERRY	BUSH '00	GORE	DOLE '96	B. CLINTON
Lee, IA	41%	57%	42%	57%	38%	58%	32%	56%
Howard, IA	36%	62%	43%	56%	43%	54%	35%	52%
Macomb, MI	45%	53%	50%	49%	48%	50%	39%	50%
Lake, MI	43%	55%	48%	51%	42%	55%	28%	60%
Ashtabula, OH	42%	56%	46%	53%	45%	50%	34%	50%
Stark, OH	46%	51%	49%	51%	49%	47%	38%	46%
Erie, PA	39%	59%	46%	54%	44%	53%	37%	53%
Luzerne, PA	45%	53%	48%	51%	44%	52%	37%	52%
Kenosha, WI	40%	58%	47%	53%	45%	51%	34%	52%
Vernon, WI	38%	60%	46%	53%	44%	50%	34%	50%

COUNTY	G.H.W. BUSH '88	DUKAKIS	REAGAN '84	MONDALE	REAGAN '80	CARTER	NIXON '72	MCGOVERN
Lee, IA	36%	63%	49%	50%	48%	44.9%	55%	43%
Howard, IA	46%	54%	56%	44%	53%	39.7%	54%	45%
Macomb, MI	60%	39%	66%	33%	52%	40.4%	63%	35%
Lake, MI	46%	53%	53%	46%	43%	51.0%	49%	49%
Ashtabula, OH	46%	53%	52%	47%	49%	42.9%	59%	39%
Stark, OH	55%	44%	60%	40%	56%	37.6%	63%	35%
Erie, PA	47%	52%	51%	51%	47%	44.5%	58%	40%
Luzerne, PA	50%	50%	54%	45%	50%	44.4%	61%	38%
Kenosha, WI	42%	58%	47%	53%	44%	47.9%	54%	44%
Vernon, WI	47%	52%	56%	44%	51%	43.1%	66%	33%

The Great Revolt Survey was conducted in August 2016 by the respected Republican opinion research firm OnMessage Inc. among an anonymous group of 2,000 self-reporting Trump voters, with 400 coming each from Ohio, Pennsylvania, Michigan, Iowa, and Wisconsin. The survey utilized a blend of both online and live telephone interviews drawn from professional third-party sample sources, geographically stratified to properly reflect the division of the actual Trump vote in 2016 based on the six county-size classifications outlined above. The weighted marginal results for the substantive questions are as follows:

The Great Revolt Survey of Trump voters in Iowa, Michigan, Ohio, Pennsylvania, and Wisconsin

Note: Totals may not add up to 100% due to rounding.

1. In the 2016 election for President of the United States did you vote for Donald Trump, Hillary Clinton, Gary Johnson, Jill Stein, or did you skip the presidential ballot and vote in other races, like Congress?

Donald Trump	**100%**

2. Thinking about the job that Donald Trump has done as President of the United States, would you say you approve or disapprove of the job he has done as President?

Approve	**86%**
Strongly Approve	40%
Somewhat Approve	47%
Disapprove	**13%**
Somewhat Disapprove	10%
Strongly Disapprove	3%
DK/Refused	**1%**

3. In general, would you say you are optimistic or pessimistic about your future career growth or financial situation?

Optimistic	**87%**
Very Optimistic	34%
Somewhat Optimistic	53%
Pessimistic	**12%**
Somewhat Pessimistic	10%
Very Pessimistic	2%
DK/Refused	**1%**

4. Thinking about multi-national organizations like the United Nations, which of the following statements comes closest to your opinion?

The United States should make our own decisions on major issues and challenge other nations to follow our example.	85%
The United States should follow the example of European nations on major issues and cooperate fully in multi-national organizations like the United Nations.	14%
DK/Refused	1%

5. I am going to read four campaign promises that Donald Trump made during the 2016 election. Please rank them in their order of importance to you, with 1 being the most important and 4 being the least important.

	% Saying Most Important	Mean Rank
Bringing back manufacturing jobs to America	34%	1.98
Protecting Medicare and Social Security	30%	2.28
Putting conservative justices on the U.S. Supreme Court	28%	2.49
Building a wall on our border with Mexico	7%	3.25

6. Which of the following ranges includes your annual household income? Would you say it is . . .

Under $20,000	7%
Between $20,001 and $40,000	19%
Between $40,001 and $75,000	30%
Between $75,001 and $100,000	19%
Over $100,000	19%
I would rather not say	6%

7. *Considering your health insurance, which of the following comes clos-est to your own personal situation? If you do not have health insurance or health care coverage, just say so.*

I pay for my own health insurance	16%
My employer pays for my health insurance	12%
My spouse's employer pays for my health insurance	11%
The cost of my health insurance is split between me and my employer, or between my spouse and their employer	23%
I am still covered by my parents' health insurance	2%
My principal coverage is Medicare	28%
My principal coverage is Medicaid	5%
I do not have health insurance or health care coverage	3%
DK/Refused	1%

8. *Thinking again about your health insurance, do you receive your coverage through Obamacare?*

Yes	6%
No	94%
DK/Refused	—

9. *Which of the following best describes your religion?*

Evangelical Protestant	18%
Fundamentalist Protestant	4%
Mainline Protestant	13%
Other Protestant	12%
Catholic	28%
Jewish	1%

Atheist/Agnostic	4%
Other	20%
DK/Refused	—

10. How often do you attend religious services?

More than once a week	9%
About once a week	30%
One or two times a month	11%
Infrequently or a few times a year	21%
Hardly ever or never	29%
DK/Refused	—

11. If you were to label yourself, would you say you are a liberal, a moderate, or a conservative in your political beliefs?

Liberal	3%
Moderate	33%
Conservative	64%
DK/Refused	—

12. Which political party are you most affiliated with?

Republican	73%
Independent	22%
Democrat	5%
DK/Refused	—

13. Did you vote for Barack Obama in either the 2008 or 2012 election for president?

Voted Obama	**21%**
2008 Only	8%
2012 Only	3%
2008 and 2012	9%
No, Neither	**77%**

Too Young	2%
Too Young 2008	1%
Too Young 2012	—
Too Young 2008 and 2012	1%
DK/Refused	—

14. Please tell me whether you agree or disagree with the following statement. Every American has a fundamental right to self-defense and a right to choose the home defense firearm that is best for them.

Agree	94%
Strongly Agree	68%
Somewhat Agree	26%
Disagree	5%
Somewhat Disagree	4%
Strongly Disagree	1%
DK/Refused	—

15. Do you or does anyone in your household own a firearm?

Yes	55%
Self	31%
Household Member	16%
Self and Household Member	8%
No	44%
DK/Refused	1%

16. Rank the following four institutions in order of your trust in them to do the right thing to benefit the country, with 1 being the most trusted and 5 being the least trusted.

	% Saying Most Trust	Mean Rank
Donald Trump	60%	1.68
Republicans in Congress	25%	2.04
Big businesses	6%	3.16
Democrats in Congress	4%	3.82
National media outlets	2%	4.29

17. Please tell me whether you agree or disagree with the following statement: Republicans and Democrats in Washington are both guilty of leading the country down the wrong track.

Agree	**89%**
Strongly Agree	44%
Somewhat Agree	45%
Disagree	**11%**
Somewhat Disagree	8%
Strongly Disagree	3%
DK/Refused	**1%**

18. Who would you say is a more patriotic American, Donald Trump or Barack Obama?

Donald Trump	78%
Barack Obama	5%
Both Equally	17%
DK/Refused	1%

19. Please tell me whether you agree or disagree with the following statement: Donald Trump stands up for the working people against powerful corporate interests.

Agree	**86%**
Strongly Agree	34%
Somewhat Agree	51%

Disagree	**13%**
Somewhat Disagree	11%
Strongly Disagree	2%
DK/Refused	**1%**

20. At any point before the presidential election did you feel uncomfortable telling friends that you supported Donald Trump because you knew that they would disapprove?

Yes	34%
No	66%
DK/Refused	—

21. When you first heard the Access Hollywood *recording of Donald Trump saying inappropriate things about women, tell me which describes your reaction at the time.*

What Trump said about women didn't bother me. It was just typical locker-room talk.	54%
What Trump said offended me, but other more important issues decided my vote.	45%
DK/Refused	1%

22. Thinking about abortion, please tell me which of the following statements comes closest to your opinion.

Abortion should be made mostly illegal	49%
Abortion should be legal but we should increase restrictions to reduce abortion	32%
All women should have affordable access to abortion doctors	18%
DK/Refused	1%

23. Please tell me whether you agree or disagree with the following state-ment: Large corporations do not care if the decisions they make hurt working people.

Agree	**72%**
Strongly Agree	27%
Somewhat Agree	44%
Disagree	**27%**
Somewhat Disagree	20%
Strongly Disagree	7%
DK/Refused	**2%**

24. Do you personally know anyone who has suffered with addiction to narcotics such as opioids or methamphetamine?

Yes	37%
No	63%
DK/Refused	—

25. Have you or a family member lost a full-time job in the past 7 years?

Yes	**31%**
Self	12%
Family Member	17%
Self and Family Member	2%
No	**69%**
DK/Refused	—

26. Would you say that your community has more or fewer job opportunities than it did 10 years ago?

More	58%
Fewer	41%
DK/Refused	2%

27. Have you ever been a member of a civic organization such as Lions Club, Kiwanis Club, Rotary Club, Sertoma Club, Ruritan Club, Civitan Club, Optimist Club, Exchange Club, Volunteer Fire Department, Rescue Squad, or a local elected board like a school board or county or town government or any similar community organization?

Yes	25%
No	75%
DK/Refused	—

28. Have you been hunting or fishing in the past ten years?

Yes	47%
No	53%
DK/Refused	—

29. Please indicate whether you have ever worked in any of the following blue-collar jobs after the age of 21.

Blue Collar	**77%**
Factory/Industrial worker, not an office job	7%
Driver or delivery or loader	2%
Physical laborer	2%
Janitorial	1%
Agricultural or forestry	1%
Construction/Building trades or landscaping or utility company	2%
Oil/Gas/Coal extraction	—
Barber, cosmetologist	—
Childcare hourly work	3%

Nursing or eldercare hourly work	5%
Mechanic or repair technician	1%
None of the above but still in a job that paid by the hour other than consulting	21%
More than one	31%
No, I have never worked a blue-collar or hourly job after the age of 21	**22%**
I am not 21 yet	—

30. Have you or your spouse ever gone bankrupt, or considered filing for bankruptcy?

Yes	**18%**
Self	9%
Spouse	2%
Self and Spouse	6%
No	**82%**
DK/Refused	—

31. Thinking about marriage, which of the following represents you?

I have never been married	14%
I am married and have never been divorced	55%
I am a widow or widower and have never been divorced	5%
Divorced	**26%**
I have been divorced once	20%
I have been divorced twice	5%
I have been divorced more than twice	1%
DK/Refused	—

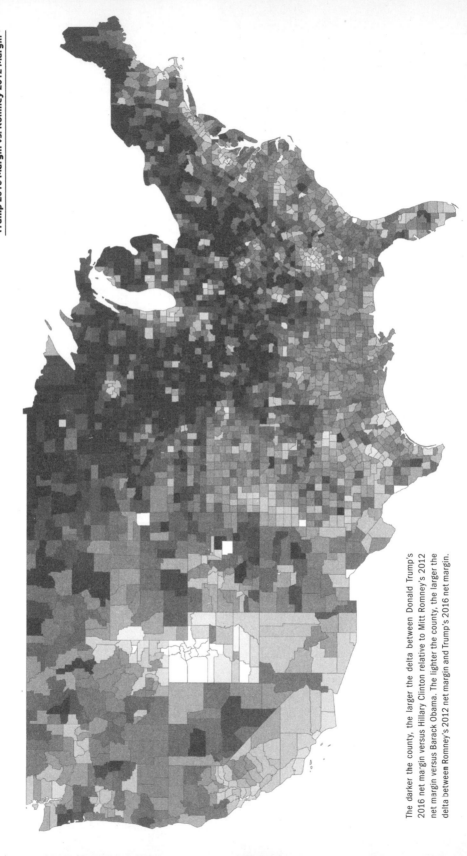

Converting the Rust Belt: Trump's Growth over Romney's 2016 Performance
Trump 2016 Margin vs. Romney 2012 Margin

The darker the county, the larger the delta between Donald Trump's 2016 net margin versus Hillary Clinton relative to Mitt Romney's 2012 net margin versus Barack Obama. The lighter the county, the larger the delta between Romney's 2012 net margin and Trump's 2016 net margin.

Notes

1. Hidden in Plain Sight

1. Paul Steinhauser, "Holding Democratic Blue Wall Was Crucial for Obama Victory," CNN.com, November 13, 2012.

2. Growth Partnership for Ashtabula County website, http://media.wix .com/ugd/358d3f_91510c27b5014ba7beee80dd7b1c60fc.pdf.

3. Bureau of Labor Statistics Data Finder, https://beta.bls.gov/dataViewer/ view/timeseries/CES0000000001.

4. "Population of States and Counties of the United States: 1790–1990," compiled and edited by Richard L. Forstall, U.S. Department of Commerce, U.S. Bureau of the Census, Population Division; United States Census Bureau Quick Facts, https://www.census.gov/quickfacts/fact/table/US,ashtabulacountyohio/ PST045216.

5. As NBC formally made its call of Trump as the winner at 3:05 a.m. in the middle of the marathon election night, MSNBC analyst Nicolle Wallace said, "Trump took down the Democratic party and the Republican party tonight." http://money.cnn.com/2017/01/05/media/election-night-news-coverage-oral -history/index.html.

6. "Here's Donald Trump's Presidential Announcement Speech," Time .com, June 16, 2015.

7. "Clinton Calls for Continuity Until January," *Los Angeles Times,* November 5, 1992.

8. Karl Rove, "More White Votes Alone Won't Save the GOP," *The Wall Street Journal,* June 26, 2013; "Republicans Can't Win with White Voters Alone," *The Atlantic,* September 7, 2013.

9. Republican National Committee, *Growth and Opportunity Project,* p. 7, https://gop.com/growth-and-opportunity-project/.

10. Dave Wasserman, "How Demographics Will Shape the 2016 Election," FiveThirtyEight.com, December 3, 2015.

11. Ronald Brownstein, "How Obama Won: Marrying Old and New Democratic Coalitions," *The Atlantic,* November 7, 2012.

12. Ruy Teixeira, John Halpin, and Robert Griffin, "The Path to 270 in 2016: Can the Obama Coalition Survive?" Center for American Progress, December 17, 2015, https://www.americanprogress.org/issues/democracy/reports/2015/12/17/127403/the-path-to-270-in-2016/.

13. Sean Trende, "The Case of the Missing White Voters," RealClearPolitics.com, November 8, 2012.

14. Stuart Stevens, "There Aren't Enough White Voters for GOP Win," *The Daily Beast,* March 17, 2016.

15. "Here's Donald Trump's Presidential Announcement Speech."

16. Ibid.

17. Ibid.

18. Brownstein, "How Obama Won: Marrying Old and New Democratic Coalitions."

19. Nate Cohn, "How Trump Could Redraw Voters' Allegiances," *The New York Times,* June 30, 2016.

20. The Upshot, "Hillary Clinton Has an 85% Chance to Win," *The New York Times,* November 8, 2016.

21. Farhad Manjoo, "Facebook's Bias Is Built-In and Bears Watching," *The New York Times,* May 11, 2016.

22. Nicholas Confessore and Karen Yourish, "$2 Billion Worth of Free Media for Donald Trump," *The New York Times,* March 15, 2016.

23. Hadas Gold, "How Donald Trump and 'Morning Joe' Made Up," Politico.com, December 5, 2016; Oliver Darcy, "Donald Trump Broke the Conservative Media," BusinessInsider.com, August 26, 2016.

24. Gabriel Sherman, "How Roger Ailes Picked Trump, and Fox News' Audience, Over Megyn Kelly," *New York,* August 11, 2015.

25. Phillip Rucker, Dan Balz, and Jenna Johnson, "Trump Says He Won't Participate in GOP Debate on Fox News," *The Washington Post,* January 26, 2016.

26. "Against Trump," *National Review,* January 21, 2016.

27. Bill Kristol, columns in *The Weekly Standard,* http://www.weeklystandard.com/author/william-kristol.

28. David Catanese, "Divided Loyalty to Donald Trump Fractures Republicans," USNews.com, October 11, 2016; Douglas Ware, "Tape Fallout: Who's Still

Supporting Donald Trump—and Who's Not?," UPI.com, October 10, 2016; "Bill Haslam: Donald Trump Needs to Step Aside for Mike Pence," *The Tennessean*, October 9, 2016.

29. Joshua Dubois, "Powerful Evangelical Women Split from Male Church Leaders to Slam Trump," *The Daily Beast*, October 10, 2016.

30. "Evangelical Leader: Trump Hurts Christian Credibility," interview with Dr. Russell Moore by Jake Tapper of CNN, http://www.cnn.com/videos/tv/2016/10/10/the-lead-trumps-comments-russell-moore.cnn.

31. Ronald Brownstein, "How Trump Could Become a 'Political Black Hole' for the GOP," *The Atlantic*, October 9, 2016.

32. Final election results in Nevada and New Hampshire, as certified by their secretaries of state: http://www.nvsos.gov/soselectionpages/results/2016StatewideGeneral/ElectionSummary.aspx and http://sos.nh.gov/2016 GenResults.aspx.

2. Red-Blooded and Blue-Collared

1. Fareed Zakaria, "Zakaria: Why Trump Won," CNN.com, July 31, 2017.

2. Eduardo Porter, "Where Were Trump's Votes? Where the Jobs Weren't," *The New York Times*, December 13, 2016.

3. Jim Tankersley, "How Trump Won the Presidential Election: Revenge of the Working-Class Whites," *Chicago Tribune*, November 9, 2016.

4. "Population of States and Counties of the United States: 1790–1990," compiled and edited by Richard L. Forstall, U.S. Department of Commerce, U.S. Bureau of the Census, Population Division; United States Census Bureau Quick Facts, https://www.census.gov/quickfacts/fact/table/luzernecounty pennsylvania,US/PST045216.

5. "History of Luzerne County," LuzerneCounty.org, http://www.luzerne county.org/living/history_of_luzerne_county.

6. *Marcellus Drilling News*, http://marcellusdrilling.com/2012/04/the -marcellus-line-of-death-in-ne-pa/.

7. Jason Brennan, "Trump Won Because Voters Are Ignorant, Literally," *Foreign Policy*, November 10, 2016.

8. Marci A. Hamiltion, "Why Are White, Uneducated Voters Voting for Trump?" *Newsweek*, November 1, 2016.

9. Pennsylvania Election Results, Pennsylvania Department of State, http://www.electionreturns.pa.gov/General/CountyResults?countyName=Luzerne& ElectionID=54&ElectionType=G&IsActive=0.

10. Denise Allabaugh, "Online Retailer Amazon Opens Fulfillment Center at Centerpoint," *The Citizens' Voice*, November 15, 2016.

11. Jennifer Learn-Andes, "Luzerne County Republican registration up by more than 6,000 voters," *The* (Wilkes-Barre) *Times Leader,* April 25, 2016

12. U.S. Election Atlas, by Dave Leip, http://uselectionatlas.org/RESULTS/.

13. Ibid.

14. CROPP, "The Choice for Organic Farmers," https://www.farmers.coop/.

15. "How Is CROPP Associated with the Organic Valley Brand Name?" Organic Valley website, http://organicvalley.custhelp.com/app/answers/detail/a_id/79/~/how-is-cropp-associated-with-the-organic-valley-brand-name%3F.

16. U.S. Census Bureau Quick Facts, https://www.census.gov/quickfacts/fact/table/WI,US,vernoncountywisconsin/RHI725216.

17. "Drug Overdose Death Data," Centers for Disease Control and Prevention, https://www.cdc.gov/drugoverdose/data/statedeaths.html.

3. Perot-istas

1. The American Presidency Project, http://www.presidency.ucsb.edu/data/turnout.php.

2. U.S. Census Bureau, American Community Survey 5-Year Estimates, February 1, 2017, https://www.census.gov/rdo/data/voting_age_population_by_citizenship_and_race_cvap.html.

3. Analysis by GOP data and analytics firm Grassroots Targeting, Inc.

4. Sheaffer Pen & Art Supply "Company History," https://www.sheaffer.com/en/help/about-sheaffer/company-history.

5. "Sheaffer Pen Factory in Fort Madison to Close in Spring," Associated Press via *Mason City Globe Gazette,* January 8, 2008.

6. Candace Smith and Liz Kreutz, "Hillary Clinton's and Donald Trump's Campaigns by the Numbers," ABCNews.com, November 7, 2016.

7. U.S. Election Atlas, by Dave Leip, http://uselectionatlas.org/RESULTS/.

8. Dan Austin, "Hudson's Department Store," Historic Detroit.org, http://www.historicdetroit.org/building/hudsons-department-store/.

4. Rough Rebounders

1. Transcript of Donald Trump interview with Marc Fisher and Michael Kranish, *The Washington Post,* June 9, 2016, https://www.washingtonpost.com/wp-stat/graphics/politics/trump-archive/docs/donald-trump-interview-with-marc-fisher-and-michael-kranish-june-9-2016.pdf.

2. Thomas C. Frohlich, Alexander Kent, Michael B. Sauter, and Sam Stebbins, "The Poorest County in Every State," Yahoo.com, January 27, 2016.

3. U.S. Election Atlas, by Dave Leip, http://uselectionatlas.org/RESULTS/.

4. Analysis by GOP data and analytics firm Grassroots Targeting, Inc., Alexandria, Virginia.

5. U.S. Election Atlas, by Dave Leip, http://uselectionatlas.org/RESULTS/.

6. Ohio Department of Job and Family Services, http://www.lmi.state.oh.us/LAUS/Ranking.pdf.

7. Shelley Terry, "Trump Makes Stop in Geneva," *Tribune Chronicle* (Ohio), October 28, 2016.

8. "Donald Trump Rally in Geneva, Ohio, October 27, 2016," on YouTube .com, https://www.youtube.com/watch?v=Sp3M6rgdcB0.

5. Girl Gun Power

1. Chuck Todd, MSNBC broadcast, November 9, 2016.

2. Alex Altman and Philip Elliott, "How Democrats Embraced Gun Control at Their Convention," Time.com, July 28, 2016.

3. "Gun Violence Prevention," HillaryClinton.com, https://www.hillary clinton.com/issues/gun-violence-prevention/ and Jackie Kucinich, "Hillary Clinton Really Is Coming for Your Guns," DailyBeast.com, August 29, 2015.

4. Ben Smith, "Hillary Hits Obama on Faith, Guns," Politico.com, April 12, 2008.

5. "2017 Report from the Crime Prevention Research Center," https://papers.ssrn.com/sol3/papers.cfm?abstract_id=3004915#.

6. Issie Lapowsky, "The Tech Skills Gap Will Test Foxconn's New Wisconsin Factory," *Wired*, July 26, 2017.

7. National Rifle Association YouTube Channel, including the ad "Classified," https://www.youtube.com/watch?v=yGc_ctmoe4w.

8. Scott Bland, "Democrats Strategize Path to Relevance Among Working-Class Whites," Politico.com, July 28, 2017.

9. Telephone interview with Wes Anderson, June 28, 2017, regarding On-Message Inc. post-election survey of presidential voters conducted November 2016 in Ohio, Pennsylvania, Indiana, Florida, North Carolina, Nevada, Missouri, and Maine.

10. Fred Barnes, "Gunning for Hillary: The NRA's Unheralded Role in 2016," *The Weekly Standard,* March 6, 2017.

11. Richard Elliott, *The Late Voice: Time, Age and Experience in Popular Music* (New York: Bloomsbury Academic, 2017), p. 160.

12. Mike Tighe, "Organic Valley Realizes $6.3 Million Profit on $1.1 Billion in Sales," *La Crosse Tribune,* March 24, 2017.

13. John R. Lott Jr., "Concealed Carry Permit Holders Across the United States: 2017," Crime Prevention Research Center, https://papers.ssrn.com/sol3/papers.cfm?abstract_id=3004915.

6. Rotary Reliables

1. Jim Tankersley, "How Trump Won the Presidential Election: Revenge of the Working-Class Whites," *Chicago Tribune,* November 9, 2016.

2. "Iowa Unemployment Rates by County, June 2016," State Library of Iowa, http://publications.iowa.gov/22594/.

3. "Population of States and Counties of the United States: 1790–1990," compiled and edited by Richard L. Forstall, U.S. Department of Commerce, U.S. Bureau of the Census, Population Division; United States Census Bureau Quick Facts, https://www.census.gov/quickfacts/fact/table/US ,ashtabulacountyohio/PST045216.

4. Rotary International, https://www.rotary.org/en/about-rotary/history.

5. "Ranking the Brands," Fortune Global 500, 2016, https://www.ranking thebrands.com/The-Brand-Rankings.aspx?rankingID=50&year=1079.

6. John David, "Massive New Iowa Fertilizer Company Plant Set to Open in Southeast Iowa," WQAD-TV, April 20, 2017.

7. Liz Allen, "Old Newsies Say Donors Surprise Them with Generosity," *Erie Times-News,* December 2, 2016.

8. Jim Martin, "Unofficial Counts: UPMC Hamot Erie County's Top Employer," *Erie Times-News,* February 19, 2017.

9. Gerry Weiss, "Erie County's Population Shrinks for Fourth Straight Year," *Erie Times-News,* March 23, 2017; United States Census Bureau Quick Facts, Census.gov, https://www.census.gov/quickfacts/fact/table/PA,US,erie countypennsylvania/AGE275210.

10. Trip Gabriel, "How Erie Went Red: The Economy Sank, and Trump Rose," *The New York Times,* November 12, 2016.

11. Nico Salvatori, "Trump's Early Visit to Erie Reflects Unconventional Approach," *Erie Times-News,* August 11, 2016.

12. "Coal Mining in Pennsylvania," Pennsylvania Department of Environmental Protection, http://www.dep.pa.gov/Business/Land/Mining/Pages/ PA-Mining-History.aspx.

13. Pennsylvania 2016 poll tracker, Real Clear Politics, https://www.real clearpolitics.com/epolls/2016/president/pa/pennsylvania_trump_vs_clinton -5633.html#polls.

14. Hillary Clinton campaign's channel on YouTube.com, including the ad titled "Doug," October 8, 2016, https://www.youtube.com/watch?v= uq4GADCWZgU&feature=youtu.be.

7. King Cyrus Christians

1. Ellen Uchimiya, "Donald Trump Insults Carly Fiorina's Appearance," CBSNews.com, September 9, 2015.

2. Wilson Andrews, Kitty Bennett, and Alicia Parlapiano, "2016 Delegate Count and Primary Results," *The New York Times,* July 5, 2016.

3. Rosie Gray, "Prominent Evangelicals Still Backing Trump After Lewd Video," *BuzzFeed News,* October 7, 2016.

4. David Green, "The History of the Jewish Temple in Jerusalem," *Haaretz,* August 11, 2014.

5. "Lance Wallnau, "Why Trump Is 'God's Chaos Candidate' and 'Wrecking Ball,'" CBNNews.com, March 21, 2017.

6. Michael Burke, "Amazon to Hire 1,000 More at Kenosha Center," *Journal-Times* (Wisconsin), July 13, 2015; Rick Romell, "Uline Adding Hundreds of Jobs in Kenosha County," *Milwaukee Journal-Sentinel,* October 24, 2016.

7. "Religious Composition of Adults in Wisconsin," Pew Research Center on Religion & Public Life, http://www.pewforum.org/religious-landscape-study/state/wisconsin/.

8. Gregor Aisch, Robert Gebeloff, and Kevin Quealy, "Where We Came From and Where We Went, State by State," *The New York Times,* August 19, 2014.

9. Eugene Scott, "Trump Believes in God, but Hasn't Sought Forgiveness," CNN.com, July 18, 2015; Maxwell Tani, "Trump on God: 'I Don't Like to Have to Ask for Forgiveness,'" *Business Insider,* January 17, 2016.

10. "Video: Allow Donald Trump to Tell You About His Christian Faith," *The Federalist,* January 20, 2016, http://thefederalist.com/2016/01/20/video-allow-donald-trump-to-tell-you-about-his-christian-faith/.

11. John Stemberger, "3 Questions Evangelicals Should Ask About Donald Trump," CNN.com, January 6, 2016.

12. Census Viewer, http://censusviewer.com/city/OH/Canton; U.S. Census Bureau Quick Facts, https://www.census.gov/quickfacts/fact/table/cantoncityohio,US/PST045216.

13. "Stark County Schools See Rise in Students Eating Breakfast and Lunch," CantonRep.com, http://www.cantonrep.com/article/20150428/NEWS/150429160.

14. "Canton, OH Crime Rates," Neighborhood Scout, https://www.neighborhoodscout.com/oh/canton/crime.

15. Stark County Mental Health & Addiction Recovery, https://starkmhar.org/help/stark-countys-heroin-epidemic/heroin-facts-figures/.

16. "Ohio, Stark County Voters Changed Party Affiliations in Primary," *Canton Repository,* May 18, 2016.

17. Dr. Roy Burris, "Remembering the 80's," https://www.drovers.com/article/remembering-80s.

18. Iowa Counties by Population https://www.iowa-demographics.com/counties_by_population

19. Exit Polls 2016 and 2012 for President, CNN.com, http://www.cnn.com/election/results/exit-polls and http://www.cnn.com/election/2012/results/race/president/.

20. Telephone interview with Wes Anderson, June 27, 2017, regarding his post-election survey in Pennsylvania, North Carolina, Ohio, Florida, Missouri, Indiana, Maine, and Nevada.

8. Silent Suburban Moms

1. U.S. Census Bureau Quick Facts, https://www.census.gov/quickfacts/fact/table/macombcountymichigan,MI/INC110216#viewtop

2. Michigan Department of State, Election Results, http://www.michigan.gov/sos/0,4670,7-127-1633_8722---,00.html.

3. Stanley B. Greenberg, *Middle Class Dreams*, pp. 37–38, http://www.democracycorps.com/attachments/article/1062/Middle%20Class%20Dreams%20-%20Chapter%202%20-%20Macomb%20in%20the%20American%20Mind.pdf.

4. Chad Livengood, "Clinton Targets Trump Battleground of Macomb County," *Detroit News*, August 10, 2016.

5. Greenberg, *Middle Class Dreams*, p. 38.

6. Ibid., p. 46.

7. Ibid.

8. "Mirrors," by Hillary Clinton for President, September 23, 2016, Clinton Campaign Channel on YouTube.com, https://www.youtube.com/watch?v=vHGPbl-werw.

9. Phillip Rucker, "Trump Has a Challenge with White Women: 'You Just Want to Smack Him,'" *The Washington Post*, October 1, 2016.

10. David Farenthold, "Trump Recorded Having Extremely Lewd Conversation About Women in 2005," *The Washington Post*, October 8, 2016.

11. "What He Believes," campaign ad, November 1, 2016, Hillary Clinton campaign's channel on YouTube.com, https://www.youtube.com/watch?v=Oy8HRdlLGCQ.

12. Exit Polls, CNN.com, November 23, 2016, http://www.cnn.com/election/results/exit-polls.

13. Exit Polls, CNN.com, December 10, 2016, http://www.cnn.com/election/2012/results/race/president/.

14. Data analysis using U.S. Election Atlas, by Dave Leip, http://uselectionatlas.org/RESULTS/.

9. A Culture Craving Respect

1. Alex Johnson, "Gore Sounds a Populist Call to Arms," NBCNews.com, August 17, 2000.

2. John Judis, "The Populist Al Gore," *The New York Times,* August 20, 2000.

3. Gwen Ifill, "The 1992 Campaign; Clinton's Standard Campaign Speech, a Call for Responsibility," *The New York Times,* April 26, 1992.

4. Transcript: Read the Full Text of Hillary Clinton's Campaign Launch Speech, Time.com, http://time.com/3920332/transcript-full-text-hillary-clinton -campaign-launch/.

5. Ibid.

6. Ifill, "The 1992 Campaign; Clinton's Standard Campaign Speech, a Call for Responsibility."

7. Charles Murray, *Coming Apart: The State of White America, 1960–2010* (New York: Crown Forum, 2012), p. 100.

8. Ibid., pp. 100–101.

9. This data comes from an analysis of two sources: the United States Census Bureau's 2016 population estimates, found at Census.Gov, and the U.S. Election Atlas, by Dave Leip, http://uselectionatlas.org/2016.php.

10. This census data excludes the counties in Alaska due to the unique lack of symmetry in that state between the census measurement area and county boundaries. In the rare states that have independent cities separated by the Census Bureau and their state elections bureau from any county, such as Virginia, those cities are treated as counties by themselves for this purpose.

11. Farai Chideya, "Nearly All of Silicon Valley's Political Dollars Are Going to Hillary Clinton," FiveThirtyEight.com, October 25, 2016.

12. Ted Johnson, "Hollywood Election Donations Heavily Lopsided in Favor of Hillary Clinton," *Variety,* November 8, 2016.

13. Nate Silver, "There Really Was a Liberal Media Bubble," FiveThirtyEight .com, March 10, 2017; The American Presidency Project, http://www.presidency .ucsb.edu/data/2016_newspaper_endorsements.php.

14. Silver, "There Really Was a Liberal Media Bubble."

15. Josh Hafner, "Donald Trump Loves the 'Poorly Educated'—and They Love Him," *USA Today,* February 24, 2016.

16. Aaron Bycoffe, "The Endorsement Primary," FiveThirtyEight.com, June 7, 2016.

17. Murray, *Coming Apart,* pp. 100–101.

18. John Gramlich, "It's Harder for Clinton Supporters to Respect Trump Backers Than Vice Versa," Pew Research Center, November 1, 2016.

19. Jens Manuel Krogstad and Mark Hugo Lopez, "Hillary Clinton Won Latino Vote but Well Below 2012 Support for Obama," Pew Research Center, November 29, 2016; Paul Waldman, "Why the Exit Polls Are Wrong on Latino Votes," *The Washington Post,* November 15, 2016.

20. Brent Johnson, "Top 20 Reactions to Trump's Call to Block Muslims from Entering U.S.," NJ.com, December 8, 2015.

21. Brent Kendall, "Trump Says Judge's Mexican Heritage Presents 'Absolute Conflict,'" *The Wall Street Journal,* June 3, 2016; Maggie Haberman and Richard Oppel, Jr., "Donald Trump Criticizes Muslim Family of Slain U.S. Soldier, Drawing Ire," *The New York Times,* July 30, 2016; Eugene Scott, "Trump Defends Inflammatory Comments, Asks 'Who Is Doing the Raping?'" CNN.com, July 2, 2015.

22. Emily Ekins, PhD, "The Five Types of Trump Voters: Who They Are and What They Believe," Democracy Fund Voter Study Group, https://www.voterstudygroup.org/publications/2016-elections/the-five-types-trump-voters.

10. Pragmatism Before Ideology

1. E. J. Dionne, Jr., "The Democrats in Atlanta; Dukakis Promising Competence and Daring at 'Next Frontier'; Party Ratifies Bentsen Choice," *The New York Times,* July 22, 1988.

2. "Text of Robert Dole's Speech to the Republican National Convention, August 15, 1996," CNN.com, http://www.cnn.com/ALLPOLITICS/1996/conventions/san.diego/transcripts/0815/dole.fdch.shtml.

3. "Here's Donald Trump's Presidential Announcement Speech," *Time,* June 16, 2015, http://time.com/3923128/donald-trump-announcement-speech/.

4. Emily Ekins, PhD, "The Five Types of Trump Voters: Who They Are and What They Believe," Democracy Fund Voter Study Group, https://www.voterstudygroup.org/publications/2016-elections/the-five-types-trump-voters.

5. Marisa Schultz, "Reason for Record Republican Voter Turnout?: Trump," *New York Post,* February 23, 2016.

6. Drew DeSilver, "Turnout Was High in the 2016 Primary Season, but Just Short of 2008 Record," Pew Research Center, June 10, 2016, http://www.pewresearch.org/fact-tank/2016/06/10/turnout-was-high-in-the-2016-primary-season-but-just-short-of-2008-record/.

7. Jason Clayworth, "Caucus Turnout: Robust, Record-Setting and Surprising," *Des Moines Register,* February 1, 2016.

8. Craig Gilbert, "Wisconsin Turnout Highest in Presidential Primary Since 1972," *Milwaukee Journal-Sentinel,* April 6, 2016; Joel Kurth, Kim Kozlowski, Chad Livengood, and Mike Martindale, "Record 2.5M Turnout for Michigan Primary," *Detroit News,* March 9, 2016.

9. Shane Goldmacher, "Donald Trump Is Not Expanding the GOP," Politico .com, May 17, 2016.

10. Lisa Mascaro, "More Than 60,000 Disgruntled Pennsylvania Democrats Switch Parties," *Duluth News-Tribune,* April 24, 2016.

11. Analysis by GOP data and analytics firm Grassroots Targeting, Inc.

12. Ekins, "The Five Types of Trump Voters."

13. Ben Shapiro, "Is Donald Trump a Pragmatist?" *National Review,* November 16, 2016.

11. Localism, Not Globalism

1. "Here's Donald Trump's Presidential Announcement Speech," Time .com, June 16, 2015, http://time.com/3923128/donald-trump-announcement -speech/.

2. "Remarks Announcing Candidacy for the Republican Presidential Nomination," June 12, 1999, The American Presidency Project, http://www .presidency.ucsb.edu/ws/?pid=77819.

3. "Public Uncertain, Divided Over America's Place in the World," Pew Research report, May 5, 2016, p. 25, http://www.people-press.org/2016/05/05/ public-uncertain-divided-over-americas-place-in-the-world/.

4. "Mondale to Labor: I'm on Your Side," June 6, 1983, United Press International, http://www.upi.com/Archives/1983/10/06/Mondale-to-labor-Im -on-your-side/3949434260800/; UnionFacts.com, https://www.unionfacts.com/ union/AFL-CIO#membership-tab; Final Certified 2016 Popular Vote Results, CookPoliticalReport,https://docs.google.com/spreadsheets/d/133Eb4qQmOx Nvtesw2hdVns073R68EZx4SfCnP4IGQf8/edit#gid=19 Final 1984 Election Results, U.S. Election Atlas, by Dave Leip, http://uselectionatlas.org/RESULTS/ national.php?year=1984.

5. Steve Greenhouse and Noam Scheiber, "Two Big Labor Unions Share Efforts to Gain Power and Scale," *The New York Times,* May 5, 2016; "How to Join," American Federation of Teachers, https://www.aft.org/join.

6. "A Database of 50 Years of *Fortune*'s List of America's Largest Corporations," Fortune.com, http://archive.fortune.com/magazines/fortune/ fortune500_archive/full/1962/; Fortune 500 list, 2016, Fortune.com, http:// fortune.com/fortune500/2016/list.

7. Nate Silver, "In Silicon Valley, Technology Talent Gap Threatens G.O.P. Campaigns," *The New York Times,* FiveThirtyEight.com, November 28, 2012.

8. Greg Gardner, "Ex-GM CEO Akerson Among 50 Leaders Endorsing Clinton," *Detroit Free Press,* June 23, 2016.

9. Thomas Edsall, "GOP Angers Big Business on Key Issues," *The Washington Post,* June 11, 1998.

10. Jim Tankersley, "What Republicans Did 15 Years Ago to Help Create Donald Trump Today," *The Washington Post,* March 21, 2016.

11. Sheryl Gay Stolberg and Gardiner Harris, "Industry Fights to Put Imprint on Drug Bill," *The New York Times,* September 5, 2003; Tom Hamburger, "Obama Gives Powerful Drug Lobby Seat at the Healthcare Table," *Los Angeles Times,* August 4, 2009.

12. Editorial board, "Trump and the CEOs," *The Wall Street Journal,* August 15, 2017.

13. Chris Cillizza, "The 64 Most Memorable Lines from Donald Trump's Alabama Speech," CNN.com, September 23, 2017.

14. Ken Belson, "Goodell and N.F.L. Owners Break from Players on Anthem Kneeling Fight," *The New York Times,* October 10, 2017.

15. "SKEDBALL: Weekend Sports TV Ratings 1.13–14.2018," ShowBuzz Daily.com, http://www.showbuzzdaily.com/articles/skedball-weekend-sports -tv-ratings-1-13-14-2018.html.

16. "Top 10 Unfavorable Brands, by Political Party," Morning Consult, January 25, 2018, https://morningconsult.com/polarizing-brands-2018.

17. Rob Tornoe, "NBC Broadcaster Al Michaels on the Eagles, NFL Ratings Declines, and Tony Romo," *Philadelphia Inquirer,* November 16, 2017.

12. What Comes Next

1. Matthew Cooper, "Will Democrats Create New Jobs? Economic Plan Has Good Ideas, but Is Anyone Listening?" *Newsweek,* July 24, 2017.

2. Ken Doctor, "Newsonomics: The Halving of America's Daily Newsrooms," NeimanLab.org, July 28, 2015, http://www.niemanlab.org/2015/07/ newsonomics-the-halving-of-americas-daily-newsrooms/.

3. Julien Rath, "*The New York Times* Wants to Fuel Political Debate Around What 'the Truth Is' with Its Latest TV Ad," *Business Insider,* February 23, 2017.

4. "See a Map That Shows Exactly How Donald Trump Won," Time.com, http://time.com/4587866/donald-trump-election-map/; "Mike Pence Says Donald Trump Won Most Counties by a Republican Since Ronald Reagan," Politifact.com,http://www.politifact.com/truth-o-meter/statements/2016/dec/ 04/mike-pence/mike-pence-says-donald-trump-won-most-counties-rep/.

5. Frederick Allen, "Howard Schultz to Anti-Gay-Marriage Starbucks Shareholder: 'You Can Sell Your Shares,'" Forbes.com, March 22, 2013.

6. Hayley Peterson, "The Target Boycott Cost More Than Anyone Expected— and the CEO Was Blindsided," *Business Insider,* April 6, 2017.

7. Ryan Rainey, "Companies See Negative Responses to Cutting Business Ties with NRA," MorningConsult.com, February 28, 2018, https://morningconsult .com/2018/02/28/firms-see-negative-responses-to-cutting-business-ties-with-nra/.

Index

About the Authors

SALENA ZITO, born and bred in Pittsburgh, Pennsylvania, worked for the *Pittsburgh Tribune-Review* for eleven years. She joined the *New York Post* in 2016 and acts as a political analyst for CNN and a staff reporter and columnist for the *Washington Examiner.* Zito's weekly syndicated column appears in more than twenty newspapers nationwide.

BRAD TODD, a sixth-generation native of rural East Tennessee, is a founding partner at OnMessage Inc., a leading national Republican advertising and opinion research agency. Todd's candidate clients have included seven U.S. senators, five governors, and more than two dozen congressmen.